Same-Sex Parenting Research: A Critical Assessment

"The bottom line is that we have an obligation to get to the truth."
Honorable Chuck Schumer, U.S. Senator from the State of New York
March 2, 2017 (Fox News)

"There is no scientific dispute....
This is ignoring science for a political agenda"
Aaron Belkin, Director of the Palm Center (Shane, 2017, p. 27)

"Is truth dead?"
Cover of Time magazine, April 3, 2017

"The trouble with people ain't ignorance – it's what they know that ain't so"
Josh Billings, cited by Milton Friedman (1983, p. 60)

He who pleads his cause first seems right,
until another comes and questions him.
Proverbs 18: 17 (World English Bible)

All truth passes through three stages. First, it is ridiculed. Second, it is
violently opposed. Third, it is accepted as being self-evident.
Attributed to Arthur Schopenhauer (Larson & Micheels-Cyrus, 1986, p. 244)

If those of us who value GLBT families are not willing to ask difficult
questions and follow the evidence where it leads us,
you can be sure that others will do so"
Professor William Doherty,
University of Minnesota, in Bigner (2006, p. xxii)

Same-Sex Parenting Research: A Critical Assessment

Walter R. Schumm

Wilberforce Publications
London

Published in Great Britain in 2018 by
Wilberforce Publications Limited
70 Wimpole Street, London W1G 8AX

Wilberforce Publications Limited is a wholly owned subsidiary of Christian Concern

ISBN 978-0-9956832-8-0

Printed in Great Britain by Imprint Digital, Exeter
and worldwide by CreateSpace

Contents

PART 2: WHAT DO WE KNOW ABOUT SAME-SEX PARENTS?

PART 3: WHAT DO WE KNOW ABOUT THE CHILDREN OF SAME-SEX PARENTS IN TERMS OF SEXUAL ORIENTATION, GENDER IDENTITY, AND GENDER ROLES?

PART 6: HOW IT ALL FITS TOGETHER

Dedication

To All Who Seek Truth
To the One Who is Truth and Life

PREFACE

In January 2010 a number of organisations in the field of marriage, family, education and counselling worked together to present a consultation: *"What can I possibly say?"* sponsored by Anglican Mainstream. The goal was to provide resources for people who wanted to respond to those who saw no problem in advising children and young people that sexuality was entirely a matter of their own choice in the light of their own claimed sexual identity.

One of the organisations involved was the Oxford Centre for Religion and Public Life (OCRPL). The consultation revealed that much "knowledge" in the field of sexuality was based on oft-repeated studies and research whose validity was open to question. These studies appeared to dominate intellectual discussion in the area of gender and family studies.

OCRPL commissioned two studies of gold standard research in the fields of same-sex relationships and same-sex parenting.

The Marriage Files by Dr Patricia Morgan was published in 2014 and contributed to the debate around the legalisation of same-sex 'marriage'.

Dr Walter Schumm's work is also most welcome and even more timely in view of the closure of the Roman Catholic adoption agencies because they would not place children with same- sex foster and adoptive parents, even though their expertise in placing difficult children was widely acknowledged. This indicated that the wellbeing of children was being sacrificed on the altar of "equality". The current lack of those willing to be foster and adoptive parents is a challenge to those who champion man-woman marriage to step forward as foster and adoptive parents.

We wish to express our deep gratitude to Wilberforce Publications for their excellent partnership in making the results of both these studies available.

We trust that this material will be an important resource to scholars and students, church leaders and church members and those in political and public life.

Dr Vinay Samuel (Director), **Dr Chris Sugden** (Secretary)
Oxford Centre for Religion and Public Life,
21 High Street, Eynsham OX29 4HE
April 2018

PROLOGUE

There are many people to whom I owe much gratitude for encouraging me in my life and even in the production of this book. I hesitate to mention them by name lest they come under attack for having any association with me. Some very Christian scholars have gone out of their way to avoid any association with this book because of the stigma or discrimination they fear. I will mention those who sponsored this book, mainly for their incredible patience because their initial hope was to have seen this book published two, three, four, or more years ago. However, research is a time-consuming process and very important research results have been reported or located in the past several years that might have made such a book premature if published earlier. I want to thank my father, Rear Admiral Brooke Schumm and my brother, Colonel Brooke Schumm, Jr. (both retired) who both encouraged critical thinking in our families. When I was a young boy, my father would take a position that I knew he disagreed with and then have me argue against it while he argued for it. I want to thank Dr. Tony Jurich for his ability to think in unconventional ways; no, Tony, I haven't picked up your habit of singing in the academic hallways, but I admire your willingness to have done so. I will always remember his example of a car mechanic who wanted to commit suicide; Tony asked him if he would junk a car just because the carburetor wasn't working well. The man said no; Tony said, "So why junk yourself?" And the man realised suicide wasn't the right answer to a smaller problem. I might not have thought of such a useful analogy. All this has led me to believe that an honest scientist has to be willing to see at least some of his or her most cherished scientific (even religious) theories or beliefs (or other assumptions) be falsified through careful research.

For example, I had a graduate student who wanted to study abortion attitudes among Roman Catholic high school students and I was very clear to her that no matter what her values were about abortion or what the Church's values were, she had to design research that could possibly show that the students were not adopting the Church's values despite being so trained in their curriculum. She did design it that way and found a complex but interesting pattern that might have been missed otherwise. While she "got it" as a scientist, she didn't "get" an academic position

13

at a Roman Catholic school as she had hoped, but that can be the price of working at being an honest scientist. I have, for example, statistical evidence that some of the religion of Islam is very problematic in doctrine and history; but are there Muslims willing to consider such evidence or will they automatically dismiss it?

My brother, for example, did a dissertation on hydrodynamics (how water moved in the wake of a propeller). He found that a third of what we had thought we knew about that was in fact incorrect. Even though I was never popular with the U.S. government for finding scientific evidence that Gulf War illnesses were associated with some of the medical treatments given U.S. soldiers, the willingness of myself and my colleagues to consider looking for unconventional findings may have helped us identify some of the causes long before other scientists confirmed our findings. That is the true nature of science.

When you start an investigation, you must not assume that you know for sure how it will turn out; you should be willing to look for unexpected findings that may not confirm your prior expectations. You cannot say "I don't like that finding, so I will pretend it never occurred". If you are not willing to do that, then I would question your credibility as an honest scientist. I think that when clergy study the Bible or the Qur'an they should adopt a similar attitude, of not knowing in advance what truths God may show them as they study. If you knew it all before, why bother to study anymore?

I think it is fair for sponsors to pay a scientist to look into certain topics but I don't think it's fair for such sponsors to expect or demand certain findings because honest research cannot guarantee "certain findings", not even "certain" findings for that matter. In social science it is particularly true because social phenomena can change over time, so even if something seemed "certain" at one time, it may have changed by a later time. For example, some of my research seems to suggest that research results associated with same-sex parenting had some important changes between the late 1990s and about 2005. There may be many who won't like this book. That's ok. Feel your anger if you need to, observe it, try to understand its sources. I have never claimed to be a good therapist, but I do hope that a few graduate schools may use parts of this book to show how research can be studied in greater depth and detail than often done, so that future graduate students will become much better at assessing scientific literature and engaging it with deeply critical thinking. Perhaps even a few newspaper or other media reporters might catch some of this scientific spirit with respect to their own investigations, even of this book.

PART 1

CRITICAL BACKGROUND ISSUES

Chapter One

Background

Scientific background of same-sex parenting research

Professor Doug Abbott once stated that "Readers assume researchers and authors are unbiased and objective and that their statistics have not been manipulated to support a personal theory; nevertheless, some researchers seek to advocate or support a social and political agenda" (2012, p. 36). Indeed, Frank (2016) has noted that "the scholarship on LGBT parenting has been heavily politicized from the start" (p. 245). To understand the *need* for this book, you need to understand the unusual background of the research associated with so-called same-sex parenting.[1] As Stacey (2013) remarked, courts, legislatures, and professional organisations "have relied heavily on the growing research literature on lesbian and gay parents and their children" (p. v). The literature has been growing. Nevertheless, I agree with Gates and Romero (2009) who stated that "A broader, as well as more abundant, research effort is needed to better inform the public controversy associated with gay and lesbian relationships and parenting" (p. 227).

More remarkably, most scholars have assessed this literature as proof that LGBT families are no different in any respects than heterosexual families except for being victims of sexual minority stress, whose source comes from "heteronormativity" (Crouch, McNair, & Waters, 2017; Few-Demo, Humble, Curran, & Lloyd, 2016, p. 74; Stacey, 2013, p. vii). For example, Trub, Quinlan, Starks, and Rosenthal (2017) state confidently that "Studies have consistently found no differences in psychosocial outcomes between children raised by heterosexual versus same-sex parents" (p. 1). Likewise, Few-Demo *et al.* (2016) state that, "Decades of research have shown that children raised by same-sex parents and children raised by different-sex parents fare equally well" (p. 74). Accordingly, Few-Demo *et al.* (2016) hope that family life educators will "start to avail themselves of LGBT-parent families research" (p. 78). Rather than merely promoting social equity (e.g., tolerance of sexual minorities), many scholars have intentionally sought, through what is labelled as "queer theory and intersectionality" among other theories and methodologies (Few-Demo *et al.*, 2016, p. 86), to challenge "the heteronormative gender order" and to destabilise and disrupt "what is known and taken for granted about families" (Few-Demo *et al.*, 2016, p. 82).

It has not been unusual for at least some scholars in this area to make statements such as, "Not a single study has ever found any results that indicated children of same-sex parents to be any different from children of heterosexual parents in any way." For example, Marks (2012) cited Patterson (2005) who said that, "Not a single study has found children of lesbian or gay parents to be disadvantaged in any significant respect relative to children of heterosexual parents" (p. 736). Cooper and Cates (2006) include a Foreword by Shay Bilchik, President and CEO of the Child Welfare League of America, who stated that, "Not a single reputable study has found that children raised by gay or lesbian parents have been harmed because of their parents' sexual orientation in any way" (p. vi). Cooper and Cates (2006) stated that, "Not a single study found any adverse effect on children's development associated with the parents' sexual orientation... These findings are therefore considered highly reliable by experts in the field. Indeed, they have led to the consensus among the major professional organizations with expertise in children's health and welfare that children of gay parents are just as healthy and well-adjusted as other children, including the American Academy of Pediatrics, the American Psychological Association, the National Association of Social Workers, and the Child Welfare League of America" (p. 31).

Later in their book, Cooper and Cates would argue that "Among social scientists, whether parental sexual orientation has an impact on children's adjustment is no longer an open question or a subject of debate. Because a well-developed body of research has answered that question, it is well-settled that children raised by gay parents are just as healthy and well-adjusted as their peers. Indeed, there is consensus among all of the major professional organisations in the social science fields.... that being raised by lesbian or gay parents does not adversely affect children's development in any way" (p. 91). Patterson (2006) noted that "the governing body of the American Psychological Association (APA) voted unanimously in favour of a statement that said, "Research has shown that the adjustment, development, and psychological well-being of children is unrelated to parental sexual orientation...." (p. 243). Likewise, Webb and Chonody (2014) stated that "research has found no emotional, developmental, or social differences between children raised by opposite-sex or same-sex parents" (p.414). Some statements are not about "harm" but about *any* differences at all. It might be possible to have differences without harm, but some statements not only deny harm, but also deny any differences. As will be mentioned later, anyone who dared to disagree with such statements for any reason was subject to being criticised in terms such as "irrational", "delusional", "fringe viewpoints", and "outliers", among others. Later, in chapter two, the issue of "harm" will be discussed in more detail.

Scholarly caution abandoned? Why?

Returning to the issue of absolute no differences claimed by many for same-sex parenting, I think that most scholars would normally be far more cautious, if only because one of the basic lessons of statistics is that 5% of the time you may get what appears to be a significant difference (half the time positive, half the time negative) that is actually only due to random chance (Herek, 2006, p. 610), if the null hypothesis is true in the population. Why would scholars take such a risk? After all, it might take only *one* study to prove such an absolute statement to be incorrect.

I am suggesting that, perhaps following the ideas of Hirschman (2016), those absolute claims were made in an attempt to impress courts with the utter harmlessness (no "difference" = no harm) of gay and lesbian parenting in order to promote the legalisation of same-sex marriage (which may have either created more inequality than it solved (Schumm, 2004b, c; 2015c) or potentially harmed heterosexual marriage (Hawkins

& Carroll, 2015; Wardle, 2015)) – and it seems to have worked! As Mezey (2015, p. 38) and Baunach (2012) have noted, U. S. public opinion (for international opinion, see Smith (2016)) about same-sex marriage became much more favourable by 2010 or so. Why? Perhaps we can note that Patterson (2006) pointed out that the research finding of no differences with respect to outcomes of gay parenting had been "used to inform legal and public policy debates across the country", had been "cited in amicus briefs filed by the American Psychological Association (APA) in cases dealing with adoption, child custody, and also in cases related to the legality of marriages between same-sex partners" and that "Psychologists serving as expert witnesses have presented findings on these issues in many different courts" (p. 243). Marks (2012, p. 736, footnote 12) noted that an APA publication on same-sex parenting (2005, p. 3) had been designed to help "parties in family law cases" (p. 3). Bos, van Balen, and van den Boom (2005) likewise stated that much of the research on same-sex families had been "designed to evaluate judicial presumptions about the negative consequences for the psychological health and well being of the children in these families" (p. 272).

More recently, Bos, Kuyper, and Gartrell (2017) stated that their findings about same-sex parenting were "pertinent" to "court officials" among others (p. 1) and that "It is also incumbent upon court officials and policymakers to be current on population-based researching concerning same-sex parenting experiences and child outcomes so that custody and placement decisions, as well as legislative and policy proposals, reflect accurate and up-to-date findings" (p. 14). Mason (2018) has argued that the U.S. Supreme Court legalised same-sex marriage because it wanted to protect the children of same-sex couples (rather than letting them remain second-class citizens) and because same-sex couples were proven by science to be just as good as heterosexual couples with respect to raising children. Thus, questions of *difference* (and if difference, then *harm?*) were foundational to arguments for or against same-sex marriage. As Mason (2018) has noted, the apparent consensus "of the social science literature" was that "same-sex marriage and parenting do not harm children" (p. 89).

As Kuran and Sunstein (1999) have noted, "Even in academic scholarship, arguments gain validity by force of repetition" regardless of their factual accuracy. Furthermore, "The objectively weaker side may triumph simply by exploiting the right cognitive biases, timing its campaigns skillfully, and pressuring the right social groups, thereby putting in motion an availability cascade in its favor" (p.714). To disagree with the arguments associated with such an availability cascade, "To call for caution in interpreting the data, even to question their validity was to risk fierce and widespread criticism" (p. 694) and to risk "being suspected of insensitivity to human suffering" (p.701). They note that "The ultimate outcome can be a widely shared judgment based on little information" (p.722). Potential critics "may choose to keep quiet, or even to join the dominant chorus, simply to be left alone" (p.725). While Kuran and Sunstein recognise that public policy "should rest on sound knowledge of relevant evidence" and "the purely factual judgments of scientific experts" (p.737), they also acknowledge that "availability cascades often spread falsehoods that overwhelm sound scientific reports" (p. 737). Thus, in the long term, "even if subsequent scientific evidence discredits the information that triggered the cascade", the "associated policies may endure" (p. 743). Ultimately, "Judges are subject to the availability heuristic, vulnerable to informational biases, and responsive to reputational incentives. All this leaves them open to the influences of availability cascades" (p.765). My point of quoting Kuran and Sunstein at length is that science can be corrupted by the repetition of limited or even false information which can lead to poor public policy decisions or even judicial decisions.

If the "no difference" scientific claims were true, then I think courts would have had few options for disagreeing with arguments in favour of same-sex marriage; my view is that social science theory would have been another consideration, as I will discuss later. It appears that, in fact, the claims were accepted by most courts in the United States and many elsewhere, both reflecting and creating public opinion and law about same-sex marriage and parenting (Armenia & Troia, 2017; Baunach, 2012; Mason, 2018, p. 94; Smith, 2016). If there has been no one willing to investigate and consider challenging such statements (and certainly there have been very few, e.g., Nock, 2001; Allen, 2015), then the courts may have felt they had no option except to accept such statements, even if they were not factually correct. This book is an opportunity for readers to determine *for themselves* the actual facts and to consider for themselves how honest or dishonest researchers have been with those facts in the past through early 2018.

Organisation of the book

What is the organisation of this book? After this introductory chapter, we will look into theory about moral development as it may pertain to issues of human sexuality and other moral decisions (chapter two). I will discuss some important methodological concerns in chapter three. After this introduction, in Part Two we will look into how same-sex *parental relationships* may differ from heterosexual parent relationships. Then in Part Three we will look into how *outcomes for children* of same-sex parents, with respect to the related topics of sexual orientation, gender identity and gender roles, may or may not differ than those for children of heterosexual parents. In Part Four, we will focus on other outcomes for children in terms of issues such as mental health and education. In Part Five, we will take a look at the question of whether same-sex marriage might have had any negative impacts on U.S. society as a whole. In Part Six, we will review the findings from the previous parts of the book and then conclude with an epilogue.

Organisation within chapters

Within each chapter, from chapters four to twelve, we will look at what has been said in the past by scholars, what the facts are, consider limitations of the research and/or counterarguments, what we do not yet know that needs further research, and what conclusions may be drawn. In many cases, it will be clear that most scholars have argued in favour of the "no differences" hypothesis, which claims that there are absolutely no differences between gay or lesbian parents and heterosexual parents or that there are no differences between the children of same-sex parents compared to children of heterosexual parents. In some cases, scholars have argued that same-sex parents and their children are doing *better* than heterosexual parents and their children (Biblarz & Stacey, 2010a; Gates, 2011). After sharing some of what scholars have argued with respect to the "no difference" hypothesis, we will look at research (if there is any) that does not support a "no difference" hypothesis, as well as some that may support it. In the limitations section, we will consider issues that limit our ability to draw firm conclusions about the research and perhaps counter-arguments that could be made against our claims. In the future research section of each chapter, we will consider issues that need further exploration or raise questions that remain to be answered about same-sex parenting or its possible outcomes for children, including things we would like to understand but do not understand at present. Finally, we will summarise what we have found for that particular area of research on same-sex parenting or the outcomes for children.

Appendices

There are five appendices to this book. Appendix A features a list of my publications in this area of research. Appendix B answers any critics who might want to argue that I have been "discredited" as a scholar (e.g., Straumsheim, 2013). Appendix C lists some examples of what has happened to some conservative scholars who dared to challenge the "no difference" hypothesis with respect to same-sex parenting, which may help the reader understand why scholarly criticism with regard to much of the same-sex parenting literature has been relatively rare, although there have been a few reviews (compared to more than 50 favourable reviews) of the literature (e.g., Allen, 2015; Belcastro, Bramlich, Nicholson, Price, & Wilson, 1993; Cameron, 2009; Destro, 2012; Marks, 2012; Schumm, 2016b; Wardle, 1997, 2015) by scholars willing to look more deeply into both sides of the issues. Appendix D lists some of the major research methodology issues that have been relevant to research on same-sex parenting. Appendix E lists some issues I have observed with how social science research has been presented in the U.S. court system during same-sex marriage or parenting trials.

Threats to Science

Before proceeding, I want to remind readers that this book is also about a theme that is much larger than anything to do same-sex parenting. Herek (2010), a leading gay scholar, has stated that "the public looks to science for answers" and it remains very important for scientists to do "everything possible to ensure that research findings are accurately communicated to the lay public and to policy makers" (p. 697; Schumm, 2013, p. 427). Yet, it will be my contention that science as an enterprise has been thrown "under the bus" in the interests of politics in this area of study, which may hint that similar challenges to the validity of science may have occurred or may be ongoing in other areas of science, especially in more controversial areas. Essentially, I am concerned that if political bias can creep into social science in this topic area (Redding, 2001, 2013), how certain can we be that similar types of bias have not crept into *other* controversial areas of science?

My opponents, however, may resort to the complaint that if research was as bad as it may seem by my standards, then "the vast majority of research in child development, and in the field of psychology more broadly, would have to be dismissed as unscientific" (Cooper & Cates, 2006, p. 90). To that I reply that I am not saying all social science research is corrupted, but I think that if it can be corrupted in one area, it is possible that it could be corrupted in others. A funny kind of situation is created in which Paul Cameron is accused of setting the bar of science too low (by Cooper and Cates, 2006, p. 30-31) while I may be accused of setting it too high (Schumm, 2010c). One has to wonder: which "bar" is worse, the bar "too low" or the bar "too high"? If we were only dealing with porridge, perhaps the "bar in the middle" would be fine, but we are dealing with *science* where the *highest* standards should be upheld rather than being excused away for the sake of expediency or politics, in my opinion. If any of my critics want to argue for lower scientific standards, go for it – let us all know where you stand!

Can science be compromised?

If science is compromised, then an important way of looking at the world, though not the only one, has been compromised. If it can be compromised in this area of controversy, how can we be sure it is not being compromised in other controversial areas?

Is science merely being sold to the most vocal or wealthy sponsor? On one occasion I was asked to be an expert witness for a trial and was told to testify to several bad things about lesbian, gay, bisexual, or transgender (LGBT) persons; I told the sponsor that I could not do that because the scientific evidence did *not* support those particular conclusions. I was immediately fired and lost, potentially, thousands of dollars in expert fees. As we shall see below, the assumption seemed to be that I was being paid, so I should say whatever the sponsor wanted me to say, the scientist being a complete servant of any political agency with enough money. I refused to take the money, but how often have other scientists accepted it, even if it meant trashing science itself in the process? Much of social science is being paid for by organisations with political objectives (from both left and right on the political spectrum). I think that means that readers need to be cautious about accepting evidence largely paid for by one side or the other. Since I have been funded by organisations on the conservative side of the spectrum you have a reasonable question if you ask how that may have biased my research. Questions need to be asked: which researcher(s) seem to have reviewed the literature most thoroughly? Which ones seem to have dissected the data more carefully? Which ones seem to acknowledge the complexity of research the most and acknowledge evidence from both sides of the fence, so to speak? Which ones cite their potential or actual critics the most? My hope is that when you compare the contents of this book in terms of breadth and depth, you will find it comparing well against similar books by scholars (e.g., Golombok, 2015; Ball, 2016) on the more progressive side of the political spectrum.

Quick overview of the book

For readers who want a quick summary of the contents of this book, the major argument over the past three or four decades has been that same-sex parents and the outcomes for their children are no different than those for heterosexual parents (as well as the idea that homosexuality itself is morally neutral and should be accepted as socially equivalent to heterosexuality)(Patterson, 2000, 2006, 2009a, 2017). In fact, some scholars have recently argued that outcomes are *better* for children of same-sex parents than for children of heterosexual parents with the idea that two mothers will parent more effectively than a mother and a father or that two gay fathers may parent well enough to prove that even a mother is not important (or at least not essential) for a child's development (Biblarz & Stacey, 2010a; Golombok, 2015, p. 198; Miller, Kors, & Macfie, 2017). Elsewhere I have detailed the many statements made by scholars that lesbians make better mothers than heterosexual couples and that children do not need a parent of each gender (Schumm, 2011a). Recently, this has been extended to the idea that "Biological links are not necessary for (nor do they ensure) normal child development" (Patterson, 2017, p. 47), despite some recent evidence to the contrary (Sullins, 2015a; Reczek, Spiker, Liu, & Crosnoe, 2016) or that homosexuality is a preferable way of life for adolescents because it would reduce unwanted pregnancies (Rosky, 2013a, b).

In this book I will examine and report those outcomes in more detail than have most scholars. The results will show, at the very least, that the situation is more complicated than many have allowed or, at the worst, that much of the way in which the research has been interpreted has been biased in favour of progressive values. I will show that there are both significant and substantial differences in a variety of areas with respect to both same-sex parenting in general and with respect to the outcomes for children, which I think overturns the so-called research consensus in this area of science and contradicts the views of hundreds, maybe even thousands, of professional social scientists as well as probably dozens of scholarly professional organisations.

How can I do that? How dare I do that? From a debate perspective, it would have been a lot more difficult if my critics had said things like "Research in this area is complex" or "The limitations of the research in this area hinder our ability to draw conclusions strong enough to influence policy". I might have agreed with my critics if they had made such careful statements. Fortunately for me, the statements were more like "No study has ever found any differences associated with same-sex parents or their parenting" – a type of statement which is much easier to refute than the former types of statements. Also, fortunately, such statements were not the realm of a few scientists on the extremes but were echoed by dozens of scholars across the globe and by many international professional social science, and therapeutic organisations. Were they right? Am I wrong? Read on!

Note
[1] Technically, two sisters who both lost their husbands and decided to pool resources into a common home would be same-sex parents. An older mother and her adult daughter who decide to foster a child together would also be same-sex parents (in one study, we found that a third of the "same-sex" foster parents were not lesbians, but mother/daughter pairs raising a foster child). It is possible that those using Census data can become confused at this point between gay or lesbian parents and other types of "same-sex" parents (Durso and Gates, 2013, p. 38; Gates, 2013a, p. 230; DiBennardo & Gates, 2014) with as many as 28-40% of "same-sex" couples in the 2000 and the 2010 U.S. Census resulting from heterosexual couples reporting one person's gender in error (O'Connell & Feliz, 2011). However, I will use the term "same-sex" parenting to refer to two lesbian mothers or two gay fathers raising children or to gay male or lesbian single parents. There is also the possibility of gay male or lesbian parents being part of a mixed-sex marriage or relationship, but the research on that type of parenting, possibly involving bisexuals, is so rare (Haney-Caron & Heilbrun, 2014, p. 20; Patterson, 2017, p. 47 referring to bisexual parents; Tasker & Delvoye, 2015) that it cannot be considered herein. The situation of transgender parents will be left to others, as well (McGuire, Kuvalanka, Catalpa, & Toomey, 2016).

Chapter Two

Social Science Theory

The Threat to Traditional Sexual Morality

Some readers may be wondering how the world got turned upside down in so many ways with respect to human sexuality in the sexual revolution or what some are calling the Second Demographic Transition (Lesthaeghe, 2010, 2014). Although this book is primarily about scientific evidence, I will try to tie in sound theory into my analysis here. In this chapter I will discuss a social science theory we developed call TPEX, for Time Preference Social Exchange Theory (Nazarinia, Schumm, & Britt, 2014). I will also discuss the theoretical issues of harm vs. difference and whether fathers are important to their children or not so much. But, first, some background on the history of and reasons for same-sex marriage.

Background – the meaning of marriage

So, *how* did the sexual revolution, especially with respect to homosexuality, succeed to date? First, there was a determined and scientifically sound effort (from a public relations perspective) to promote homosexuality and then same-sex marriage (Kirk & Madsen, 1990), using a variety of psychological and public relations techniques to influence public opinion (Morgan, 2014, p. 77). One of the key methods was to marginalise anyone who dared challenge the science in this area, making critics look like simple, ignorant bigots, perhaps even mentally ill (e.g., a *homophobic* bigot). However, the basic premise was the promotion of homosexuality.

As Mason (2018) notes, the promotion of same-sex marriage was not so much intrinsic but as a means to an end – "The vast majority of their respondents [pro-gay activists] instead cited marriage as a *tool* for achieving other political aims such as protesting discrimination and publicly denouncing heteronormativity and homophobia" (p. 87). As she noted again, for many, the goal was not to promote inclusion of same-sex couples in traditional marriage but rather to help "*queer* that institution – that is, to upend its conservative traditions and radically reshape it" (p. 5). These techniques appear to have succeeded in terms of changing public opinion in favour of same-sex marriage (Baunach, 2012; Smith, 2016), even though for many the real goal was making homosexuality more acceptable to the public and changing the very nature of marriage itself. One might say: well, I am not keen on homosexuality itself, but I don't see how legalising same-sex marriage will harm anyone. But, what might it mean to "queer" marriage? Green (2010) illuminates this question by discussing how many of his LGBT research participants looked forward to marriage because marriage would give them the security to have sex with other persons with less risk of breaking up their relationships. In other words, it was not about the right to marry as much as using marriage as a tool to make the practice of the sexual revolution more acceptable and less risky.

The incongruity of this is seen if a heterosexual man were to tell his female fiancée, "Honey, I just can't wait to marry you, so I can feel more secure in having sex with lots of other women. If I get any of them pregnant, I'm sure you'll be delighted to share your hard-earned salary (and mine, too, of course) with these other women because you love new babies so much, especially if they are mine but not yours." Does anyone think the average heterosexual woman (if any of them) would be delighted with hearing that? For myself, I doubt it. That means that two different definitions of the purpose of marriage are being created, one for LGBT persons and another for heterosexual persons: one group "free" in terms of sexual freedom and the other not, because of the risks of pregnancy, inside or outside of marriage.

The meaning of happiness

Elsewhere (Schumm, 1999), I postulated that there were four types of positive emotional affect: pleasure, satisfaction, happiness, and joy, in that order, with the lasting impact of each type of effect being longer for those to the right (e.g., joy longer than pleasure). I suggested that pleasure was most often related to tangible inputs (food, drink, sensual touch, etc.). Satisfaction as a term is derived from Latin for "do enough" and pertains to getting what you expect out of a transaction or deal; if you get what you think you deserved in the trade, you will be satisfied. Happiness was keyed to having positive relationships with others while joy was related to more transcendent, often spiritual, experiences. The idea was not that some of these were bad and others good, but that you would gain more in the long run if you traded pleasure for joy or satisfaction for happiness. On the other hand, giving up joy to gain pleasure would often yield a long-term loss for yourself.

TPEX theory

However, second, in the contest between pleasure and joy, pleasure is a tough competitor. Without a long-term view of the rewards and costs of human sexuality for yourself and others, individual pleasure and the perceived individual civil *right to short-term pleasure* may easily become a dominant factor in ethical and legal decision-making. Elsewhere, my colleagues and I (Nazarinia-Roy, Schumm, & Britt, 2014) have presented an exchange theory-based mathematical model of morality (a theory often used in guiding research with sexuality and/or LGBT issues in which one key element is time (which is why we labelled it Time Preference Exchange Theory or TPEX), (Peplau, 1993, p.405; Patterson, 2013b, p.660; Peplau & Beals, 2004; Tolman and Diamond, 2014, pp. 12-13). Time preference refers to delayed gratification in that people makes choices based to some extent on how long it will take for the rewards or costs they expect to occur. If you are willing to wait longer for the expected rewards you may have a longer time preference; or otherwise, you might have a shorter time preference. While it appears that a majority (73%) of research papers on same-sex parenting have not included any major theoretical perspective (Farr, Tasker, & Goldberg, 2016), I wanted to present a framework (TPEX) that has guided my interpretation of much of the literature.

Type A and D decisions

In TPEX theory (Figure 1), there are some decisions (type A) that result in positive outcomes in both the short run and the long run for everyone concerned. Eating healthy foods that taste good now and promote your better health in the long run would represent a Type A decision. There may be some decisions that are precisely the opposite (Type D). Those two types of decisions are pretty straightforward and seldom controversial.

Type B decisions

However, what makes life interesting are the other two types. One type of decision (Type B) provides apparent positive *short term* benefits but often has *long-term* negative outcomes, even if the decision-maker was led to believe that the long-term outcomes would be neutral or positive. Using illegal drugs would be a type B decision – you may feel wonderful in the short run but run a higher *probability* (i.e., not a certainty) of adverse long-term outcomes, not to mention possible addiction to the drug(s). Proving the harm of type B decisions is a challenge because some individuals may make type B decisions (e.g., smoking three packs of cigarettes a day for fifty years) and not seem to suffer any harms in the short term, perhaps not even after a period of several decades.

Notably, however, Hofmann and Vohs (2016) have stated that "In fact, the consequences of poor desire regulation" (i.e., from a TPEX perspective, type B decision-making) "can be enormous, especially viewed from a societal level. It has been suggested, for instance, that 40%

of deaths in the United States each year are associated with behaviors that are at least partially due to the way people deal with desires, including those for unhealthy foods, tobacco, alcohol, unprotected sex, aggressive urges, and illicit drugs" (p. 76).

Type of Decision	Short-term Outcomes	Long-term Outcomes	From a Short-Term Perspective	From a Long-Term Perspective
"A"	Positive	Positive	A = B	A = C
"B"	Positive	Negative	B = A	B = D
"C"	Negative	Positive	C = D	C = A
"D"	Negative	Negative	D = C	D = B

Figure 1. TPEX Typology

That list covers a lot of type B decisions! And it shows how type B decisions are often very costly in a very personal sense to individuals, to their neighbours, and to the larger society, even if a few individuals appear to escape any negative consequences of such decisions. Type B decisions, especially in contrast to Type A or C decisions, are probably related to lower levels of self-control. Laird, Marks and Marrero (2011) defined self-control as "a person's capacity to override and inhibit socially unacceptable and undesirable impulses and to regulate one's behaviors, thoughts, and emotions" (p. 78). They go on to state that "individuals with low self-control are expected to engage in more antisocial behavior than individuals with high self-control because they tend to consider immediate benefits for themselves while failing to consider the long term consequences of their actions and how their actions may affect others" (p. 78).

Type C decisions

Another type of decision (Type C) involves short-term sacrifices or costs but yields long-term positive benefits, even if some of the time those benefits turn out to be posthumous; you may need to have positive expectations with respect to future outcomes in order to be willing to accept such short-term risks associated with type C decisions. Saving or investing for the future would be a type C decision – you cannot enjoy the money now, but you will probably have more money in the future when you may need it more. Type C decisions may be a major key to what distinguishes humans from other animals. Balter (2008) has stated that "our ability to trade immediate gratification for long-term rewards sets us apart from other, more impulsive animals. Without patience, activities from planting crops for later harvest to sending space probes to Mars would be impossible" (p.404). In other words, our ability to make difficult type C decisions is what largely sets us as humans apart from other animals.

Even Mason (2018) implicitly acknowledged the importance of type C decision-making, describing the ideal of (heterosexual) parenting in which "this ideal demands that people in the present make sacrifices, often to the detriment of their own [present] freedom, on behalf of imagined future generations. And in the legal system, the appeal to child well being lets courts weigh – even favour – the State's hypothetical future interests (embodied in its future citizens, children) over and against the actual interests of its marginalized citizens" (p.89). Mason probably did not realise it, but she was describing the difference between type C and type B decision-making. In other words, those foolish courts were trying to privilege type C decision-making over type B decision-making – how unjust of them (in Mason's apparent opinion)! Was not the point of Aesop's fable about the ant and the grasshopper (see Sowell, 1993, pp.5-6) that the wise ant made a type C decision to store up food for winter while the grasshopper lived a type B lifestyle, enjoying life in the "now" but forgetting to plan for the future? Of course, the grasshopper did not think it was "fair" that the ant hesitated to equalise their benefits and help the grasshopper escape the natural consequences of its earlier decisions when the ant had done all the work as well as the long-term planning. From the grasshopper's perspective, equality was a matter of equal outcomes, regardless of unequal risks taken, work done or advance planning made. Mason (2018) seems to be saying, in my view, that courts should focus on equality of outcomes, catering to the grasshopper's perspective rather that of the ant in that fable.

Application of Type C decisions in understanding marriage

Because of the inherent gender differences between the parties in heterosexual couples, their willingness to enter into marriage may well be a type C decision (Schumm, 2005, p. 460; McGraw, 2000, pp. 40-43). McGraw, for example, stated that "there are serious limits to how successful mixed-gender couples can become at being compatible because of their biologically and socially determined gender differences" (pp. 41-42). Likewise, Judith Stacey (2003), a very progressive scholar, acknowledged that "same-sex couples tend to be more compatible than heterosexual couples" and that they "share more interests and time together than married [opposite-sex] couples" (p. 164) (Schumm, 2004c, p. 1205). Books such as *Men are from Mars, Women are from Venus* (Gray, 1992) and *You just don't understand: Women and men in conversation* (Tannen, 1991) sell well because they reflect actual and perceived gender differences in communication between men and women.

Boon and Alderson (2009) interviewed women who had been married to men and then left their husbands for other women; those women reported greater freedom from restrictive gender roles and more equal sharing of responsibilities because of some of the benefits they gained by becoming attached to another woman rather than to a man. The same women also reported enhanced sexual satisfaction and greater emotional intimacy, as well as greater sexual freedom, in their same-sex relationships. Gender inequities in heterosexual marriage, especially in terms of sexuality, have been thought to detract from marital satisfaction for women since Bernard (1972) published her book on gender differences in marriage (as noted by Balsam *et al.* (2008), Leckey (2014), and Waller and McLanahan (2005); Schumm, 2015c, p.11). There are important differences between men and women in how they respond to conflict, how they view conflict, and how they respond to conflict physiologically, leading Kurdek (2001) to conclude that mixed-gender relationships often become "bastions of inequality, unfairness, and clashing perspectives" (p.729) (Schumm, 2015c, p.14).

It seems clear that men and women differ substantially in terms of their attitudes about sexuality and their sexual behaviours (Peplau, 2003), with men desiring sex more than women, which creates a loss of relational power for men (Baumeister, Catanese, & Vohs, 2001; Santilla, Wager, Witting, Harlaar, Jern, Johansson, Varjonen, & Sandnabba, 2008). Baumeister *et al.* (2001) indicated that "if one gender differs from the other in average strength of sex drive, pervasive patterns of potential conflict could result" (p.242), while Elliott and Umberson (2008) report that it is common for opposite-sex couples to experience much "conflict around sex" (p.391). Solomon *et al.* (2005) found that married heterosexual women significantly more frequently reported "refusing to have sex" with their husbands than did lesbians with their partners, while married men reported "refusing to have sex" much less frequently than did gay men. Peplau, Fingerhut, and Beals (2004) concluded that gay men and lesbians may have greater sexual satisfaction because of gay males having sex more often than heterosexual men or because of lesbians have higher quality sex than heterosexual women. Shechory and Ziv (2007) summarised literature (p.631) to conclude that women were more likely to feel underbenefitted in heterosexual marriage while men felt overbenefitted; either way, inequitable conditions can lead to depression or reduced marital satisfaction. In their study, Shechory and Ziv found that lesbians tended to see their relationships as equitable in contrast to heterosexual couples and to gay male couples for which there was more frequent inequity. Mezey (2008, p.71) reached similar conclusions that LG persons were better off than heterosexuals because they could side-step many gender-related conflicts and avoid costs inherent in pregnancy or at least unwanted pregnancy. Kaesar (1999) quoted one gay man as saying that the difficulty in having children was "the only truly negative thing about being gay" (p.65). Actress Cynthia

Nixon, who lived as a heterosexual for decades and then developed a relationship with a woman in her 40s, stated that, "I've been straight and I've been gay, and gay is better" (Diamond & Rosky, 2016, p. 382).

In summary, biological differences, as well as social differences, between men and women tend to present their own challenges in a number of ways, putting heterosexual marriage into more of a type C decision in which society may accrue long-term benefits at the short-term expense of the opposite-sex individuals involved. In the past, courts recognised the inherent sacrifices that biology and society virtually forced upon heterosexuals, especially those who wanted children, and were open to providing them with various forms of compensation for those risks, costs and limitations on their freedoms. But, by deciding to reward everyone equally, regardless of the risks, costs or loss of freedoms, the courts, in my assessment, have *created* inequality (in terms of legal benefits relative to risks and costs) for the many in order to create an apparent equality of outcomes for a few. From the progressive perspective, it is easy to claim that society has denigrated "same-sex sexuality as inherently inferior to heterosexuality" (Diamond & Rosky, 2016, p. 380). What such claims overlook is that perhaps society was not "denigrating" homosexuality as much as attempting to recognise the greater inherent costs and risks involved for heterosexuals who, after all, on average, are providing society with a critically necessary and greater fertility benefit (enabling the society to continue down the generations) relative to homosexuals.

For example, Mason (2018) described a court's sarcastic view that "Homosexual couples do not produce unwanted children; their reward is to be denied the right to marry. Go figure" (p. 91). What the court missed was right under their nose – that heterosexuals inherently, because of natural biology, entertain the risk and costs of unwanted pregnancy (and the costs and risks associated with the time, cost and effort to avoid unwanted pregnancies; as well as the risks a heterosexual woman faces if her husband impregnates other women) unlike homosexuals; the legal benefits of marriage compensated them (in the past) in part for having to bear those types of risks, among many others. Denying the costs and risks of heterosexuality may well have the effect of turning heterosexuals and their children into the actual "second-class citizens" in terms of no longer getting the respect they deserve for the extra risks they take and costs they assume, ultimately for the sake of society's long-term outcomes. Another way of looking at such issues is the "playing by the same rules" approach. When a man marries a woman, it is not in her financial or biological interest for him to have sex with other fertile women because any births by him to other women will detract from the first wife's resources (financial and emotional most likely). Therefore, I believe that societies tended to develop a rule about sexual fidelity in order to minimise the long-term downsides of sexual infidelity (itself looking pretty much like a type B decision). Along come same-sex couples who want the same benefits as heterosexual couples but want to play (and biologically can play) by different rules because, for them, there are no risks of pregnancy. Thus, they don't want to play by the same rules or take the same risks, but they want the same benefits of the game. Isn't the whole point possibly of teaching sports to young people to train them in playing in systems using the same rules and having rewards for following those rules and penalties for not following those rules?

This may be why Mason (2018) wants to *queer* marriage, to make things the same for all by changing the rules for all – for example, making sexual fidelity optional and sexual infidelity acceptable (also see Morgan, 2014, pp. 24, 101, 107). On the surface, this looks like greater equality due to more similar rules. However, the consequences of violating the rules would appear to put heterosexuals at greater risk than gay men or lesbians due to the fertility risks for heterosexual encounters. The rules may appear more equal, but the risks remain unequal. The net result is that some may feel that greater equality has been attained, but in reality, more inequality may have been created by same-sex marriage legalisation. Similarly to Mason (2018), Bosisio and Ronfani (2016) see the legalisation of same-sex parenting as contributing in a positive way to "deconstructing the primacy of the biogenetic connection as the fundamental element of kinship and family ties" (p. 460). As one of the Italian children they interviewed, a 12-year-old girl who had two lesbian mothers, put it, "Having two moms is better than having a mom and a dad" (p. 462). Some may think that I am opposed to same-sex marriage because I am a conservative or because I am somehow "religious", but my view is that my primary concern is when courts create inequality by treating things that are different as if they were the same in terms of short and long-term costs, risks, and benefits. If it were possible to have legal same-sex marriage and not create such inequalities, I might well be fine with it. My challenge to others would be to ask "How will you create equality for heterosexuals given the greater risks and costs they entail for the sake of providing greater fertility (and other) benefits for their societies?" It remains an open question whether access to legal marriage will improve the mental health of same-sex couples or parents. LeBlanc, Frost, and Bowen (2018) recently found (Table 3, p. 404) that three separate aspects of mental health were not significantly related to whether same-sex couples were legally married; even the effect sizes were very small, less than .20 (.16, .10, and .06), though in the direction of predicting better mental health. At the same time, when same-sex couples were in legal unions other than marriage (registered domestic partnerships or civil unions), that status was significantly (p < .01) associated with worse mental health with an effect size of 0.46 for all three measures of mental health. It is also possible that having better mental health is itself selective for getting married, so the causality could be operating in either or both directions with opposite effects cancelling each other out.

Importance in TPEX theory of long-term perspectives

If you do not look at life from a long-term perspective, Type A and B decisions (as well as Type C and D decisions) will look identical; yet if you look at life from a long-term perspective, Type A and C decisions are similar while Types C and D are very different (Figure 1). Human sexuality is an area for which type B decisions come very easily because the short-term benefits of sex, which can have the power and pleasure similar to a drug addiction, can easily outweigh (emotionally, at least) most long-term (more cognitive) considerations. In some sense, marriage may have developed as a way to convert sexual interaction from a Type B issue into a Type A issue. Cultures that required dowries or other pre-marital sacrifices may have been trying to convert Type B issues into Type C issues. One of our cultural conflicts is whether human sexuality in general (and perhaps homosexuality in particular as a part of human sexuality) is, on average or in most cases, a Type B or a Type A or C process. This impacts social science research in that looking at a decision only in the short run may mean overlooking long-run consequences. In terms of parenting, what seems to work for a few years when children are younger may not work so well in the long run, when children have become adolescents or young adults.

Our cultural struggle

Thus, I think we are engaged in a great cultural struggle over which types of decisions are optimal for society and which types of decisions society should encourage among our citizens – Types A and C versus Types B and D. This struggle is more than accepting or rejecting our TPEX model. This model doesn't require "religion" to order to be a logical model, so we think it is independent of religion even if many religions would see its value. However, some civil libertarians may want society to equate the various types of decisions, regardless of their long-term outcomes.[1] If considerations of long-term outcomes are ruled "out of order" or a mere product of "bias" or "religion", then, in my opinion, decision-making for that society is going to become far more complicated and far less effective in the long run.

Distinguishing harm versus difference

A second important theoretical issue involves the distinction between difference and harm. Difference is a scientific word that can be clearly defined as a small to large effect size, which might be as low as 0.10 or as high as 5.00 or more. If professor X says there is no difference and I show there is an effect size of 0.25, then I have found evidence that professor X was incorrect, even if the result was not statistically significant (remember Cuijpers (2017) identified an effect size of .24 or larger as clinically relevant). That is pretty clear cut. If professor X can show that when that effect is entered into a meta-analysis with other effects and the overall result is not significant according to the meta-analysis, then professor X could rebut my claim. That is pretty clear cut, too. In other words, there are relatively clear scientific criteria for determining "difference".

But if professor X and I agree that the effect size is 0.50 and significant, but he/she argues there is no harm in that difference, now we are in much more difficult territory. Proving difference is relatively easy and straightforward but proving harm is much more problematic, mainly because there is no clear answer or criteria for what level of difference, if indeed any, would "prove" harm. For example, consider the use of illegal drugs. What level of illegal drug use would it take to prove "harm"? If the children of same-sex parents used 20% more illegal drugs at age 17 than a comparable group of children of heterosexual parents, would that "prove" harm? What about 50% more? What about 200% more? What about 60% versus 21%, nearly triple the rate?

I would not be surprised if some scholars would argue that if *every* child of same-sex parents used illegal drugs before turning age 18 that would not prove harm, even compared to *no use ever* among children of heterosexual parents, bringing out arguments such as (1) illegal doesn't mean harmful, (2) any harm was only due to stigmatisation for using drugs, (3) any harm would cease once the drug use ceased, so any harm was only minor or temporary, (4) drug use was "normative" within the culture, so it was not really a problem, (5) the harmfulness of drugs might pertain to children of heterosexual parents but not necessarily to the children of same-sex parents, (6) drug use was permitted by the government for some religions, so how can it be harmful for anyone else? (7) drug use is only a problem if done while operating equipment unsafely, (8) making illegal drugs legal would solve any issues of harm, (9) if more people die in vehicle crashes while under the effects of illegal drugs, that is the fault of not having crash-proof cars, or (10) showing how some people can use drugs without any apparent effects (if so, why would they use them?) so why imply that they are harmful to all if they are harmful only to a few? I am sure there might be some that would argue that use of illegal drugs was a protected constitutional right, even if such use caused physical harm or increased risks to the user or to others. That list is just for starters – I could concoct many more similar counter-arguments making illegal drug use look acceptable from a social science and/or legal point of view.

Evelyn Hooker (1957, p. 30; see Schumm, 2012b, p. 470) may have begun this sort of tradition in the 1950s when she argued that if 29 of her 30 homosexual men had been mentally ill compared to only one of her 30 heterosexual men, that would have proven that there wasn't any intrinsic association between homosexuality and mental illness and therefore it was essentially of no "harm".

My point is that once "proof of harm" becomes the standard for the judiciary, hardly anyone could ever prove harm scientifically because the side claiming "no harm" could put forth a list of excuses or exceptions essentially forever and there would be no firm criteria by which "harm" could be demonstrated or not demonstrated as agreed upon by both sides (maybe not even by the judge) in the case. If no degree of evidence can be agreed upon as evidence of "harm", then any statements about "harm" become essentially meaningless except to keep the opposing side from ever being able to win their case.

In summary, I question the scientific credibility of the use of "harm" as an outcome measure, because it is difficult to define in the first place in a way that would be acceptable to all sides of a debate and because some harms are a matter of probability and mainly in terms of long-term outcomes. In other words, a person could get drunk and drive a car wildly down a road. But until he hits something or someone, is any harm done? If he does damage something or hurt himself, was it his fault or was it the fault of his car not having the right type of bumpers or air bags? Perhaps some nights, he gets home safely, ostensibly showing that driving drunk is not intrinsically or inevitably harmful. Despite such counter arguments, most States have laws against drunk driving as it is considered to be a risky (type B) action for both the drunk driver and other nearby drivers (and their friends and families if they are injured or killed). Consequently, the focus of this book will be on assessing "difference" rather than "harm".

Conclusions

So, what are the implications of these theoretical issues? First, I think you need to distinguish between issues of difference and issues of harm. The former can be tested scientifically and clearly so, while the latter may be far more difficult to define or to prove. Second, TPEX theory suggests that just because there appear to be no differences in the short run, does not mean there may not be differences in the long run. There may even be adverse results in the short run but much better results in the long run. Applied to raising children, some techniques might look good in the short run or even seem effective, but might prove to be a disadvantage in the long run. Some outcomes of parenting may not "show up" until the child is older. Furthermore, TPEX theory would suggest that an important goal of parenting is teaching children about decision-making along TPEX lines and that what seems pleasurable for the moment may have negative long-term consequences that should be taken into account when making decisions. One important goal of parenting may be to teach children greater self-control, to manage their emotions in ways that promote building positive relationships in the long run. A considerable body of research suggests that learning delayed gratification as a child is a key factor in better outcomes as an adult (Nazarinia, Schumm, & Britt, 2014). This ties into research on same-sex parenting because what is *missing* from research may be as critical as what has been studied. In the case of same-sex parenting, very little research has focused on children learning skills such as delayed gratification, self-control, or emotional regulation, despite the great importance of such skills. Finally, many of the contributions of fathers may have been overlooked in the research literature since their contributions from a TPEX theoretical perspective have seldom been studied.

Note

[1] Those who do not agree with TPEX theory have several options open for "discrediting" it. One would be to redefine B decisions as A decisions. Another would be to minimise the long-term negatives associated with type B decisions or attribute them to a failure "to take precautions" rather than making an unwise or high risk decision in the first place. Since matters of social science are rarely 100% determined but appear to be a matter of probability over time, some type B decisions may not immediately lead to negative outcomes, supporting the idea that perhaps the anticipated "negatives" are not really there. A third approach would be to blame negative outcomes on societal or religious bias rather than the decision itself as if the adverse outcomes were due to discrimination or stigma imposed on the person (Hatzenbuehler, 2013; Hatzenbuehler, Bellatorre, Lee, Finch, Muennig, & Fiscella, 2014; Hatzenbuehler, Bellatorre, Lee, Finch, Muennig, & Fiscella, 2018; Regnerus, 2017) rather than natural or logical consequences of type B decisions (Morgan, 2014, pp. 29-30). A fourth approach would be to argue that there is really no choice (no decision) involved at all, that the person is unable to decide any other way and cannot help but make type B decisions. A fifth approach is to translate all decision-making into a "liberty" or "freedom of choice" issue, negating any right or responsibility of society to encourage some types of decisions more than others or to stigmatise/punish some types of decisions. If you think about it, all of these approaches have been used by progressives to advance their agendas.

Chapter Three

Methodological Questions

How is Science Done?

What is science? What do we expect scientists to be doing? I think there are at least four things that should characterise good science. If these are sacrificed for the sake of politics, then I think science has been diminished. If these things are not being done, then I think you, the reader, should be skeptical about "scientific" claims.

Comprehensive knowledge

First, I think that scientists should have a well-developed knowledge of their field. When you hear a so-called scientist argue that every piece of research ever done by anyone in any country has supported their view of the world, I think you should be *skeptical*. The chances of that actually being the case are very low. It is far more likely that such a critic is either ignorant of much of the research or knows about it but does not want to advertise differences in order to protect their political or legal view of the world. One example comes to mind – when Biblarz and Stacey (2010a) published a progressive review of the literature on same-sex parenting, they reported only one study (MacCallum & Golombok, 2004) that had found a lower stability rate for same-sex parents. However, if you look at the credits they gave to other scholars who had reviewed their draft manuscript (e.g., Charlotte Patterson), some of those scholars had done research that had *also* found lower stability rates for same-sex parents. In other words, Biblarz and Stacey (2010a) had access to further research

(Fulcher, Chan, Raboy, & Patterson, 2002; Chan, Brooks, Raboy, & Patterson, 1998) that would have supplemented their discussion of the stability of same-sex parents but somehow omitted that information even though it would have bolstered some of their conclusions about relationship instability among lesbian mothers. While I hope that most scholars would have been more hesitant than to derive a conclusion from only one study, Biblarz and Stacey (2010a) did not demonstrate a comprehensive knowledge of the field in that area since they omitted at least one research study of which at least their reviewers were aware as well as some other studies that were available in the field (i.e., those reported by Schumm, 2010e), as well as others discussed later in chapter five. Another recent example similar to Biblarz and Stacey (2010a) is the literature review by Diamond and Rosky (2016). They concluded that same-sex parents might indeed influence the sexual orientation of their children, based on results from only two studies. What is *missing* from their review is that fact that there have been over fifty studies on whether same-sex parents might influence the sexual orientations of their children, not just two (Schumm & Crawford, 2018a). Similarly, Frank (2017) criticised Sullins' research (2016b) and noted how his research group had compiled data from nearly 80 studies on same-sex parenting. What is missing is that my research group has compiled data from over 330 studies on same-sex parenting, but reading Frank (2017) you would never realise that discrepancy in comprehensiveness.

Awareness of conflicting research

Second, I think that scientists should be able to point to research that does and does not support any given research question. I hope you note that I *do* point to some research that does *not* support some of my perspectives in this book. When a so-called scientist cannot point to research or a researcher with whom they disagree without somehow feeling obligated to "discredit" that researcher, I think you should be *skeptical*. Straumsheim (2013) stated that "there is a consensus that same-sex parents aren't better or worse than other parents, and that only a few outliers disagree" (p. 1). Straumsheim could have said only a "few" disagree but chose to add the term "outliers", perhaps as a way of further marginalising those who might disagree. Ball (2016) discusses how one court described those who disagreed with the "no difference" hypothesis as representing a "fringe viewpoint" (p. 139). As another example, recently Patterson and Goldberg (2016) argued that the researchers who had disagreed with them about same-sex parenting had (presumably all) been *discredited*. Why cannot a good scientist allow others to disagree without feeling, apparently, an urgent need to "discredit", "marginalise", or, to invent a new term, to "outlier" them? If someone is so concerned about minorities (of any type) being marginalised, why would you be so eager to join in *that same sort of process* with respect to others with whom you might disagree?

Being a good scientist means, in my opinion, being aware of more than one side of an issue – and giving opponents credit in your works. For example, Golombok (2015), in her popular book on new family forms, mentioned only one conservative critic (Allen, 2013), leaving an impression for the average reader that there are virtually no scholars who have ever disagreed with her assessment of the literature about new types of families. Similar lack of detail has occurred in other popular books (e.g., Ball, 2016; Mezey, 2015). I suspect if one of my readers wanted to check this, you would find that I am far more likely to quote progressive scholars than they are to quote either myself or other conservative scholars. Furthermore, if you check my writings, I do not think you will find me labelling my critics as "discredited" or "outliers" or even "bad people". Nor do I accuse them of being irrational or delusional. It is easy to throw around accusations against those you do not like but sometimes these may not be valid, if you check them out carefully.

As another example, Dr. Paul Cameron is a favourite whipping boy of progressives and his research has many limitations. Canning (2005) in his dissertation drew upon comments by Stacey and Biblarz (2001, p. 161) about Cameron (pp. 41-42; see Schumm, 2015b, footnote 8, p. 23) in which Cameron had been accused of research malfeasance. However, after Cameron complained, and presumably because Canning and his dissertation committee could not find support for the accusations, Canning and his committee retracted their comments and stated that "Paul Cameron was not expelled from the American Psychological

Association or the American Sociological [Association], nor is there any evidence that he "willfully misrepresented research". Toby Canning and his dissertation committee (Malcolm Gray, Bob Jacobs, Cyd Strickland, and Thomas Vail) sincerely regret these inaccuracies. We acknowledge that Dr. Cameron's extensive research on homosexuality and homosexual parents (e.g., 38 articles listed on PubMed) appears in peer-reviewed journals." (p. 119). I cannot rule out the possibility they recanted in order to avoid legal entanglements, but I would have hoped that if what they had claimed about Cameron were true, they would have stuck to their guns, so to speak, and not recanted.

Deeper research

Third, I think that scientists need to be willing to dig deep into research and to not be content with superficial analyses of what may be very complicated. When you hear a so-called scientist state that research is simple and clear, without much in the way of complexity, I think you should be *skeptical*. Seeking empirical truth can take a lot of courage, resources and support because of the potential complexity of most scientific issues. Making the case that "good science is easy" is about as foolish as underestimating your enemy in military operations. What do I mean by deeper research, specifically? To me, it means that if you have looked at factors A, B, C and D but not E, perhaps you should look at E; at least you should not claim you have looked at all possible factors. It means that predicting one factor from several others is not enough to understand something. You need to consider mediating and moderating factors as possibilities. Mediation means that it may not be enough to predict factor C from factors A and B but perhaps you should see if factor A predicts factor B which predicts factor C – because A may influence C through B indirectly, even if there is not a direct effect of A on C. Moderation means that A may influence C differently, depending on the level of B. You need to consider the size of an effect, not just its significance level, as I will discuss in more detail shortly. Even progressive scholars have lately admitted that most research on LGBT issues, presumably including same-sex parenting, has not involved the testing of complex models (van Eeden-Moorefield *et al.*, 2018) as has been occurring for some time in other areas of family social science.

Dismissal of common sense

Fourth, I think you should be skeptical when public viewpoints are dismissed by a presumably elite group of scientists who presume they know better than everyone else. For example, Biblarz and Stacey (2010a) admitted there was an "overwhelming public consensus" that children need both a mother and a father (p. 6). Yet they conclude that "social science research does not and cannot support the claim that children need both a mother and a father parenting together" (2010b, p.42). Others appear to have concurred that the absence of a father is "really not important" (Biblarz & Savci, 2010; Gartrell & Bos, 2010). Lamb (2012) has argued that there is no evidence "that children *need* relationships with parents of both sexes in order to develop normally" (p.101).

Sometimes I think such elitists trap themselves in their own logic. For example, Biblarz and Stacey (2010a) stated that "scholars have achieved a rare degree of consensus that unmarried lesbian parents are raising children who develop at least as well (i.e., possibly even better) as their counterparts with married heterosexual parents" (p.5), suggesting that fathers are less effective parents than lesbian co-mothers. Think about that for a moment. If unmarried parents can do as well as married parents, then why all the fuss about same-sex marriage being important for children; what is it going to do? Make the outcomes for children of same-sex parents even *better* and therefore *superior* to those of married heterosexual parents? Likewise, Gartrell, Rodas, Deck, Peyser, and Banks (2006) argued that the small differences in break-up rates between their lesbian mother parent couples and those lesbians' heterosexual sisters' relationships had shown that "being denied access to marriage has not fostered relationship instability in lesbian families" (p.197). While others have disagreed (Wald, 2006), it would seem that if lesbian parents have relationships that are just as stable as other parents and their children are doing as well or better without parental access to legal marriage, why the rush to obtain legal marriage? If lack of access to marriage has not harmed same-sex families, why would attaining access to marriage benefit them? It would not seem that legal marriage would help the children of same-sex parents, if those children are doing as well or better than different-sex parents' children. Such statements could have been taken to argue against the need for same-sex marriage in terms of outcomes for children. More specifically, gay fathers might have made the better case for their need for same-sex marriage because the claim was that two mothers provided superior *and* more stable parenting, compared to two fathers or a mother and a father. My sense is that same-sex parent relationships are less stable (see Gates, 2015, who concurs) and that might have been used as a valid scientific argument for same-sex marriage, but most arguments in courts leading up to the *Obergefell* decision were based on the idea that same-sex parent relationships were just as stable as heterosexual ones.

How dare anyone challenge scientific "consensus"?

You might ask, how dare anyone, much less you, do that? Well, St. Athanasius of Alexandria, a short Black man, (296-373 C. E.) (Cornish, 2005, pp. 58-60) was known as "Athanasius Contra Mundum" (against the known world) but that did not stop him from promoting his world view. St. Telemachus (d. 401 C. E.?) opposed gladiatorial contests in Rome and died protesting them, but did public support for killings in the arena stop him? In contrast to them, I have the considerable advantage of being a scientist with a large amount of social science data upon which to draw to reach scientific conclusions. All I ask my readers is this: both I and the other hundreds of scholars have had the same data upon which to build their conclusions. How is it that I am able to draw conclusions at substantial variance from their conclusions? That decision should not be based on personal values, political views, or the law but upon which side has studied the literature more widely and more in depth, with the most careful statistical analyses. There was once a book published to discredit Einstein, called *100 authors against Einstein* (Israel, Buckhaber, & Weinmann, 1931). But Einstein noted that if his ideas were wrong, it would have taken only one scientist to disprove them. Maybe I happen to be that scientist at the moment, with respect to this particular, relatively narrow issue. You might ask, well, if there are literally *no* studies that differ from the scientific *consensus* (Adams & Light, 2015), how can this fellow possibly show otherwise?

If that is an interesting question for you, you may enjoy reading this book. If what other scholars and professional organisations have said is true – that there are *absolutely no differences whatsoever* – then it should be *impossible* for me *or anyone* else to find *any* evidence that might differ from such a conclusion – and such an absolute and definitive scholarly "consensus". I would ask you to consider other popular books on same-sex parenting and ask yourself, after reading them, which of them has featured the most current references from scholars on both sides of the issue and the most detailed arguments (regardless of whether you agree with them or not)?

Scholar – not a lawyer or politician

I am a scholar, not a lawyer or a politician. That means that I try to mainly address issues of fact and social science theory, not issues of law or politics. Facts can have different interpretations, different legal implications, and different political implications – or perhaps none at all. But that does not negate *the value of facts*. By facts, of course, I mean empirical evidence from ideally numerous studies with different strengths and weaknesses. Of course, part of science is developing theory and, as you have seen, I have developed ways of theoretically interpreting research that may be new to you, even if they seem to have been familiar to some of the ancients (e.g., Aesop). This book is not designed to address legal or political questions to the same extent that it deals with research issues.

Lebow (2014) has cautioned that in a politicised and media-driven (often to exaggeration) academic environment, there remains a temptation to inflate results to gain scholarly or media attention. Patterson (2013a) has stated, with regard to facts, that "social science research on children who have been reared by lesbian and gay parents can be useful to the court by providing information about issues that are central to their decisions" (p. 29). While I recognise that facts can be disputed and have different interpretations, my main concern with the way same-sex marriage and parenting were treated judicially is that I do not think both sides of those arguments got to fully express their assessments of the research literature. If you are inclined to disagree, just ask yourself if any of the conservative expert witnesses at those trials ever presented material as detailed as that within this book or within my numerous articles dealing with same-sex marriage and same-sex parenting? *If not*, then might not you wonder *why not*? (See Appendix C).

Methodological caveats

While I leave the discussion of most methodological questions to Appendix D, a few must be explained so you can understand the rest of the book.

Effect Sizes
Many scientists rely upon statistical significance to determine whether to count a result as important. However, Cohen (1990) has stated that "I have learned and taught that the primary product of a research inquiry is one or more measures of effect size, not *p* values" (p. 1310). Since 1994, the American Psychological Association (APA, 1994, p. 18; 2001, p. 25; 2010, p. 34) has insisted that scholars report effect sizes as well as significance levels. In 1999, the APA Task Force on Statistical Inference stated that scholars should "Always provide some effect-size estimate when reporting a *p* value" (Wilkinson & Task Force on Statistical Inference, p. 599). Effect sizes are often calculated by the difference between average scores divided by a composite measure of the standard deviations of the groups being compared. For example, suppose group A has an average score of 120 with a standard deviation of 10 while group B has an average score of 100 with a standard deviation of 10 as well (assuming the sample sizes are the same). The difference between the average scores would be $120 - 100 = 20$ while the average of the standard deviations would be 10, leading to an effect size of $20/10 = 2.0$. Most of the scores (75%–95%) within a group will usually fall within

two standard deviations of the average score. In this example, most of the scores for group B would fall below 120 points while only about half of the scores for group A would fall below 120.

In essence, effect sizes, often measured by Cohen's d (for consistency, I have converted zero-order correlations (r) into d, from Cohen's (1988) table on page 22), tell us more about the impact of a factor than the significance level. With large samples, you can get significant results that have trivial effect sizes; with small samples, you can get substantial effects that are not significant statistically. Thus, significance level is often more an indicator of your sample size than much else. As another scholar has stated, "We should in general be more concerned with estimating the sizes or magnitudes of effects (i.e., effect sizes) than with the outcome of statistical tests" (Kline, 2011, p. 13). That is why I (in agreement with the APA, Cohen, and Kline) will focus, in contrast to much of the literature on same-sex parenting, on effect sizes more than significance levels in interpreting research results. Cohen (1992) indicated than an effect size of .20 was small, .50 was medium and likely to be detectable by a careful observer without using statistics, and .80 was large. Amato (2012) suggested using less than .20 as weak, .20 to .39 as moderate, .40 to .59 as strong, and greater than or equal to .60 as very strong. If I report an effect size of .20 to .50, you should think "small to medium" impact. If I report an effect size of .50 to .80, you should think "medium to large" impact. If I report a larger effect size (.80 or larger), you should think "large to very large" impact. Cohen (1988) observed that "Many effects sought in personality, social, and clinical-psychological research are likely to be small effects as here defined, both because of the attenuation in validity of the measures employed and the subtlety of the issues frequently involved" (p. 13). Likewise, Lebow (2014) has noted that the impact of smoking on health, presumably a sound scientific outcome, involves an effect size of only 0.33 (and think of all the ways that smokers are treated unequally by the law over a small effect size) but he notes that "large effect sizes are not necessary for impacts to be considerable" (p. 175). Cohen (1992) indicated that "My intent was that medium ES represent an effect likely to be visible to the naked eye of a careful observer" (p. 156). Effect sizes between .20 and .50 can be very important, even if deemed "small" for technical reasons. Effect sizes between .10 and .19 are probably worth noting, though they are no doubt weaker; however, consistent findings of positive (or negative) effect sizes can signal importance as well, even if some of the effect sizes are below 0.10. Effect sizes of .50 or greater should be strong enough that you might not need statistics to detect the effect. Cuijpers (2017, p. 8) claims that an effect size of only 0.24 should be deemed to have clinical relevance, reaffirming the idea that even a "small" effect size may have substantial importance in terms of potential impact on, in his focus, depression or mental health in a larger context.

What many scholars do not seem to appreciate is that you can easily have a medium size effect in a population but, upon doing random samples of that population, many of the studies will not detect any significant findings. For example, Hunter and Schmidt (2004, p. 9) assumed a population effect size of 0.70 ($r = 0.33$) with a standard deviation of 0.14 for the correlation using sample sizes of 40 and found that 31% of random samples from such a population *would not* be expected to yield significant results. If the population effect size were reduced to 0.41 ($r = 0.20$), then 65% of the random samples would yield non-significant results; if reduced to 0.20 ($r = .10$), then 84% of samples would not yield significant results, creating a ratio of five non-significant outcomes for every significant outcome (Biblarz & Stacey, 2010a, reported four non-significant outcomes for every significant outcome in their review of the literature). In other words, it is quite possible to have a medium to large effect in a population and yet find that a *majority of studies* indicate a *non-significant* effect, even though it would have been correct to reject the null hypothesis as false in every test (because there was not sufficient statistical power).

Extensive Research
A second note is that, unlike some authors in this area, I have published extensively in peer-reviewed journals. Therefore, to spare readers some of the details of the research, I often cite some of my own previously published material, leaving further investigative work to the reader who is most interested in that level of detail. Some might say that I am merely repeating my previous material in this book. I am repeating some of it by necessity in order to be able to explain how the science has developed

over time, but I have also added material published within the past year or two (and working papers, not yet published) that were not included in my previous articles. I hope to strike the right balance between making a point and overwhelming the reader with more detail than is needed.

Not Dogmatic

A third approach that I am using is this. I have no intention of even trying to prove that 100% of the children of same-sex parents are X, Y, or Z. That is because I do not think such a statement would ever be correct. I also have no intention of trying to make a case of some percentage value (plus or minus some percent) being the correct and final value for any issue with respect to same-sex parenting. I do not think our research is strong enough to permit such pinpoint assessments. What I do think is feasible is to consider a statement such as "There has never been a study anywhere by anyone that found anything different about the children of same-sex parents compared to the children of heterosexual parents" and determine if it is correct or not. I think that *is* feasible! All that is needed is to produce one such article to disprove such an absolute statement. However, my critics would be correct to argue, so what? Perhaps there are 39 other articles out there that did not find any differences and yours only represents the 2.5% chance of a difference in one direction simply due to random chance. That would be a valid rebuttal if I had only found one article. However, I intend to, in some areas, produce perhaps ten or twenty articles that have found an apparent difference; if my critics want to produce 390 (10/400 = 2.5%) articles that have found no differences in any one specific area, to prove me wrong, please go for it! Better yet, if they can find 780 (20/800 = 2.5%)! I could, of course, run more meta-analyses but at least one scholar is already working on that and may want to publish the results, if accepted, in the journal *Marriage & Family Review*, for which I serve as editor, so I am happy to leave that process (meta-analysis) to others, even readers of this book if you want to beat others to the punch.

Some may ask if my look at the research may harm the children of same-sex parents or their parents themselves. As an example, my review of the literature will suggest that the children of same-sex parents seem more likely to at least experiment with same-sex relationships compared to the children of heterosexual parents. Will this research make them feel bad or encourage others to stigmatise them? I hope not. Some criticism of same-sex parenting may actually come from childfree lesbian, gay, or bisexual persons. However, it appears that the children of same-sex parents have worried about this for far longer than this book has been out. Their friends have often been teasing them that they might become gay long before this book was available. Same-sex parents, as well as their children, have often worried about this. Some scholars have responded by telling everyone that there is no such effect. But if the effect does exist, at least some children or parents will be aware of it, no matter what the research "says". And "no difference" research may not ring true to them. But the point of this book is not to condemn same-sex parents or their children, but to showcase weaknesses in the extant research, so the "target" (if you must have one) is not individual persons of any type or persuasion but rather invalid or misinterpreted research.

Science can change its conclusions over time. If the public consensus is one thing and science seems to indicate something else, perhaps a little humility is needed by scientists. Have all relevant variables been measured and tested? Have all subpopulations been studied? Have the best statistical models been tested appropriately? If not, perhaps some caution is in order.

With these preliminaries out of the way, it is time to delve into the research on same-sex parenting. In Part Two, the research on same-sex parents will be examined.

PART 2

WHAT DO WE KNOW ABOUT SAME-SEX PARENTS?

Introduction to Part Two

First, in Part Two of this book, we will consider same-sex parents themselves – do they differ from heterosexual parents? In chapter four, we will consider the issue of how many same-sex parents are raising children together – or as single parents. In chapter five, we will consider the stability of same-sex relationships, especially same-sex parental relationships. In chapter six, we will consider the issue of sexual abuse of children. Finally, in chapter seven, we will consider what little is known about the characteristics of or values associated with same-sex parenting. Of course, it is quite possible that the characteristics of same-sex parents might influence how their children grow up, but outcomes for the children themselves will be considered in Part Two of this book. It has been relatively rare for scholars to look for linkages between same-sex parenting *per se* and outcomes for the children of same-sex parents, perhaps because if there really were no differences in either area, why would anyone want to bother to see if they might be related?

I hope that readers consider in this section how *so-called* facts were promulgated over time and how those differed from what we now know to be more likely to be the *actual* facts. One must keep in mind, for both areas, that in science we are talking about general trends, not things that are true of each and every person within a larger sociological group. You might find that on average, religious persons were more likely to attend religious services or meetings at least once a month, but you almost certainly would find some religious persons who did not attend at all and some non-religious persons who did attend. In fact, some non-religious persons might attend religious services more often than some religious persons. Those apparent exceptions to the sociological generality would not disprove the idea that religious persons tend to attend religious services more often than non-religious persons. In social science, a few counter-examples do not disprove the general trend from a scientific perspective.

In social science, my sense is that, because of the complexity of human beings and of our societies, the laws of (social) science are not nearly as perfect or as predictable as in physics or the "hard" sciences, although some have disagreed (Hunter & Schmidt, 2004, p. 20). For example, if I claim there is a general trend for same-sex parents to raise children who grow up to be involved in same-sex sexual activity, that cannot be disproven by merely citing a few examples of children who had same-sex parents but grew up to be heterosexual. It cannot be disproven by even showing that a majority of the children of same-sex parents grow up to be heterosexual. To disprove my claim, you need to show either (1) *no* children of same-sex parents *ever* grow up to be anything other than heterosexual in attractions, behaviours or identity, or (2) that there are *no* studies showing a higher rate of same-sex attractions, behaviours or identity among children of same-sex parents beyond statistical chance results, or (3) there are some studies showing higher rates but when the entire range of studies are included in a meta-analysis, the overall results are *not* statistically significant. I am confident that the results presented in this book will be impossible to disprove in some areas in terms of options 1 or 2. Possibly, in some areas option 3 might be feasible. However, most meta-analyses to date (e.g., Crowl, Ahn, & Baker, 2008; Fedewa, Black, & Ahn, 2015; Miller *et al.*, 2017; Schofield, 2016) have included only a small number of studies and may not reflect the larger literature (or a larger set of child outcomes) that could have been used. In looking at the issue of whether same-sex parents are more likely to raise children who grow up in some nonheterosexual sexual ways, Crowl *et al.* (2008) and Fedewa *et al.* (2015) never looked at more than five studies to develop their conclusions, whereas in chapter 8 we, in contrast, will consider dozens of such studies.

As a further example, the Columbia Law School (2017) has listed 79 studies on same-sex parenting, while my research suggests something much closer to 400 or more studies on same-sex parenting. Despite their limited selection of studies they claim 75 of the 79 studies found that the children of same-sex parents fared no worse than the children of heterosexual parents, while the other four studies had been criticised by many scholars as "unreliable assessments" (p.1), concluding that "this research forms an overwhelming scholarly consensus, based on over three decades of peer-reviewed research, that having a gay or lesbian parent does not harm children" (p. 1). Frank (2016) cited the Columbia Law School What We Know Project and echoed their conclusions and those of Biblarz and Stacey (2010a) that there is a rare degree of scholarly consensus that children raised by same-sex parents do at least as well as children raised by heterosexual parents. Indeed, Frank (2016) goes on to state that "The scientific debate over the politics of gay parenting is over, and equal treatment has won" (p.246). Keep in mind – if that were truly correct – then it would be virtually impossible for anyone to present much in the way of disagreement with that science.

Again, in the next four chapters of Part Two, we will look into several questions. First, how many same-sex parents are raising children? Second, how stable are same-sex parenting relationships? Third, are same-sex parents more likely to sexually abuse children? Fourth, are same-sex parents different in any other ways from heterosexual parents? For each of these questions, we will look at what has been said by scientists and how that fits the actual scientific facts. If you assume no scientific differences have ever been found, you might be in for a surprise. In fact, if you assume that scientists are pretty good at estimating basic demographic information without making major errors, you might also be in for a surprise.

At the very least, there has been more complexity involved in dealing with these four questions than you might have guessed from the confidence with which some social scientists have discussed them.

Chapter Four

How Many Same-Sex Couples are Raising Children?

What has been claimed?

You might surmise that determining the number of same-sex couples raising children or the number of gay men or lesbians raising children in the United States would have been an easy thing to discover. However, it has been not so easy. We have elsewhere discussed in far more detail the history of estimates of the number of children being raised by same-sex parents in the United States (Schumm, Seay, McClish, Clark, Asiri, Abdullah, & Huang, 2016). Some early estimates of the number of lesbian mothers raising children in the United States ranged between 1.5 million (Hunter & Polikoff, 1976, p. 691; Davies, 1979, p. 21) to five million (Sutton, 1980, p. 1007), which led to estimates of five to seven million children being raised by lesbian mothers (Rivera, 1979, p. 23; Wittlin, 1983, p. 78). The issue of estimates of children being raised by same-sex couples in other nations will not be discussed here.

A *USA Today* newspaper article in 1984 (Peterson) estimated the number of children of same-sex parents to be as many as 14 million. In 1987, Bozett (p. 39) estimated the number of LGB parents to be between six million (Schulenburg, 1985) and 14 million (Peterson, 1984). The Editors of the Harvard Law Review in 1989 cited "three million gay men and lesbians in the United States" as parents and "between eight and ten million children" (p. 1629) being raised in gay or lesbian households. Patterson (1992) cited, though incorrectly (page 30 rather than 3D), the 1984 news story in the prestigious social science journal *Child Development*; after that, her estimate of the number of children of gay and lesbian parents (6-14 million, p. 1026) was widely accepted as scientifically accurate, despite its humble origin in a newspaper story and despite Patterson (1992) admitting that there was "no accurate answer" (p. 1026) to the question of how many children of same-sex parents there might be. Later, Patterson and Friel (2000) admitted that the estimates of six to fourteen million children of same-sex parents had been widely cited but "no empirical studies [had been] cited in connection with them. Hence, it is difficult to be certain about the origin of these figures or to evaluate their reliability" (p. 242). That major limitation, of course, did not stop Patterson (1992) or many others from continuing to cite them as scientifically sound evidence, even before courts of law.

For example, Stacey and Biblarz (2001) noted, without citing the original newspaper article, that "Since 1984, most research.... had estimated '6 to 14 million children of gay or lesbian parents' (e.g., Patterson, 1992, 1996)" (p. 164), although they preferred an estimate of one to nine million such children. Flaks (1994) was one of the first authors to cite the 6-14 million estimate in a law review article. Jacobs (2002) cited estimates by the American Bar Association of "as many as ten million children within the United States currently" living "in families with same-sex parents" (p. 342). Cooper and Cates (2006), representing the ACLU, accepted estimates between one and nine million children being raised by gay parents (p. 2), an estimate echoed by Rosato (2006, pp. 74, 82) and Ruffini (2017, p. 310), although Rosato (p. 82) also noted that the one to nine million estimate did not include children being raised by single gay or lesbian parents. With highly regarded social science and law review articles having cited the estimate of up to 14 million children of same-sex parents, it was off to the races, with one estimate as high as 28 million (Selekman, 2007, p. 454). Estimates of 14 million were reported by scholars as recently as 2012 (Kintner-Duffy, Vardell, Lower, & Cassidy) and 2013 (Davis, p. 393; Raley). Kintner-Duffy *et al.* attributed their estimate to the Census Bureau (p. 208), without a factual basis for that attribution. One scholar estimated that 14 million children had been *adopted* by same-sex parents (Mabry, 2005), which if true, might have suggested far more than 28 million children under the parentage of same-sex parents through adoption, birth into a prior heterosexual family, or other means. As recently as 2015, Baiocco *et al.* continued the high estimates, claiming that in the USA there were up to 7 million lesbian or gay parents raising up to nine million children (p. 202).

Few-Demo *et al*. (2016) estimated that LGBT adults were raising "around two million children younger than age 18" (p. 74). Bonander (2016) stated that estimates as to the number of "children being raised by gay or lesbian parents could be as high as 14 million" (p. 1).

How did these estimates come about? Generally, it was assumed that ten percent of the population was lesbian, gay, or bisexual (an overestimate) (Patterson, 1992, p. 1026, footnote 1 includes the estimate of 10% of 250 million; Patterson & Friel, 2000). Then it was deduced that if the USA had a population of 250 million adults there would be twelve million adult lesbian or bisexual women and twelve million adult gay or bisexual men, of whom perhaps 50% of the lesbians or bisexual women would have had a child and perhaps 20% of the gay or bisexual men (both possibly overestimates at the time, although close to the percentages of 49% and 19% found in the 2008 General Social Survey, per Richards, Rothblum, Beauchaine, & Balsam, 2017, p. 1, citing Gates (2011)), which would yield an estimate of 8 million or more children if each adult had only one child; with two children each (probably an overestimate, too), the estimate would easily reach 16 million.

Yet, considering that the number of children (under age 18) in the USA since 1984 has never exceeded 75 million and was less, under 63 million, in 1984, would one really think that as many as over 44% of all children in the USA had gay or lesbian parents (28/63 = 44.4%; 14/75 = 19%; 14/63 = 22%)? Yet, for many decades, dozens of law review and social science journal articles argued for several "millions" of such children. Schumm, Seay, *et al*. (2016, p. 297) found that there were at least 90 law review articles and 71 social science journal articles that cited the number of children being raised by same-sex parents in the several millions. These numbers peaked between 1996 and 2005, with 44 law review articles and 26 social science journal articles reporting several "millions" during those years alone. In the ten years after 2005, the numbers decreased to 18 and 25 respectively. However, from one book chapter in 1987 (Pennington) to eleven articles since 2006 (see Schumm, Seay, *et al*., 2016 for details), more recent social science articles have rejected such estimates as too high. Our analysis of changes in the estimates of same-sex parents over time indicated that, although some high estimates dated back to the 1970s, the popularity of estimates, in both legal and social science journals, in the millions peaked in the first half of the first decade of the 21st century, possibly to meet the needs of legal teams arguing in favour of same-sex marriage (if legal marriage helps parents, which helps children, then the need is much greater if there are millions of same-sex parents and millions of children of same-sex parents than if there are only a couple hundred thousand same-sex parent couples with children at home in the United States). Overby (2014) stated that "greater numbers of openly gay parents – including adoptive parents – would presumably further the goal of 'normalizing' the public view of homosexuals and homosexuality" (p. 571). In other words, exaggeration with respect to the numbers of gay parents and their children might well be expected to work to promote homosexual civil rights in terms of marriage, parenting, and adoptive parenting.

What we know now

In stark contrast to estimates in the 6-28 million range, Gates (2013b, 2015), a scholar (now retired) from the pro-gay Williams Institute of the University of California at Los Angeles (UCLA), concluded that in terms of same-sex couples raising children under age 18 in the USA there might be 200,000 such couples while there might be 2 to 3.7 million children under age 18 with a lesbian, gay, or bisexual (LGB) parent, which we think either implies a great deal of instability among same-sex parents or a large number of single lesbian or gay parents or quite a few mixed-orientation marriages (where one or both partners may not be heterosexuals despite being of opposite genders). One recent source estimated 6 million children (and adults) who have ever had an LGBT parent (Harris, 2016, p. 116). Tornello and Patterson (2016, p. 550) have estimated that there are currently about 2.8 million sexual minority persons with grandchildren.

It seems clear that Gates' recent estimates imply that the children of stable same-sex parent couples, married or not, are a small subset of all children of lesbian or gay parents. In other words, not many children with lesbian, gay, or bisexual parents are experiencing a stable home life with two consistent lifelong same-sex caregiver parents (as few as

400,000/1.6 million = 25% at best; 200,000/3.7 million = less than 6% at worst). Aside from the numbers, other research has suggested that many same-sex parents are part-time parents at best. Henehan, Rothblum, Solomon, and Balsam (2007) reported that only 39% of lesbian mothers lived full-time with their children, compared to 71% of heterosexual mothers in their comparison group; for fathers, the respective percentages were 18% and 62%. Perrin, Pinderhughes, Mattern, Hurley, and Newman (2016) found that 18% (12/68) of gay fathers spent half-time or less with their children, among those who chose to answer the question (N = 8 refused to answer) while 78% spent half time or more. Robitaille and Saint-Jacques (2009) interviewed eleven adult or near-adult children with same-sex coupled parents and found that on average the children had only spent 32% of their life before age 19 with those same-sex parents. Their criterion for selection as a child of same-sex parents was that the child spent at least 8 days a month for at least one year with their same-sex parents, a pretty low bar. Comparing lesbians and their heterosexual sisters, Rothblum and Factor (2001) found only 7.1% of the lesbians living with children, compared to 36.4% of their heterosexual sisters ($p < .0005$).

For science, the good news is that eventually, I think we arrived at more accurate estimates of the number of children (under age 18) actually being raised by LGB parents and LGB parent couples within the United States. The bad news is that for *decades*, unreasonably high estimates of such children were promulgated as correct facts in both legal *and* social science scholarly works, but were actually very *inaccurate* estimates that probably influenced a number of court decisions (favourably) on same-sex marriage. If you believe that the end justifies the means, perhaps that was a good thing. If you think science should have done better, maybe not so much. Once the ball got rolling on the 6-28 million estimates, it took a long time to stop it. I think it was just too much easier for progressive, and perhaps even conservative, scholars to cite previous estimates than to inquire about those estimates or to try to assess their accuracy.

Even though the Southern Poverty Law Center has listed his Family Research Institute among its hate groups, Paul Cameron (2004) was one of the first scholars to argue that the "millions" estimates were too high, although Pennington (1987) did so even earlier. Wardle (2004a, b;

2005) was one of the first legal scholars to make a similar argument. By then, whatever damage had been done to science (or in the courts) by the inaccurate estimates had probably already been done. The larger issue here is the question of how useful is an extremely inaccurate social science that can't even give us, for several decades, the correct *demographic* information on the types of parents that children have? How could supposedly good science get such inaccurate estimates so wrong for so long? In other words, scientists were *not* accurately communicating with the lay public and policy makers, despite Herek's (2010) view of science. Can this type of substantial, though basic, error be occurring in *other* areas of science today?

Limitations

One basic limitation that continues is that we do not have much of a handle on mixed-orientation marriages (sometimes abbreviated MOMs) and how children develop with that type of parenting arrangement. As Few-Demo *et al.* (2016) noted, "little research exists on these families" (p.83). However, some recent sources of information on MOMs are articles by Legerski, Harker, Jeppsen, Armstrong, Dehlin, Troutman, and Galliher (2017), Schwartz (2012), Tornello and Patterson (2012), and Wolkomir (2009); a recent book on lesbian, queer, and bisexual women in heterosexual relationships is by Tabatabai (2016). Patterson and Farr (2017) found two bisexual women married to heterosexual men in their sample of 50 "heterosexual" parents, suggesting that heterosexual samples may often contain some mixed-orientation marriages. Some, but far from all, children of now-single same-sex (attracted) parents may have been born into mixed-orientation marriages.

One of the problems with interpreting the previous literature was that it was sometimes not made clear how adult children (that is, those over 18 years of age), whose parents (possibly now deceased) were same-sex parents, were being counted. The use of the word "children" implied that the issue pertained to children under the age of 18 but some estimates may have included anyone, regardless of current age, whose parent or parents had been lesbian, gay or bisexual.[1]

Another limiting factor is that it is also possible that the advent of legal same-sex marriage may reduce a perceived need for same-sex attracted persons to marry someone of the opposite sex, which could tend to reduce the number of children being born into mixed-orientation marriages and, therefore, the number of children being born to same-sex parents in general (Gates, 2011; Patterson, 2017, p. 45).[2]

Another major concern that I have, which pertains to all of the issues in this book, is that when you look into research on same-sex families, the parents are often highly educated and White, often being more educated and of higher socioeconomic status than the participants in any heterosexual comparison group. This is often true of lesbians compared to heterosexual women, including their sisters; Rothblum and Factor (2001) found that lesbians had more education (generally college or graduate degrees) than their heterosexual sisters who generally had some college to a college degree ($d = 0.65, p < .0005$). Yet when Gates (2011) looked into *national* data on same-sex families, he found *the opposite*. Not only did he find that the percentage of apparent same-sex couples with a child under age 18 in the home (relative to all same-sex couples) had declined from 18.8% in 2006 to 16.2% in 2009, but he found that different-sex couples with children under age 18 in the home tended to have much higher levels of education than did same-sex couples with children under age 18 in the home.

For example, only 10% of same-sex couples with a college degree (15% for those with a graduate degree [UK: higher degree]) had a child in the home, compared to 47% (and 44%) of different-sex couples. For those couples with less than a high school diploma ('A' levels in UK), on the other hand, the percentages were more similar (43% versus 48%). For same-sex parents with respect to an adopted child, the pattern reversed, with an 8% rate of having an adopted child for those with a high school degree or less, compared to 18% for college graduates and 33% for those with a graduate degree. Gates (also see Compton, 2013, p.271) also reported research from the 2000 U.S. Census that found children of same-sex couples to be twice as likely to be living in poverty (20%) as children of heterosexual couples (9.6%). Patterson (2017) has stated that "lesbian and gay adults are more likely than those who are heterosexual to have low incomes or to be unemployed" (p.47). I am concerned that therefore much of the published research on same-sex couples (i.e., highly educated, wealthy same-sex couples), which is what was provided to most courts, may not generalise to less educated or poor same-sex couples. I am also concerned that some "same-sex" couples may not be lesbians or gay men but heterosexual persons of the same gender who have chosen to live together to help raise a child together.

Future research

It has been difficult for researchers to locate random samples of stable same-sex parent couples, especially gay male couples. The situation has improved in recent years, but it is still a challenge. For example, Potter and Potter (2017), using a national random sample of parents with young children, only found about 72 same-sex parent couples within a sample of more than 11,000 families. Golombok *et al.* (2003, p. 22) obtained a random sample from England and initially only found 18 lesbian parent couples from the larger sample of almost 14,000 families (with snowball sampling, a few more were later added to their survey). Regnerus (2012a, b) used a panel sample designed to emulate a random sample of the USA and only found two or three lesbian parent couples (of nearly 3,000 respondents) that had been stable since the birth of the adult child. I think it is essential that Census and other government survey data include sexual orientation, measured in terms of attraction, behaviour, and identity, if only to allow the public and scholars to obtain an accurate estimate of how many types of same-sex parent families there are in a given nation at a given time. Where parents are involved, I think data on the duration of their current parenting partnership(s), as well as the ages of each child at home or elsewhere, should be obtained in the same surveys so scholars can determine if children were born before or after the start of the current relationship, regardless of its type. Research is also needed on same-sex parenting among less formally educated same-sex parents and among same-sex parents living on lower incomes or living in poverty, which might provide some different perspectives on the challenges of same-sex parenting compared to the challenges faced by very highly educated or high income same-sex parents.

Conclusions

For decades, remarkably high estimates of the number of children being raised by same-sex parent couples were promulgated in dozens of both social science and law review articles.

It may have been a case of "if you say it often enough, true or not, people (and judges) will start believing it". At least some of the higher estimates did not make any sense by any standard scholarly estimation approach. Rather than there being as many as 28 million or more children in the United States being raised by stable same-sex parent couples, the actual number of such couples is more like 200,000 with fewer than 400,000 children. The highest estimates appear to have been incorrect by a factor of 50 or more! If you believe in the end justifying the means, perhaps you might conclude it was not such a bad idea to bring exaggerated claims before courts in the United States or elsewhere in order to promote the legalisation of same-sex marriage and same-sex parenting. Even if those decisions helped same-sex couples and parents, I think they damaged the reputation of social science, which may not be trusted or perhaps should not be trusted as much in the future by the public or other courts. Politics, rather than facts, were certainly in play. For example, Ruskola (1996) – as noted by Schumm and Crawford (2015, p. 93) – scolded the courts of the United States for not realising that "it is a fact... that between six and fourteen million children" were being reared in gay and lesbian households. Thus, an unfounded estimate that could not be substantiated by social science went from being reported in a newspaper in 1984 to being a virtually uncontested *judicial* "fact" by 1996, only to be discredited ten or more years later. However, if government agencies were to collect detailed information on sexual orientation in their surveys, social scientists could do a much better job of reporting the facts.

Notes

[1] Another minor error is that in Schumm, Seay, *et al.* (2016) in Appendix I in the row of 1986-1990, the copy editors put a 10 and 7 one column to the left of their correct position, so there should have been 10 law and 7 social science papers listed in that group of years rather than what appears as 7 and 1 under the columns for law and social science article counts.

[2] Ocobock (2018) reports that same-sex parents are much less likely than heterosexual parents to want to have children (p. 371), citing a figure of 28%, which is much lower than some previous estimates.

Chapter Five

Family Stability

What has been claimed?

Many, if not most, scholars accept the idea that parental stability (i.e. fewer caretaker transitions) is helpful for children (Amato, 2010, p. 657; Ball, 2013, p. 727; Fomby & Bosick, 2013; Fomby & Sennott, 2013; Lansford, 2009; Rosenfeld, 2015; Strasser, 2010, p. 18). On the reverse side of this same coin, parental/caretaker instability is generally deemed bad for children. Amato and Anthony (2014) found "multiple negative outcomes among children" (p. 370) as a function of parental divorce. Moore and Stambolis-Ruhstorfer (2013, p. 499) noted that family instability may be detrimental to children's academic outcomes, regardless of family structure, for which Potter and Potter (2016) found some empirical support. That may be why Kurdek (2005) stated that "perhaps the most important 'bottom-line' question asked about gay and lesbian couples is whether their relationships last" (p. 252). Ruffini (2017) cited Supreme Court Justice Anthony Kennedy's concern in the *Obergefell* decision that marriage would afford "the permanency and stability important to children's best interests" (p. 307, also see p. 310).

So, what do we know about the stability of same-sex parent relationships? Those looking for a consensus answer will be disappointed. Arguments have been made on every side (lower, higher, no difference) with respect to family stability for lesbian, gay, and heterosexual parents (Schumm, 2015a, b; Schumm, 2016b, pp. 649-655), while some scholars have said we do not know that answer. Ball (2003, p. 726) was not aware of any study comparing the stability of lesbian and heterosexual parents while Peplau and Fingerhut (2007) indicated that "we currently know little about the longevity of same-sex relationships" (p.412). Mezey (2015, p.105) concluded that there had been little research on the stability of LGBT families, so that we did not know how their stability compared to heterosexual families, even though others had found some research on the issue (Biblarz & Stacey, 2010a; Patterson, 2013a; Rothblum, 2009; Schumm, 2010e; Stacey & Biblarz, 2001).

Arguments for the same or greater stability

Despite such uncertainty, Goldberg (2010, p. 26) and Rohrbaugh (1992, p.471) argued that lesbian parent couple relationships should be *more stable* than heterosexual parent relationships. If women are better at communication and parenting skills than men, two mothers should be able to communicate better and parent better than heterosexual couples – and therefore, be more stable, an idea also advanced by Joyner, Manning, and Bogle (2017). Ross, Gask, and Berrington (2011) reported lower instability rates for same-sex civil unions compared to heterosexual marriages using data from Britain. Badgett and Herman (2013, pp. 351-352) reported, using State data from States with legal recognition of same-sex couples, lower divorce rates for same-sex couples than for heterosexual couples (about 1% instability per year compared to 2% for heterosexual married couples). Manning *et al.* (2016, p. 938) argued both ways, citing theories that might support more instability for same-sex couples as well as theories that might support less instability.

On the other hand, Baetens and Brewaeys (2001), Cooper and Cates (2006), Diamond and Butterworth (2009), Hartz (2010), Lubbe (2007), Lin (1999), Redding (2008), Rith and Diamond (2013), Short, Riggs, Perlesz, Brown, and Kane (2007), Golombok (2017, p. 78) and Ruffini (2017, p.308) have all argued that lesbian and gay relationships were *as stable* as heterosexual ones. Cooper and Cates (2006) unequivocally stated that "Not a single study has found anything unstable about the families created by lesbian and gay parents" (p. 87). I surmise that was regardless of how they were created, but it was nonetheless an astonishingly absolute statement! Perhaps that is why, in the case of *Perry v. Schwarzenegger* (2010), Dr. Peplau testified that opposite-sex and same-sex couples were indistinguishable in terms of relationship stability (Schumm & Crawford, 2015, p. 71).

On the other hand, Stacey and Biblarz (2001, p. 177), Biblarz and Stacey (2010a), and Patterson (2013a) argued that some research had indicated higher rates of instability for same-sex parents. Some scholars did not distinguish between rates of stability as a function of parenthood status – it is possible that same-sex couples without children might have higher rates of stability than same-sex or perhaps even heterosexual parents (Kurdek, 2006, p. 513).

Arguments for lower stability

Rothblum (2009) decided that "same-sex couples do not stay together as long as married heterosexuals, and this may be the result of lack of legal marriage, less likelihood of having children, greater autonomy, or less stigma attached to being single than among heterosexuals" as well as "less social support" or "less resistance to breaking up" (p. 135). Biblarz and Stacey (2010a) concluded that same-sex relationships were less stable than heterosexual relationships, although citing only one study (MacCallum & Golombok, 2004) for evidence. Diamond (2013) concluded that same-sex couples had lower stability than heterosexual couples but believed that difference was related to "the absence of structural barriers to dissolution, such as legal marriage, joint property, and the presence of children" (p. 599). If so, same-sex parents might well have similar rates of stability to heterosexual parents, especially if they could legally marry or obtain children. Riggle, Rothblum, Rostosky, Clark, and Balsam (2016) drew the conclusion that same-sex couples "were also slightly more likely to dissolve their relationship over time" (p. 321), even though their levels of commitment and relationship satisfaction were similar to those factors among heterosexual couples. Citing only Kurdek (2004), Zrenchik and Doherty (2017) concluded that the committed relationships of GLBT couples were "more likely to be unstable and strained" (p. 2). Joyner *et al.* (2017) also argued that the relative lack of marriage might lower the stability of same-sex relationships. However, Joyner *et al.* (2017), though they found higher rates of relationship instability for same-sex couples compared to heterosexual couples (Figure 1, p. 2365), were comparing apples and oranges to some extent because 39% of the heterosexuals were parents compared to only 7% of the lesbians and 1% of the gay participants. Nonetheless, it seems that many scholars consider this issue to be an important question, even if they disagree on how relationship stability relates to sexual orientation.

Domestic violence and relationship stability

A related issue is domestic violence (which might predict lower stability). Elliott (1996), Murray and Mobley (2009), Redding (2008) and many others have argued that domestic violence rates for same-sex couples were equivalent or lower than for heterosexual couples. In *Goodridge v. Department of Public Health* (2003) it was contended that the idea of greater domestic violence in same-sex relationships was "utterly baseless" (Schumm, 2013, p. 323). Thus, we have seen "no difference" arguments for both relationship stability and for domestic violence.

What do we know?

Schumm (2016b), after reviewing empirical evidence on relative family stability, concluded that same-sex couples with children were probably less stable than same-sex couples without children, the opposite of the pattern for heterosexual couples for whom having a child tends to stabilise the couple relationship (stability rates for couples without children may not differ much by sexual orientation). While more details are available in Schumm (2010e, 2015b, pp. 18-19; Schumm, 2016b, pp. 643, 649-657), studies comparing instability rates for lesbian mothers versus heterosexual parents included the following differences: 39% vs. 6% by age 7 of their child (odds ratio = 10.1, p < .05)(Fulcher, Chan, Raboy, & Patterson, 2002; Chan, Brooks, Raboy, & Patterson, 1998), 43% vs. 13% over six years (odds ratio = 4.95, p < .05)(MacCallum & Golombok, 2004), 45-48% vs. 30% over ten years (odds ratio = 1.91, p<.07, two-tailed; one-sided Fisher's Exact Test, p < .05)(Gartrell, Rodas, Deck, Peyser, & Banks, 2006),[1] 56% versus 36% (p < .001) (Gartrell, Bos, & Goldberg (2011, p. 1201), and 10% vs. 4% by age 5 of the child (not significant even though the odds ratio = 3.26)(Brewaeys, Ponjaert, van Hall, & Golombok, 1997).

Studies without a heterosexual comparison group

Studies that looked only at lesbian mothers, without a comparison group, found breakup rates as follows: 13% by age 6 of child (Patterson, 2001), 25% over five years (Vanfraussen, Ponjaert-Kristoffersen, & Brewaeys, 2002), 40% by age 7 of the child (Stevens, Perry, Burston, Golombok, & Golding, 2003), 61% over 4 years (Stevens *et al.*, 2003), up to 75% by age 18 of the child (Tasker & Golombok, 1997), at least 30% over a few years (Brown & Perlesz, 2007, citing Gabb (2005)), 56% by age 17 of the child (Gartrell & Bos, 2010), 33% by age 6 of the child (Golombok, Tasker, & Murray, 1997), and 53% by the time the child was an adolescent (Kuvalanka & Goldberg, 2009). Gottman, Levenson, Gross, Frederickson, McCoy, Rosenthal, Ruef, and Yoshimoto (2003) found significantly different break-up rates for lesbian couples (7/18, 38.9%) than gay male couples (1/22, .5%) over 12 years ($d = 0.95, p < .05$, two-sided Fisher's Exact Test). Manning, Brown, and Stykes (2016) reported slightly higher instability rates for lesbian couples (33%, probably 21/65) than for gay male couples (24%, probably 14/59), results that were not significant but involved effect sizes between .17 and .20 (or odds ratios between 1.46 and 1.57).

On the other hand, Bos, Gartrell, van Galen, Peyser, and Sandfort (2008) only found a 3% break-up rate among 74 Dutch lesbian families between their initial study and their follow-up (notably, the ages of the children at the time of the initial study ranged between 8 and 12, so the initial study started with a sample of lesbian parents who had been stable for many years already).

Comparative relationship duration

Some studies have compared the duration of current romantic relationships as a measure of relative relationship stability as a function of sexual orientation. Rothblum and Factor (2001) compared lesbians and their heterosexual sisters on the length of current romantic relationship for those who were in a romantic relationship and found a significant difference ($d = .29, p < .0005$), lesbians having an average of 6.9 years compared to 11.4 years for their heterosexual sisters. Shechory and Ziv (2007) found their heterosexual couples had been in their current relationship longer than lesbian women ($d = 0.67, p < .05$) as had gay men ($d = 0.58, p < .05$, using the number of individuals rather than the number of couples); duration times for heterosexual couples and gay male couples did not differ significantly. However, most of the couples studied by Shechory and Ziv were not parents. Rothblum, Balsam, and Solomon (2008) did not sample heterosexual couples but did obtain data from lesbian and gay male couples in three States. Consistently, gay men reported longer relationships than lesbian women (California, $d = 0.64, p < .05$; Massachusetts, $d = 0.08$; Vermont, $d = 0.71, p < .05$); however, most of their participants were *not* parents.

Population-based studies on stability

However, relatively few random sample-based longitudinal studies have reported stability rates for same-sex parent couples. For example, Potter and Potter (2017) controlled for number of family transitions in their multivariate analyses but did not specify how transitions differed for different family structures. However, it appeared from their weighted data that approximately 57% (6,462/11,314) of married, two-parent families who were together when the focal child was in kindergarten were still in that structure when the child was in the fifth grade (usually age 10-11). The comparable percentage for same-sex parents was 31% (22/72). Reczek, Spiker, Liu, and Crosnoe (2016) used a national U.S.

sample to compare married and cohabiting parent families for both same-sex and heterosexual parents. If one credits, as an indication of stability, the percentage of married parents in each group of the total number of same-sex families, it would appear that a much smaller percent of heterosexual families were cohabiting than were same-sex families (14,976/166,414 = 9.0% versus 417/633 = 66%; this would, in a sample of 100 for each type of gendered family, yield an odds ratio of 19.06 (95% CI, 8.82 – 43.69, p < .001), although the relative percentages might be expected to change in the future with the increasing availability of legal marriage). In their revised report, based on Sullins' (2017) critique, Reczek $et\ al.$ (2017) reported new figures of 14,542/138,835 (10.5%) versus 321/393 (81.7%), yielding an even larger odds ratio of 34.9 (95% CI, 15.7 – 77.8, p < .001). It is also possible that the meaning of marriage may be different for some same-sex parents, which might alter the role of parental stability in a child's development (Schumm, 2016b, p. 658). Wiik $et\ al.$ (2014) in a population sample of Norwegian couples with legally recognized unions found, over ten years, break-up rates of approximately 37% for lesbians, 30% for gay couples, and 20% for heterosexual couples.

Breaking from the consensus pattern of no differences, Gates (2015) accepted the idea that same-sex parents had lower levels of stability, using it to account for this conclusion: "I argue that the research on same-sex parenting is remarkably consistent. It shows that children raised by same-sex couples experience some disadvantages relative to children raised by different-sex married parents. But the disadvantages are largely explained by differences in the experiences of family stability between the two groups" (p. 74). Farr (2017b) suggested that lower stability among lesbian couples might occur, suggesting that "when lesbian women cannot effectively manage conflict, or when disagreements become too difficult, lesbian couples may have a lower threshold for dissolution" (p. 99). Sarantakos (1996a) seemed to attribute higher rates of instability for gay and lesbian couples to their view that their relationships were based on freedom rather than commitment (Schumm, 2015b, p. 18).

Adoptive same-sex parent stability

Some research has focused on adoptive couple stability. For example, recent articles (Farr, 2017a, b; Sumontha, Farr, & Patterson, 2016, p. 990) found a significantly higher rate of instability among lesbian adoptive mothers than among heterosexual adoptive parents (30-31% versus 7-8% over only five years, $p < .05$; gay adoptive fathers, however, only experienced a 6-7% breakup rate). Remarkably, 30-31% closely aligns with results from Gartrell *et al.* with lesbian mothers: 31% of lesbian mothers of five-year-olds had broken up with their female partners since the birth of their child (Gartrell, Banks, Reed, Hamilton, Rodas, & Deck, 2000, pp. 542, 545) while Golombok, Tasker, and Murray (1997) found that 33% of their lesbian parent couples had broken up by the time their child was six years old. On the other hand, Goldberg and Garcia (2016) found no significant differences in breakups over 5-6 years for adoptive parents (12.3%, lesbian mothers; 2.0%, gay fathers; 8.3%, heterosexual parents), although lesbian mothers had the highest rates, gay fathers the lowest.

Effects after same-sex parent breakups

Gartrell *et al.* (2006) while finding a 48% breakup rate for lesbians who had been parents for ten years also noted that, among the lesbians who broke up, their children had been exposed to as many as six new partners over the same ten years or fewer. Tasker and Golombok (1997; see Schumm, 2011a, p. 103, footnote 164) found that 24% of their lesbian mothers had five or more sexual partners over the fifteen years of their longitudinal study; also having more partners had consequences – adolescent children were less likely to accept their mother's lesbian identity if she had been with multiple partners and yet were more likely to develop nonheterosexual attractions, behaviour, or identity. Specifically, 100% (6/6) of the children of lesbian mothers who broke-up and went on to have five or more sexual partners as the child grew up developed nonheterosexual attractions, behaviour, or identity compared to 16% (3/19) of the other children whose mothers had fewer partners ($p < .001$, $d = 2.23$). That result, while isolated, suggests a possible link between lesbian parent instability and the intergenerational transfer of sexual orientation from parent to child.

While the evidence may not be conclusive, since not all studies feature the same outcomes, it seems to be trending in the direction: that same-sex parents, especially lesbian mothers, have less stable relationships than heterosexual parents, although the rates may depend on whether the children are from the current or a prior relationship (Wiik *et al.*, 2014). Furthermore, once lesbian relationships break up, at least some lesbian mothers seem to engage in multiple subsequent partnerships in relatively short time periods, which may represent fairly rapid multiple caretaker transitions for their children, which of course might not be beneficial for those children, especially if the children were expected to treat each new partner as a new co-mother. On the other hand, Goldberg, Moyer, Black, and Henry (2015) in a small qualitative study of lesbian and heterosexual parents who had divorced or separated found that heterosexual women who had divorced seemed to report shame and emotional distress more often than lesbian women who had separated from their partners, which might translate into fewer difficulties for the children of lesbian mothers who break up.

Parent instability and children

One might ask "But does greater lesbian couple parent instability translate into lower levels of mental health for their children"? That is a great question but the answer depends on whether you focus on effect sizes or significance levels. The significance level of that pattern was reported to be $p < .09$ (Gartrell & Bos, 2010), which is not significant at the conventional .05 level, but the effect size was approximately medium (0.49 or so)(Schumm, 2015b, p. 20). One possibility is that losing a co-mother to a same-sex parental breakup might not have the same impact on a child as losing a biological mother or father to a heterosexual parent divorce (Goldberg, Moyer, Black, & Henry, 2015; O'Leary, 2010). An argument could be made that higher instability rates for lesbian mothers might not, therefore, translate into disadvantages for their children. However, a recent report by Reczek, Spiker, Liu, and Crosnoe (2016) seems to find that the mental health of children is better when their parents are more stable (i.e., married versus cohabiting), regardless of the parents' gender composition.

Domestic violence as a factor

With respect to domestic violence, a number of studies have found higher rates for same-sex couples, though not necessarily for same-sex couples who are also parents, as discussed in more detail elsewhere (Schumm, 2013, pp. 323-326; 2015b, pp. 19-20). Higher rates of domestic violence might translate into or explain part of higher instability rates among lesbian couples or parents. Walters, Chen, and Breiding (2013) in a random national U.S. study found higher rates of interpersonal domestic violence for lesbian, gay, and especially bisexual persons. In general, LGBT youth, especially bisexuals, have reported greater sexual and physical victimisation as children and in adolescence from other LGBT youth, including higher levels of violence from same-sex partners than from other-sex partners (Freedner, Freed, Yang, & Austin, 2002; McLaughlin, Hatzenbuehler, Xuan, & Conron, 2012; Schumm, 2013). Mezey (2015) discussed interpersonal violence among same-sex partners but believed that any higher rates could be attributed to stigma or discrimination.

Limitations

One of the studies cited as having proven that same-sex parents have no less stable relationships than heterosexual parents is Rosenfeld's (2014) study. For example, Umberson *et al.* (2015) stated that his research (Rosenfeld, 2014) showed that "same-sex and different-sex couples have similar break-up rates once marital status is taken into account" (p. 98). Joyner, Manning, and Bogle (2017, p. 2354) concurred with Umberson *et al.* (2015) in Rosenfeld's conclusions. I suspect that some scholars think that settles the question. What casual readers may not realise about Rosenfeld's (2014) study is that: (1) his response rate was only 13%, a very low rate, (2) he appears to have included 96 couples as stable even though one of the two partners had died over the first four years of his study, and (3) there were only 4 married (non-dead) same-sex parents in his sample of over three thousand families, hardly enough to prove anything about stability for same-sex parents or their being married (their breakup rate over four years was 25% compared to about 8% for married, heterosexual parents in the study). Those limitations did not hinder the American Psychological Association in their amici brief before the U.S. Supreme Court in *Obergefell v. Hodges* from claiming that Rosenfeld's (2014) study had proven that "break-up rates were not significantly different between heterosexual and same-sex couples in marriages or marriage-like relationships" (Schumm & Crawford, 2015, p.74). Not to slight the American Sociological Association, the ASA claimed that studies such as Rosenfeld's (2014) and Wainright and Patterson's (2006, 2008, with 61% of their "same-sex" families actually being heterosexual families; Patterson, 2009b; Sullins, 2015b) represented "the highest standards of social science research" (Schumm & Crawford, 2015, p.77). One has to wonder when a 13% response rate became the highest standard in terms of response rates for social science research.

Until recently, many random-sample longitudinal studies have not measured parental sexual orientation, making the assessment of the relative stability of same-sex and heterosexual parents difficult, if not impossible. The use of smaller, non-random convenience samples of same-sex and heterosexual parents, even if longitudinal, might find substantial differences in stability without reaching the .05 level of statistical significance. Some studies have collected data on parental gender, marital status, and sexual orientation but have not reported stability rates as a function of the combinations of those variables. For example, Rostosky, Riggle, Rothblum, and Balsam (2016) reported a 10.4% (28/269) instability rate for same-sex couples between 2002 and 2013 (not counting couples in which one partner had died), but did not break down that rate by gender of parents (versus non-parents), although a one-sided Fisher's Exact Test was significantly different ($p < .05$) compared to the breakup rate (4.2%, 4/96) for marriages of siblings of the same-sex couples (Clark, Riggle, Rostosky, Rothblum, & Balsam, 2015). Likewise, Manning *et al.* (2016) did not differentiate instability rates as a function of parenthood status when they compared the stability rates of same-sex cohabiting couples with rates for different-sex cohabiting and married couples (though, notably, the same-sex cohabiting couples had significantly higher incomes, levels of education, rates of both partners being White, and rates of not having a minor child in their households). Other studies have changed the denominators of their stability measures from one study to the next, yielding different estimates of stability for more than one type of family pattern for each separate study (even though essentially the same families participated in all of the studies).

Future research

Many scholars, on both sides of the conservative/progressive fence, agree that parental or caretaker instability is problematic for young children (Morgan, 2014, p. 14). However, there is a possibility that loss of a non-biological step-parent, whether heterosexual or not, may impact a child less adversely than losing a biological parent to separation or divorce. The circumstances of parental instability may also matter.

Better analytical models are needed that assess family transitions as a mediating factor between family type and child outcomes, so that the direct and indirect effects of family structure can better be evaluated rather than merely controlling for marital status (Rosenfeld, 2014) or instability (Rosenfeld, 2015). While we have some direct comparisons in nonrandom samples of relationship stability comparing lesbian and heterosexual parents (Schumm, 2010e; 2015a, pp. 8, 17-20; 2015b, pp. 4-5; 2016b, pp. 643, 649-657, 661), we have fewer random multivariate studies – and those have often not mediated the effects of instability, nor have they reported the basic percentage differences in stability among different types of parents (Rosenfeld, 2014, 2015; Schumm, 2015b, p. 5). Furthermore, to understand how instability influences child outcomes, we need to know more about its context, for both heterosexual and same-sex parents. We also need to take into account that not only might some lesbians and gay men have experienced a heterosexual divorce in the past (for example, Sasnett (2015) found that 70% of her sample of 20 adult children of same-sex parents had seen their biological parents divorce) but since that divorce they might have experienced break-ups with same-sex partners, which might have a more proximate influence on their children (Schumm, 2015b, p. 6). Nonetheless, it is remarkable that highly regarded scholars (as well as the American Psychological Association) testified at U.S. federal trials that lesbians had relationships that were just as stable as heterosexual couples (Schumm & Crawford, 2015, pp. 71, 74), without reference to the numerous studies indicating that, among parents at least, lesbians had substantially higher rates of instability than heterosexual parents. It is also remarkable that lesbian mothers, who were presumed to have greater social, communicative, emotional, and parenting skills, seem to have greater difficulty maintaining long-term parent couple relationships when some have expected them to have more stable relationships than either gay male parent couples or heterosexual parent couples. It may be surprising for many that a number of studies have found higher stability rates for gay parents than for lesbian parents, sometimes as good or better than for heterosexual couples.

Conclusions

While many scholars have claimed that same-sex relationships are just as stable as heterosexual relationships (e.g., Manning *et al.*, 2016), that may not be a valid claim for same-sex coupled *parents*, especially for lesbians. Herek (2006) argued that if there were differences between same-sex parents and heterosexual parents (or their children), then at least some studies should have shown such differences. He noted that "the more realistic standard is that repeated findings of no significant differences should be accepted provisionally as a basis for concluding that the groups, in fact, do not differ" (p. 612). In this area, we have not had "repeated findings of no significant differences"; therefore, is it not more appropriate to draw a different conclusion than to accept a "no difference" conclusion? Indeed, several studies have found that same-sex parent couples tend to be less stable than heterosexual parent couples while lesbian parents may be less stable than gay male parents. If Biblarz and Stacey (2010a) were free to conclude that lesbian parent relationships are less stable, based on only one study, does it not make more sense to draw the same conclusion, based on many more similar studies?

The legalisation of same-sex marriage might reduce those disparities over time. However, stepfamilies tend to be less stable if they have children than intact biological parent families, so only time will tell if the stability of same-sex parents will at least improve to the level of stability for heterosexual stepfamilies. Otherwise, it seems that while children may not improve the happiness of many heterosexual couples (Roy, Schumm, & Britt, 2014), they do seem to increase the stability of those couples, while children seem to decrease the stability of same-sex couples (compared to same-sex couples without children). It is possible (*speculation* only) that such differences might be reduced over time with the advent of same-sex marriage; even so, this would not be an easy problem to evaluate statistically. It is likely that once same-sex marriage is legalised that the most committed same-sex couples will be more likely to marry earlier, if not to have more children already living in the household. Comparing stability as a function of children for same-sex and heterosexual couples would require controls for level of commitment at and after marriage, the degree of biological connection between parent and child, as well as the presence of a child in the household before the parents obtained a legal marriage. Another possibility is that genetic factors might predict both sexual orientation (of parents) and relationship instability (Bailey, Ellingson, & Bailey, 2014, p. 1676), though evidence is sparse. However, if it were so, controlling for genetic factors might reduce the strength of any relationship between the sexual orientation of parents and their relationship stability.

Note
[1] Gartrell *et al.* (2006) reported that 30 of 67 lesbian couples broke up by ten years, which seems to be 45% but they reported the percentage as 48% (p. 182). They said that 54% of the 137 mothers had heterosexual sisters who were a mother (.54 x 137 = 74) and that 30% of those heterosexual sisters had divorced (.30 x 74 = 22). Comparing the difference of 30/67 versus 22/74 yields the results shown, with $d = 0.32$. If the 48% result is used (32/67), then a two-sided Fisher's Exact Test is significant ($p < .05$), the odds ratio is 2.16 ($p < .05$), with $d = 0.38$. However, Bos, Gartrell, van Balen, Peyser, and Sandfort (2008) reported that the percent of breakups was 44%, obtained from this statement: "Thirty-seven biological mothers were still together with the original comother, 34 mothers no longer lived with the comother, and seven mothers who were originally single continued to be single" (p. 213) with $34/(37 + 34 + 7) = 34/78 = 43.6\%$. However, counting never coupled singles as stable couples does not seem reasonable. Among the 71 couples, 34 had separated, yielding $34/(34 + 37) = 34/71 = 47.9\%$, close to the 48% reported in Gartrell *et al.* (2006). If one compares 34/71 versus 22/74, that yields a significant ($p < .05$) Fisher's Exact Test, and an odds ratio of 2.17 (95% CI, 1.10 to 4.30, $p < .05, d = 0.38$). It appears that the statement by Gartrell *et al.* (2006) that "Thirty couples had split up by T4" (p. 181) overlooked four of the couples who had apparently (according to Bos, Gartrell, van Balen, Peyser, & Sandfort, 2008, p. 213) split up by T4. Acceptance of that error has persisted (e.g., cited by Goldberg, Moyer, Black, & Henry, 2015, p. 143; Bos, Knox, van Rijn-van Gelderen, & Gartrell, 2016, p. 185).

Chapter Six

Same-Sex Parents as Sexual Abusers?

What has been claimed?

Cooper and Cates (2006) made the case that there was "not a shred of evidence" to support the myth that gay men or lesbians were more likely to sexually abuse children (p. 88), in agreement with Baptiste (1987, p. 129), Bozett (1985, p. 342; 1987, p. 47), Davis (2013, p. 386), DiLapi (1989), Herek (1991), McClellan (2006), Perrin and Kulkin (1996), and Schlatter and Steinback (2013). Harder (2016a) noted that "A common stereotype of gay parents is that they will sexually abuse the child. This belief does not have any credibility in scholarly research that addresses gay men's parenting" (pp. 899-900). Mezey (2015) has argued that children raised in same-sex families were at *lower* risk of being sexually abused by their parents than were children raised in heterosexual parent homes (pp. 61, 64). The American Psychological Association (2004) recognised that "Another common fear is that children living with gay or lesbian parents will be more likely to be sexually abused by the parent or by the parent's friends or acquaintances" (p. 2), but went on to state that "Fears about children of lesbian or gay parents being sexually abused by adults... have received no scientific support" (p. 2). I think it is fair to say that most scholars have rejected any idea that same-sex parents would be more likely to sexually abuse their children than would heterosexual parents. Attempting to disagree with the apparent scientific consensus in this area is a particularly daunting challenge. I have found that even conservative scholars are hesitant to discuss research in this particular area due to its extremely controversial nature. When I was in the Florida trial, the State's lawyers did not want me to bring up the topic of sexual abuse, even if it might have helped their arguments, because it was such a sensitive topic.

What do we know?

Some research has found that same-sex foster parents appear more likely to sexually abuse same-sex children but that *might* include cases of heterosexual foster parents engaging in sex with children of the same gender (Cameron, 2005), although my own analysis of the Illinois data suggested that same-sex parents were probably more likely to have abused foster children than were opposite-sex parents (Schumm, 2005, pp.455-457) if one could assume that less than two-thirds of same-sex sexual abuse was perpetrated by heterosexuals or if fewer than 20% of foster families had involved gay or lesbian parents. Many States do not track sexual abuse cases closely enough to permit a determination whether rates differ by the sexual orientation of the parent (Schumm, 2005).

The Jenny *et al.* study

The Jenny, Roesler, and Poyer (1994) study is often cited as evidence of the "no difference" hypothesis here. Yet, that conclusion depends on how one approaches the data. The data came from 352 patient records from July 1, 1991 to June 30, 1992 at a child abuse clinic or emergency room of a children's hospital, each child having been evaluated for suspected sex abuse. The children ranged in age from less than one year to age 17, with an average age of 6.1 years; 78% of the children were girls. Only 269 children had been allegedly abused by adults (50 boys, 219 girls). There were 50 children sexually abused by same-gender adults, 8 girls and 42 boys. Jenny *et al.* reported that only one lesbian woman was identified as having sexually abused a daughter for a rate of 0.4% (1/219). However, of the 8 female offenders, one was lesbian and the sexual orientation of only six were "known" to be heterosexual. Thus, two were either lesbian or not known to be heterosexual. For the boys, 38 male offenders were labeled heterosexuals, with 4 others of unknown sexual orientation (n = 3) or gay (n = 1). Thus, of the 50 children abused by a same-sex adult, 4% (2/50) of the cases involved a known lesbian or gay man, compared to none of the 209 cases of sexual abuse by an opposite-sex adult, a significant ($p < .05$) difference.

Another way to slice the data is to note that of those of unknown sexual orientation or homosexual sexual orientation (n = 34), 33% (2/6) involved homosexual adults abusing a child of the same gender compared to none of the 28 cases of opposite-sex child sexual abuse, again a significant ($p < .05$) difference. That suggests that if lesbian or gay adults select a child for sexual abuse, they seem more likely to select one of the same gender which, as we will see later, might correlate with the tendency for same-sex parents to prefer children of the same gender.

The point is that given a case of same-gender sexual abuse, while the majority of cases would seem to have involved heterosexual adults, a significantly greater percentage of childhood same-sex sexual abuse was by lesbian or gay male adults compared to lesbian or gay male adults involved in opposite-gender child sexual abuse. Thus, the conclusions of the Jenny *et al.* (1994) study are more ambiguous than often stated.

Other research

Sedlak and colleagues (2010) found that the family form with the lowest rate of child sexual abuse was that of two biological married parents; all other family forms had rates five to twenty times higher, though same-sex parenting was not cited as a separate family form (Schumm, 2013, p. 306). Morgan (2014, pp. 59, 103) has noted that heterosexual step-parents are more likely to abuse children in general than are biological parents. Cameron, Cameron, and Proctor (2017) have argued that sexual molestation rates have been found to be higher for same-sex parents, but their research has been criticised for a variety of reasons (Schumm, Crawford, Childs, Ateeq, Koochel, & Alshalan, 2017). Tomeo, Templer, Anderson, and Kotler (2001) reported in their non-random sample that gay men (46% vs. 7%) and lesbian women (22% vs. 1%) were more likely to have been sexually abused by same-sex older adults compared to heterosexual men or women. Furthermore, they found that at least some gay men (32%) and lesbian women (38%) were sexually abused before they said they had self-identified as gay or lesbian, leaving open the possibility that late childhood/early adolescent sexual experiences in some cases might facilitate subsequent self-identification as a gay or lesbian person. In a later study, Steed and Templer (2010) found that, in a convenience sample of 280 LGB adults, over 36% had been sexually molested under the age of 16 by adults (age 16 or older) at least five years older than the victim; over half of the victims said that their molestations had influenced their eventual sexual orientation. With data from Swedish adolescents, Donahue, Langstrom, Lundstrom, Lichtenstein, & Forsman (2017) found higher rates of sexual abuse ($d = 0.53, p < .001$) and sexual assault ($d = 0.52, p < .001$) among sexual minority youth than among heterosexual youth. McLaughlin *et al.* (2012, p. 649), using national random data from the National Longitudinal Study of Adolescent Health, found that gay, lesbian, and bisexual youth reported nearly twice the rate of childhood sexual abuse as heterosexual youth (8.2% vs. 4.2%). A more recent study of LGB youth (ages 15-35) in the Netherlands (Dewaele, van Houtte, Symons, & Buysse, 2017) found that 36.4% of LGB youth experienced pain in their sexual debut compared to 4.4% of heterosexual youth (p < .001), a situation suggestive of sexual abuse (sex is not supposed to hurt). They also found that LGB youth were more likely to have had an older partner at their first sexual experience (23.9% five years older versus 2.2% for heterosexual youth, p < .001; for two years or more older, the percentages were 42.8% versus 11.3%). McWhirter and Mattison (1984) found that nearly 61% of their gay men had experienced their first homosexual sex between the ages of 11 and 14, compared to only 13% who had experienced their first heterosexual in that same age range (pp. 269-271). Perhaps same-sex parents can protect their LGB children from such situations, but research on those conditions as a function of parental sexual orientation has not been done to the best of my knowledge. Sullins (2015b) in a reanalysis of data from Wainright and Patterson (2006) found that 100% of the sexually active daughters of married same-sex parents had been forced to have sex at some point (p. 14), while 38% indicated that a family caregiver had forced them to have sex prior to the sixth grade (compared to zero to 7% for all other parental categories, p. 15). Roberts, Glymour, and Koenen (2013), using

U.S. national (NESARC) data, stated that sexual minorities (measured in terms of attraction, partners, and identity) reported higher rates of childhood sexual abuse. Further information on sexual orientation and childhood sexual abuse is available elsewhere (Schumm, 2013, pp. 296-304) where information is presented that suggests that there may be a cycle of abuse for those who experience childhood sexual abuse, though we have no evidence (either way) that such a cycle applies to same-sex parents. However, Edwards and Sylaska (2013) reported that LGBTQ college students were more likely to indicate they had abused their own sexual partners if they had been victimised earlier, with each type of abuse best predicted by the same type of past abuse; sexual abuse victimisation and sexual abuse perpetration were correlated ($r = 0.42, d = 0.93, p < .001$) significantly and substantially. We should not forget that the absence of evidence is not the evidence of absence (Alderson, 2004; Alderson, Altman & Bland, 1995). Because childhood sexual abuse is illegal for the perpetrator, it will be difficult to determine the exact role of sexual orientation, if any, in it.

Limitations

The issue of definitions makes research difficult in this area. Some scholars redefine a person who sexually abuses young children as a paedophile, regardless of their sexual orientation with respect to adults. On the other hand, if you define a paedophile as someone who is *only* sexually attracted to children, you leave other options (e.g., adults who enjoy sex with both other adults and with children, adults who are sexually attracted to both adults and children) open. Even so, there may be some adults who are not sexually attracted to young children but who might be sexually attracted to post-pubescent adolescents under the age of 18.

Given the seriousness of the issue, there has been surprisingly little recent research on the perpetration of child sexual abuse by self-identified homosexuals. Some studies that I have reviewed, because they seemed to be trying to connect homosexuality with the perpetration of sexual abuse of children, did not appear to be internally consistent, so I have not given them much weight. When I examined the New Family Structures Study (NFSS) in detail, it did not appear that children of same-sex parents who had been sexually abused were being abused by their parents (when they were living with those same-sex parents) but it seemed that the sexual abuse that was experienced was more likely to have occurred if and when the child left home in their early or middle teens and was probably abused "on the street". However, I have not compared rates of sexual abuse across different family types as carefully as I would prefer, so at this point, I must state that my analysis of the NFSS data has not yet yielded conclusive results.

It would be remarkable, in my opinion, if the cycle of abuse that is ascribed elsewhere to many conditions would, by some twist of science, be voided in the case of sexual abuse. It is possible that perhaps *only heterosexuals* who have been abused sexually would have a greater tendency to sexually abuse children while homosexuals having suffered similar abuse would be less likely to continue the same dysfunctional cycle. That would be a very interesting statistical interaction effect. I do not think we can rely upon parent reports of sexual abuse by themselves against their own children (Gartrell, Bos, & Goldberg, 2011, p. 1202; Gartrell, Deck, Rodas, Peyser, & Banks, 2005, p. 521) – social desirability and fear of legal repercussions would probably prevent honest answers by most parents, heterosexual or otherwise.

A substantial help to improving our research would occur if States would track sexual abuse of foster children, adopted children, and other children by the gender, relationship to the child, and sexual orientation of the abusive adult (or possibly peers), which would require retaining that information on all foster or adoptive parents. Cameron, Cameron, and Proctor (2017) have tried to use innovative methods such as newspaper reports to track such abuse, but the validity of such methods remains questionable. The researcher's quandary is that if you ask directly if study participants have sexually abused a child, you are asking them to admit to illegal behaviour, which means your very question might not be approved by a human subjects committee, and even if the question were approved, very few perpetrators might admit to their behaviour. If you rely upon evidence from convicted child sexual abusers, the data will be suspect (how can you trust a convict?). If you rely upon news reports about trials of alleged child sex abusers, numerous questions could be asked about bias in accusations, bias in which cases were selected for prosecution, bias in which cases led to convictions, all perhaps related to the resources, legal or financial, or the lack thereof, of the accused.

Conclusions

In my opinion, there have been insufficient high quality studies in this area to draw much in the way of firm conclusions about same-sex parents abusing their children, although there is much more evidence that early childhood sexual abuse seems to have occurred frequently in the backgrounds of adult LGBT persons (Balsam, Rothblum, & Beauchaine, 2005; Schumm, 2005, p.457; Schumm, 2013, pp.296-304; Mustanski, Kuper, & Greene, 2014, pp.609-610), even though it is sometimes claimed that we don't know much about the origins of homosexuality in adults. It would seem logical that those who are abused sexually as children might be more likely to abuse sexually as adults, but that logic has not been supported by what I would consider high quality studies. However, if same-sex parents are not more likely to sexually abuse their children, what harm would it be to prove this – by having government agencies maintain more accurate records of parental sexual orientation and rates of sexual abuse of foster or adopted children, making the data available to independent researchers?

Chapter Seven

Values and Behaviours of Same-Sex Parents

What has been claimed?

There have been many claims that same-sex parents are not different from heterosexual parents in any important aspect, although some may be disadvantaged from discrimination and be more likely to live in poverty (Harris, 2016). Some scholars have asserted that same-sex parents are probably more open to their children finding their own way in terms of sexual orientation or sexual expression (Schumm, 2013). However, most studies have focused so much on outcomes for children that they have less often considered differences between same-sex and heterosexual parents.

What do we know?

Biblarz and Stacey (2010a, pp. 7-8) summarised much of the literature here; they reported only studies with significant findings and stated that there were "four or more findings of no significant difference" (p. 8) that they did not report for every significant result which they did report. It seems clear that same-sex parents try to achieve a more equitable division of labour within their households for child care and many other issues than do heterosexual parents, who may be more content to allow for gender specialisation. They reported that lesbian parents rated themselves higher on relationship satisfaction than did heterosexual couples. Same-sex parents often have spent more time thinking about ways to have children, perhaps because of the difficulties involved.

In terms of time spent with children, warmth, affection, attachment, and parenting skills (as rated by parents), Biblarz and Stacey (2010a) found same-sex parents (mainly lesbian mothers) to score better than heterosexual parents (citing Bos, van Balen, & van den Boom, 2007; Brewaeys, Ponjaert, Van Hall, & Golombok, 1997; Flaks, Ficher, Masterpasqua, & Joseph, 1995; Golombok, Perry, Burston, Murray, Mooney-Somers, Stevens, & Golding, 2003; Golombok, Tasker, & Murray, 1997; MacCallum & Golombok, 2004). They also found that same-sex parents placed less emphasis on gender conformity in their children (Fulcher, Sutfin, & Patterson, 2008), and they placed less emphasis on social conformity (learning self-control), and limit setting (citing Bos, van Balen, & van den Boom, 2004; Bos, van Balen, & van den Boom, 2007; MacCallum & Golombok, 2004). They viewed most of these differences as advantages and concluded that female gender seemed to predict better parenting, more so than marriage itself. Two lesbian mothers would give a child the benefit of a double dose of "a middle-class 'feminine' approach to parenting" (p. 11) and that such mothers would "parent better on average than a woman and a man" (p. 17). They concluded that "Lesbian coparents seem to outperform comparable married heterosexual, biological parents on several measures, even while being denied the substantial privileges of marriage" (p. 17). They found that lesbian mothers preferred to adopt daughters (citing Ciano-Boyce & Shelly-Sireci, 2002; Shelley-Sireci & Ciano-Boyce, 2002); and daughters rated their relationship with their lesbian mothers better than did sons (citing Vanfraussen, Ponjaert-Kristoffersen, & Brewaeys, 2003) and gay fathers preferred (relative to lesbian mothers) to have sons (pp. 12-13). They did raise the issue of co-parental jealousy (p. 12), that a non-biological mother might resent the stronger claims of the biological mother for the child's affections, creating jealousy between the two women which others have also reported (Gartrell, Rodas, Deck, Peyser, & Banks, 2006; Goldberg, Downing, & Sauck, 2008; O'Leary, 2010; Pelka, 2009; Sullivan, 2004).

I would contend that many of their studies did not control for socioeconomic and mental health differences between the two types of parents. It might be that more equitable divisions of labour were related to higher levels of education for both parents, rather than sexual orientation *per se*. The lower parental emphasis on gender conformity might not represent gender flexibility but gender confusion to children. The lower emphasis on teaching self-control or setting reasonable limits might not be an advantage for children. Recently, Bos, Knox, van Rijn-van Gelderen, and Gartrell (2016) studied children of lesbian and heterosexual parents in the U.S. and found that on the variable of "coping behaviour" which reflected a child's ability to self-control emotions under stress, the children from heterosexual families were rated by their parents better than were the children from the lesbian parents ($d = 0.34$, $p < .05$), a possible indication that differences in parental emphasis on self-control might influence children in this important area. Another interpretation would be that if same-sex parents value self-control less, social desirability may have less of an effect on their responses to self-control issues in questions about their children, meaning that comparisons with heterosexual parents' reports might be more valid than in other areas. Sarantakos (1996b) found in his Australian research that same-sex parents seemed to grant children more autonomy, tried to control them less directly, and placed less emphasis on their education (Schumm, 2015b, p. 7). However, a number of studies have found that lack of self-control in one's youth tends to predict a number of behaviour problems later in life (reviewed in Schumm, 2013, pp. 337-339; Bickel & Marsch, 2001, p. 83; Chamorro, Bernardi, Potenza, Grant, Marsh, Wang, & Blanco, 2012; Chen & Vazsonyi, 2013; Moffitt, Arseneault, Belsky, Dickson, Hancox... Caspi, 2011).

Another interesting, but isolated, result was that Erich, Leung, and Kindle (2005) found that parental sexual orientation was related to family functioning (measured by the Family Assessment Measure III, General Scale, p. 48; see Skinner, Steinhauer, & Sitarenios, 2000; also www.mhs.com) with lower rates of functioning for same-sex parents ($b = 0.17$, $d = 0.36$, $p < .07$)(Schumm, 2015a, p. 19), although Ryan (2007, p. 112) and Averett, Nalavany, & Ryan (2009, p. 14) cited it as evidence of no differences (because $p > .05$). While I explained this in more detail elsewhere (Schumm, 2015a), the gist is that the same-sex parents had higher levels of education than the heterosexual parents but Erich *et al.* (2005) did not control for education in their analyses. If education had from a small (.20) to medium (.50) effect on family functioning, then adding education to the regression model should have changed their results so that parental sexual orientation would then significantly ($p <$ .05) have predicted family functioning, with same-sex parents reporting lower family functioning. This is one area where my proposition could be checked and perhaps disproven if Erich *et al.* (2005) wished to re-analyse their data including education in their model. Notably, Averett *et al.* (2009) also found that gay and lesbian adoptive parents scored lower on family functioning ($d = 0.14, 0.24$ in two different samples), even though their children scored better on measures of mental health.

Limitations

The values and behaviours of same-sex parents, as opposed to the values and behaviours of heterosexual parents or of childless parents in general, is still largely an overlooked area of research, despite what Biblarz and Stacey (2010a) argued. I think it should be given more importance. Elsewhere I have quoted Frank Luntz (2009) who said "two-thirds (66 percent) of nonreligious Americans agree with the statement 'If it feels good, do it,'" despite its selfish, dangerous undertones. By comparison, fully 71% of religious Americans disagree with the concept of instant gratification. What we have here is a chasm between the value systems of these two American camps" (p. 261). That effect is at the "large" level ($d = 0.79, p < .001$, if N = 200) (Schumm, 2011b, p. 68). In one study I was able to convince the sponsors to include measures of delayed gratification but not measures of sexual orientation, thus preventing me from investigating any connections myself. When there are only one or two studies about any given issue as related to same-sex parenting, it is difficult to draw much in the way of firm conclusions. Hunter and Schmidt (2004) stated that "no single study is adequate by itself to answer a scientific question" (p. 12). Likewise, Henson and Roberts (2006) noted "Findings in a single study seldom 'prove' anything" (p. 400). Herek (2006) also noted that it was not wise to "draw conclusions from one or a few studies because random variations in sampling can be expected to produce some heterogeneity of findings" (p. 612). In particular, I would like to see more research on how same-sex parents and heterosexual parents deal with children in terms of teaching them self-control and delayed gratification. Bos, Knox, van Rijn-van Gelderen, and Gartrell (2016) have provided a hint that emotional self-control might be lower in children from same-sex parents but, as noted, basing firm conclusions on one study is problematic.

Future research

I think that much more research is needed in this area. For example, Stettler and Katz (2017) have called for more research on emotional regulation (another term for emotional self-control) among LGBT youth, but their recommendation could pertain to children of same-sex parents, regardless of the sexual orientation of the youth. Other than the Bos *et al.* (2016) report, I am not aware of research looking (other than perhaps Sullins, 2015a) at intergenerational transfer of emotional self-control. Another issue is how well same-sex parents and heterosexual parents get along with their own parents or in-laws. Rothblum and Factor (2001) compared how far lesbians and their heterosexual sisters lived from mother and father and found significant results for both ($d = 0.32$, mothers; $d = 0.36$, fathers, both $p < .0005$), with heterosexual sisters living closer to their parents. Rothblum and Factor did not break down distance from parents by the participants' own parental status, but if distance counts as a (weak) measure of getting along with one's parents, the lesbians may have been doing less well with their own parents than siblings from the same family of origin.

Another area for future research concerns whether the non-monogamistic tendencies of gay and lesbian couples carries over to same-sex parents. Sarantakos (1998) found that only 10% of his gay male partners and 17% of his lesbian partners studied were intentionally monogamous. Elsewhere, the issues of monogamy and nonmonogamy have been discussed in much more detail (Rambukkana, 2015; Schumm, 2015b, pp. 20-22; Schumm, 2016b, pp. 657-660; Ziegler, Conley, Moors, Matsick, & Rubin, 2015). Sarantakos (1998) worried that "sexual pluralism and promiscuity can cause confusion to young children and retard their social and emotional growth and development" (p. 33).

Research might prove that polyamory is mostly irrelevant to same-sex parenting, so we cannot at this time generalise from non-monogamy among same-sex couples to same-sex parenting, even if such non-monogamy might be harmful to children, which itself is being debated in academia (Rambukkana, 2015). On the other hand, Gartrell (1999, p. 32) hoped that polyamory would become common and accepted among lesbians. Likewise, Bernstein (2015) noted that same-sex marriage would allow for "the possibility of nonmonogamy for some same-sex couples by providing a secure and trusting environment through which other intimate possibilities" could be explored (p. 323), only one of a variety of "nonnormalizing results of same-sex marriage" (p. 323).

Conclusions

Progressive scholars have begun to argue that same-sex parents, especially lesbian mothers, may be better parents than heterosexual parents in a number of ways (Biblarz & Stacey, 2010a; Miller, Kors, & Macfie, 2017). To me it is not as clear since socioeconomic or educational advantages may be responsible for observed differences, rather than sexual orientation *per se*. In addition to controlling for socioeconomic differences, controls might be useful with respect to any parental jealousy. A major gap in the research literature is the near-total absence of studies comparing same-sex parents and their children in terms of delayed gratification or self-control, especially with respect to sexuality, even though we have evidence that problems with self-control in general can extend to issues of self-control with respect to sexuality (Gailliot & Baumeister, 2007). One study that looked into parental assessment of their parenting goals for their children in terms of self-control found lower scores for same-sex parents compared to heterosexual parents, while one study found the children of same-sex parents scoring lower on emotional self-control in terms of parental-report. Likewise, the former study found same-sex parents placing fewer limitations on their children. However, one should not make too much of a study here or there. Even if differences were found, they might reflect a difference in religious engagement since same-sex parents seem to be less involved with religion than heterosexual parents, on average. However, this sets the table for looking at outcomes for children in Part Two of this book. If same-sex parents are so much better at parenting than heterosexual parents, despite lacking access to marriage (at the time of most of the research so far) and having to deal with anti-gay discrimination, should not their children prove to have far better outcomes than the children of heterosexual parents?

Summary for Part Two

It is dismaying to me that exaggerated estimates of the number of same-sex parents were maintained for so many decades when the facts were quite otherwise. I do not see how science was well served by its slowness in correcting the estimates. On the other hand, at the present time, I think we do have reasonably accurate estimates, though I wish that the U.S. Census and other U.S. government agencies would measure sexual orientation more explicitly in all of their surveys.

In terms of parental relationship stability, arguments have been made in every direction, with most scholars making the case that same-sex parents have relationships as stable as heterosexual parents. However, the evidence seems contrary to the "no difference" hypothesis and some scholars are now indicating that same-sex parents do have less stable relationships, though it is hoped that access to legal marriage might reduce disparities in parental stability. Lesbian mothers seem to have less stable relationships than gay fathers, which seems counterintuitive, if indeed they have such superior parenting skills, though co-mother jealousy might be a factor. The risk to children by sexual abuse from same-sex parents remains unproven, even though LGBT individuals (little research on same-sex parents) have much higher rates of sexual abuse as children or adolescents, as much as two or three times higher than for heterosexuals (Mustanski, Kuper, & Greene, 2014, p.609). Rather than assuming there is no need for further research in this area, I think that better research is needed, especially in terms of data from government records on foster or adopted children.

While most scholars seem to believe that parental stability is important for a child's welfare and same-sex parents seem to have higher rates of instability than heterosexual couples, some research seems to suggest that same-sex parents engage their children more effectively than heterosexual parents, contradicting the dictum that children need a mother and a father rather than merely two parents of any gender combination. The ability of same-sex parents to excel, as summarised in numerous articles, despite a lack of access to legal marriage and despite anti-gay discrimination would seem remarkable. One might therefore expect that their children would also excel, if better parenting does make a difference for them. Nevertheless, the relative instability of lesbian parent relationships remains a concern since such instability might impact their children adversely in the long run despite any other advantages. In this author's view, much more research is needed in terms of intergenerational transfer of delayed gratification skills or time preference skills (which may be associated with a greater tendency to make type C decisions rather than type B decisions) as a function of parental sexual orientation. It is remarkable that such an important outcome of parenting has been overlooked by most scholars who have studied same-sex parenting.

PART 3

WHAT DO WE KNOW ABOUT THE CHILDREN OF SAME-SEX PARENTS IN TERMS OF SEXUAL ORIENTATION, GENDER IDENTITY, AND GENDER ROLES?

Introduction to Part Three

In Part Three, in chapters 8, 9 and 10, we will look into sexual and gender-related outcomes for children as a function of the sexual orientation of their parents. Davis (2013) argued that "The consensus is that there are no negative consequences evidenced by children" (p. 385) from same-sex parent families. Ball (2014) has stated that "The vast majority of the studies have found no differences between the children of lesbians and gay men and those of heterosexual parents" (p. 84). That does not mean there are no studies that found differences, but there should be few. More importantly, that statement implies that the area of inquiry does not matter, whether mental health, drug abuse, sexual orientation, gender identity, gender role behaviour, or peer relationships, even though Ball delves more deeply into some of those areas in the same chapter. Ball concludes there are absolutely no differences in mental health and any differences in gender roles or sexual orientation are constitutionally irrelevant. As I noted before, I am not a lawyer, so I am not here to argue law but to investigate empirical research. Ball (2014, pp. 125-128) has reviewed a number of arguments, which I will not repeat, that claim that social science research should *not* be relevant to litigation about same-sex marriage or same-sex parenting (see Stacey & Biblarz, 2001, p. 179, and Amato, 2012, for similar arguments about the alleged irrelevance of social science). However, many social scientists it seems have tried to argue about law from the perspective of social science.

As described by Golombok (2015), we will consider issues of gender development, which she describes as "generally examined in terms of three components: gender identity, which is a person's sense of being male or female; gender role behaviour, which refers to behaviour that is typical for males and females in a particular culture; and sexual orientation, which is a person's identity as lesbian, gay, or bisexual or heterosexual" (pp. 38-39). In contrast to much other scholarly comment, Stacey and Biblarz (2001) argued that "The burden of proof in the domain of gender and sexuality should rest with those who embrace the null hypothesis" (p. 177) because "A diverse array of gender theories (social learning theory, psychoanalytic theory, materialist, symbolic interactionist) would predict that children with two same-gender parents, and particularly with co-mother parents, should develop in less gender-stereotypical ways than would children with two heterosexual parents" (pp. 176-177). We will also consider other issues, though there has been far less research in those areas. Numerous professional organisations have staked out claims that there are no differences between the children of same-sex compared to heterosexual parents (Harris, 2016). For example, the American Psychological Association (2004) recognised concerns that "children brought up by lesbian mothers or gay fathers will show disturbances in gender identity and/or in gender role behavior" (p. 1), but claimed that "Results of social science research have failed to confirm any of these concerns about children of lesbian and gay parents" (p. 2) with virtually no differences across children in terms of gender identity, gender-role behaviour, and sexual orientation. We shall examine each of those three areas of concern in separate chapters in Part Three of this book, asking the question "Are there really no differences in those areas as a function of parental sexual orientation?" One reviewer of this book asked what methodology was used to find the research cited. Over the past ten years, I have attempted to find most of the research conducted on same-sex parenting, not that I have not missed some on occasion (Schumm *et al.*, 2017). At the present time, I have nearly 400 research articles, book chapters or dissertations on hand dealing with the issues covered in this book. It is primarily from those sources, as well as texts on same-sex parenting, that I have developed the literature reviews presented in each chapter in this book. Readers are welcome to compare my coverage of the literature against that provided by other reviewers, but I think the coverage in this book is comparable or better.

Chapter Eight

Sexual Orientation and Children

What has been claimed?

Anderssen, Amlie, and Ytteroy (2002) claimed that "Sexual preference is one of the outcomes of most concern in debates about children growing up with a lesbian mother or gay father" (p. 344). Many in the public and some court officials have believed that children of same-sex parents might be more likely to grow up to engage in or identify with same-sex sexuality (Allen & Burrell, 1996; Goodman, Emery, & Haugaard, 1998; Morse, McLaren, & McLachlan, 2007). Judith Stacey (2011) asked "How do children raised by lesbian or gay parents turn out? Are they more likely to be gay?" (p. 14), a question she did not answer in her 2011 paper though she suspected the answer was "yes" in 2001 (Stacey & Biblarz, 2001). Formerly many courts, as noted, believed the answer was "yes" and sometimes denied lesbians custody of their children on the basis of that assumption (Schumm, 2013, p. 275). However, that assumption has been declared a myth by many scholars. For decades some, if not most, scholars have denied *any* relationship between parental and child sexual orientation (Armesto, 2002; Bosisio & Ronfani, 2016, p. 455; Bozett, 1985, p. 342; 1987, p. 47; Davis, 2013; Falk, 1994; Fitzgerald, 1999; Herek, 1991; Lobaugh, Clements, Averill, & Olguin, 2006; McNeill, 1998; Patterson, 1995a, b; Riley, 1975; Rosato, 2006, p. 79; Trub *et al.*, 2017, p. 3), often specifically because some courts had assumed there to be a connection (Elovitz, 1995; McNeill, 1998; Patterson, 2005). Cooper and Cates (2006) summarised such research stating that "Parents' sexual orientation does not determine the sexual orientation of their children" and that "it is clear that children's sexual orientation is not determined by the sexual orientation of their parents" (p. 30). Language is a challenge because in social science I doubt that *anything* is in a strict sense "determined" by anything else, so the statements by Cooper and Cates (2006) may actually have little real meaning.

Folgero (2008) claimed that "Children of homosexual parents are neither more nor less likely to identify as homosexuals than the offspring of heterosexual parents" (p. 138), even though they might be more accepting of such differences. Folgero acknowledged that if research had found that children of homosexuals had been more likely to become LGBT then such a result would have supported heteronormative assumptions and led to less support for legislation extending rights to homosexual families. Davis (2013), for example, stated that "multiple studies show that children raised by gay male and lesbian parents have the same rates of homosexuality as do those raised by heterosexual parents" (p. 386). Patterson (2013b) stated that "rates of homosexuality are similar among the offspring of lesbian, gay, and heterosexual parents" (p. 669). Golombok (2015) concluded that "the commonly held assumption that children brought up by lesbian mothers will themselves grow up to be lesbian or gay is not supported by the evidence" (p. 68), though she acknowledged such children might be more likely to engage in same-sex relationships because of their accepting home environment. Rosario and Schrimshaw (2014) discussed familial causes of homosexuality but did not mention LGBT parents as a familial factor, possibly because they believe that one's sexual orientation in terms of sexual attraction is not under the individual's control nor is it affected by external conditions (p. 558). Mustanski, Kuper, and Greene (2014) mentioned childhood sexual abuse as having a partial association with later adult homosexuality, but did not mention the role of LGBT parents in the development of a child's sexual orientation. Diamond (2014) reported that female and male same-sex sexuality differed considerably but did not discuss that difference in the context of same-sex parenting. Bernstein (2015, p. 325) blamed the homophobic fears of opponents of same-sex marriage for the idea that children of LGBT parents might grow up to be nonheterosexual.

Recently, Duncan (2016) concurred with Patterson and Redding (1996), stating that "Children who are raised by lesbians and gay men.... are not more likely to be gay than children raised by heterosexual parents" (p.45). Patterson and Farr (2016) concluded their review of the literature on parental and child sexual orientation as "In summary, there is no reliable evidence of associations between sexual orientation of parents and children" (p.131).

Likewise, Harder (2016a, b) stated that "research shows that children raised by same-sex parents are no more likely than children raised by heterosexual parents to be gay, lesbian, or transgender" (pp. 900, 1295) with which Bowen (2014), Dempsey (2013), Dundas and Kaufman (2000, p.67), Gilmore, Esmail, and Eargle (2016, p. 1291), Tasker (2013), Titlestad and Pooley (2014, p. 334), Robitaille and Saint-Jacques (2009, p.424), and Bailey, Vasey, Diamond, Breedlove, Vilain, and Epprecht (2016, p. 84), among many dozens of others (Schumm, 2013), appear to have concurred.

Ronner (2010) noted how court testimony by scientific experts refuted "each and every delusional belief about gay and lesbian parents" (p.5) and especially refuted the notion "that homosexuality is contagious. Essentially, there are people who believe, despite reliable studies to the contrary, that children raised by gay and lesbian parents are more likely to become homosexuals themselves" (pp. 22-23). Likewise, Ritter (2010, p.384) has discussed how the court in *Perry v. Schwarzenegger* concluded that the idea that children might be more likely to become gay because of having gay parents was a myth, without any basis in scientific evidence. Meta-analyses by Crowl, Ahn, and Baker (2008) and Fedewa, Black, and Ahn (2015, citing 4 studies) found little evidence to contradict the "no difference" hypothesis here, although Crowl *et al.* (2008) found an overall effect size of $d = .20$ in their meta-analysis that drew upon only five research studies to reach that outcome. Any who disagreed with the "no difference" hypothesis in this area were stated to "have been discredited by reputable social scientists" (Lev, 2010, p.270). Clarke (2001) argued that the real problem was not gay parents having gay children but heterosexual parents suppressing their children's homosexual potential with compulsory heterosexuality.

Thus, among the many areas of study with respect to same-sex parenting, perhaps none features as many denials of any relationship between parental and child characteristics as this area. Schumm (2013) was able to list over 150 scholarly statements that supported the "no difference" hypothesis in this area. In addition, denials of any patterns here have continued since 1975 (Riley) up to 2016 at least (Duncan, Harder). Even the U.S. Government (Child Welfare Information Gateway, 2011), at least under President Obama's administration, officially agreed with the "no difference" hypothesis with respect to this research. U.S. courts got involved with the debate, being told, for example, that "There is, however, no scientific basis to conclude that same-sex parents somehow 'cause' children who do not otherwise feel same-sex attractions to have such feelings, or to enter romantic relationships with members of the same sex" (Schumm, 2013, p.274). One might well assume that with so many absolute denials in place for over forty years of scholarship (not to mention the imprimatur of the U.S. government, if not U.S. courts) that there would be *absolutely no evidence* of *any* association (much less a causal connection) between parental and children's sexual orientations in the research literature, other than random chance results. As noted, certainly that is what U.S. courts were told upon sworn testimony by scholarly experts in social science, so how could such clear-cut conclusions possibly be incorrect? Keep in mind that experts *could* have said that there was an association, even a causal connection, but that it did not matter because homosexuality itself was a morally neutral phenomenon of no *harm* for children; yet, although some have made that argument (Schumm, 2010a), most of the time scholarly discussion didn't go that far – it dead-ended at the point of saying there was no association whatsoever, even if any such association would have been harmless. Redding (2008) was one exception as he changed his earlier position (Patterson & Redding, 1996) and concluded that children raised by same-sex parents were more likely to grow up to be LGBT, although he felt that such developments were of no harm to the children. One factor that might be fueling such denials is the idea that, if homosexuality is biologically determined rather than "transmitted" to children, there should be no cause for alarm with gay adoptions or gay parenting (Overby, 2014, p.569). On the other hand, if parents can "transmit" their sexual orientation to children, then more people might see a problem with gay adoption, gay parenting, or perhaps even same-sex marriage, though many would not care, thinking sexual orientation to be a harmless matter in any event. Such transmission could occur via genetics or social environment; some research supports a genetic component (Alanko, Santtila, Harlaar, Witting, Varjonen, Jern, Johansson, von der Pahlen, & Sandnabba, 2010; Bailey, Dunne, & Martin, 2000; Burri, Cherkas, Spector, & Rahman, 2010; Langstrom, Rahman, Carlstrom, & Lichtenstein, 2010).

However, at the same time, a relative minority of scholars have argued that the research was too scant to be able to answer this question or that children raised by same-sex parents might more often feel less uncomfortable exploring options beyond heterosexuality (Short, Riggs, Perlesz, Brown, & Kane, 2007, p. 22). Moore and Stambolis-Ruhstorfer (2013) did not totally accept the "no difference" hypothesis here, noting that daughters of lesbian mothers might "hold less rigid ideas about their own sexuality" (p. 499). Likewise, while Haney-Caron and Heilbrun (2014) accepted the general conclusion that the research literature did *not* suggest "that lesbian and gay parents are more likely than heterosexual parents to raise children who identify as lesbian or gay" (p. 21), they did acknowledge the existence of two studies (Bos, van Balen, Sandfort, & van den Boom, 2006; Tasker & Golombok, 1997) that indicated higher rates of same-sex sexual attraction among daughters of lesbian mothers and one study suggesting higher rates of gay identity among sons of gay fathers (Bailey, Bobrow, Wolfe, & Mikach, 1995). Interestingly, Kuvalanka (2013) cited two of those studies (Bailey *et al.*, 1995; Tasker & Golombok, 1997), among others, as evidence in *support* of the null hypothesis regarding same-sex attraction. Even so, Kuvalanka (2013) explained that LGB parents might well teach their children "less rigid and more flexible notions and ideas about sexuality" (p. 166) so that their children would be aware of and perhaps open to "options beyond heterosexuality" (p. 166) or that "LGBTQ parents' experiences of having nonheterosexual and/or gender nonconforming identities may influence their intentions to teach their children more diverse notions of sexual orientation... Sexual minority parents may be more cognisant of the potential for their children to eventually assume a sexual orientation identity other than heterosexual" (pp. 166-167)(Schumm, 2013, p. 426). For example, Goldberg, Gartrell, and Gates (2014) concluded that "Although adolescents and young adults reared by LGB parents are no more likely to self-identify as exclusively lesbian/gay than those reared by heterosexual parents, having a lesbian mother was associated with a greater likelihood of considering or having a same-sex relationship, and more expansive, less categorical notions of sexuality" (p.3). Goldberg *et al.* (2014, p. 23) did call for more research on reasons for differences in sexual orientation or related issues as a function of parental sexual orientation. In 2014 Ball looked at a mere five studies by four groups of researchers to reach the conclusion that "Much of the social science literature, then, fails to show an association between the sexual orientation of lesbian mothers and that of their children" (p.105). Just two years later Ball (2016) tried to make it clear that he was not "suggesting that the social science evidence shows an association between parents' and children's sexual orientation" (p.103), but he was (now) aware of a few, a minority of studies that differed from the "no difference" hypothesis. Thus, while the vast majority of scholars accepted the "no difference" hypothesis here, a few seemed hesitant to endorse it completely or at least felt that more research was needed to make firm conclusions about it. Some even thought that same-sex parents might encourage their children to explore options beyond heterosexuality.

What do we know?

Some scholars have argued from social science theories that one might expect parents to influence the sexual orientations of their children (Baumrind, 1995; Golombok & Tasker, 1994, 1996; Kirkpatrick, 2004; Perrin, 2002; Stacey, 2003; Stacey & Biblarz, 2001; Tasker & Golombok, 1991, 1997, pp.30-35; Wald, 2006; Schumm, 2013, pp.270-273). For example, Stacey and Biblarz (2001) stated that "Yet it is difficult to conceive of a credible theory of sexual development that would not expect the adult children of lesbigay parents to display a somewhat higher incidence of homoerotic desire, behavior, or identity than children of heterosexual parents" (p.163), even though they also indicated that they recognised "the political dangers" (p.178) of saying that. Despite the extensive theory suggesting a possible connection between parental and child sexual orientation, it was usually argued that research had not supported any such hypothesis. Despite such assurances, some gay or lesbian parents worried that "we are hurting our children because we are queer, especially regarding the development of their sexual and gender identities" (Berkowitz & Ryan, 2011, p. 329), while some children of same-sex parents worried they might become gay themselves (Doolittle, 2009, p. 692). Jedzinak (2004) discussed the issue of second generation LGBT children noting that "Additionally, there is the homophobic stereotype that gay or lesbian individuals raising children will make their kids gay. Therefore, some gay and lesbian parents may hope their children are not gay because, sadly, that argument has been used for so long against them for why they should not be able to raise children" (p. 94). Hequembourg (2007) said that lesbian or gay parents felt pressure to "deny the possibility that their children will be anything except heterosexual" (p. 131). Thus, it was not always clear that same-sex parents or even their children truly believed the "no difference" hypothesis themselves even if they viewed its opposite as an unfair stereotype. However, in a recent analysis of data from 72 reviews of the literature on same-sex parenting published since 2001, we found that 90% of those literature reviews concurred with the "no difference" hypothesis in terms of whether same-sex parents would be more likely to raise LGBT children (Schumm & Crawford, 2018a). Thus, even our own evidence suggests a scientific "consensus" in this area of research. I think that empirical evidence will show that such a consensus is incorrect, however.

Schumm (2010a) reviewed material from books written about the children of same-sex parents, considered previous research on sexual orientation outcomes for children of same-sex parents, and analysed anthropological data on prevalence of homosexuality and tolerance of homosexual behavior in multiple societies. It appeared that children of same-sex parents were more likely, on average, to grow up LGBT than were children of heterosexual parents; furthermore, a gender factor seemed important whereby female gender of either the mother or the child (or both mother and daughter) in same-sex families seemed to increase the association between same-sex parenting and the child's nonheterosexual sexual orientation. It seemed that daughters of lesbian mothers were most likely to become involved in same-sex sexual activity while sons of gay fathers were least likely. Schumm (2013) later reviewed 38 studies that had assessed the sexual orientation of the children of same-sex parents. Of those studies, most found elevated rates of nonheterosexual interest or behaviour. Additional studies located since 2013, also found elevated rates (Schumm, 2015b, pp. 10-11; Schumm, 2016b, pp. 662-665; Schumm & Crawford, 2018a).

Reviewing studies with heterosexual comparison groups

Restricting studies to those involving at least 20 adult children (at least 12 years old) of LGB parents, studies done since 1995, and studies involving a comparison group of at least 20 adult children of heterosexual parents, there are at least twelve: Golombok and Tasker (1996; replicated parts of Tasker & Golombok, 1995), Sirota (1997, Schumm, 2008), Kunin (1998), Zweig (1999), Sarantakos (2000), Murray and McClintock (2005), Bos and Sandfort (2010), Regnerus (2012a, b), Gartrell, Bos, and Goldberg (2011), Gartrell, Bos, and Goldberg (2012), Swank, Woodford, and Lim (2013), and Richards, Rothblum, Beauchaine, and Balsam (2017). Each article will be considered in sequence of publication. First, I will mention Javaid's (1993) research with 26 children of lesbian mothers and 28 children of heterosexual mothers. None of the children (average age 13-14 years) identified as LGBT but 27% (7/26) of the children of the lesbian mothers did not want or were unsure about their plans to marry heterosexually and have children compared to 11% (3/28)($d = 0.43$) of the children of heterosexual mothers; among daughters only, 73 % (11/15) of those with lesbian mothers compared to 45% (5/11) of those with heterosexual mothers reported having homosexual fantasies ($d = 0.59$). The results reported by Tasker and Golombok (1995, 1997) will be subsumed under the results for Golombok and Tasker (1996). Canning's (2005) research is not included below because his sample included only children of ten gay fathers and 21 heterosexual fathers, although $d = 0.55$ (10% versus 0% of the children were nonheterosexual, respectively). MacAtee's (2005) dissertation is not included because his research only involved 17 children of LGBT parents compared to 33 children of heterosexual parents. Bailey *et al.* (1995) are often cited, but they measured children's sexual orientation from the son's and the father's perspectives, which did not always agree and they did not have a comparison group of sons of heterosexual fathers. Kirkpatrick, Smith, and Roy (1981) compared 20 children of lesbian mothers versus 20 children of single heterosexual mothers on a variety of clinical measures, but the children were as young as five years of age with an average of about 8.5 years, mostly too young to have identified a probable or certain future sexual orientation; Fedewa, Black, and Ahn (2015) reported an effect sizes of magnitude .71 for each gender of child across the two groups but their results pertained to a test of gender identity rather than to sexual orientation. Rees (1979) is not included because his data predate the 1980s.

Golombok and Tasker (1996) compared children from 25 lesbian mother homes with 21 children from heterosexual mother homes when the adult children were on average 23-24 years old. Only 8% (2/25) of the children of the former identified as LGB compared to none of the other group, but the difference was not significant (though $d = 0.39$). In terms of Kinsey scale ratings, the average score for the children of lesbian mothers was 0.80 (SD = 1.73) versus 0.15 (SD = 0.37), which was significant ($d = 0.49$) by a separate variance one-tailed t-test (Schumm, 2005, p. 443). Children of the lesbian mothers were more likely to report same-sex attraction (36%, 9/25 versus 20%, 4/20, $d = 0.36$), a non-significant difference (also see Tasker & Golombok, 1995). The children of lesbian mothers were more likely to have considered the possibility of a same-sex relationship (63.4%, 14/22) versus 16.7% (3/18, $p < .01$, $d = 1.07$); for daughters the rates were 10/15 (66.7%, 10/15, $d = 1.21$, odds ratio = 14.0, $p < .05$) versus 12.5% (1/8) while for sons the rates were 57.1% (4/7, $d = 0.83$, odds ratio = 5.33, n.s.) versus 20.0% (2/10). The former were also more likely to have engaged in a same-sex relationship (24%, 6/25) versus none (0/20)($p < .05$, $d = 0.75$) (also see Tasker & Golombok, 1995). Furthermore, if the analysis was restricted to children who had experienced same-sex attraction, the children of lesbian mothers were significantly more likely to have acted on that attraction and engaged in a same-sex relationship (66.7%, 6/9 versus 0/5, $d = 1.57$, $p < .05$)(also see Tasker & Golombok, 1995). Because only 9 of the children of lesbian mothers reported same-gender attraction while 14 had considered having a gay/lesbian relationship, at least five of the children of lesbian mothers had or were considering an LGB relationship even though they had experienced only opposite-sex sexual attraction (Schumm, 2004a).

Sirota (1997), as described in Schumm (2008, p. 290), found that the adult daughters of gay fathers were significantly more likely to identify as lesbian or bisexual (34.3%, 23/67) compared to daughters of heterosexual fathers (3.0%, 2/67)($d = 0.87$, $p < .001$). Likewise, among daughters who became heterosexual, they were also more likely to report having questioned their sexual orientation while growing up (69.8%, 30/43) compared to 23.3% (14/60)($d = 1.32$, $p < .001$). Sirota's results could be challenged on the basis of the high divorce rate (57%) among the gay fathers, but one must question why having a divorced father (of any sexual orientation) would encourage a daughter to become bisexual or lesbian at such a high rate. Furthermore, when Schumm (2008) controlled for divorce differentials between Sirota's gay and heterosexual fathers, the results did not totally explain the differences Sirota had found.

As noted in Schumm (2008, p. 291), Kunin (1998) surveyed children between the ages of 12 and 17, and found that child sexual orientation did not differ significantly as a function of LGB (8.5%, 4/47) versus heterosexual parents (2.1%, 1/47)($d = 0.28$) but the child's having questioned their sexual orientation did differ significantly (44.7%, 21/47 vs. 21.3%, 10/47)($d = 0.52$, $p < .05$). Such a result suggests that one useful model might be to predict child sexual orientation from child's sexual questioning, predicting sexual questioning from parental sexual orientation.

Zweig (1999) used the Kinsey Scale to measure sexual orientation and found that among the 154 adult children of heterosexual parents, 1.9% were LGB and a total of 3.9% were not exclusively heterosexual, compared to 25.0% ($d = 0.79$, $p < .001$) and 57.5% ($d = 1.55$, $p < .001$) of the 80 children of lesbigay parents. Zweig's study is notable because it is evidence that not all studies have found that a majority of the offspring of lesbigay parents would become exclusively heterosexual as Patterson and Redding (1996) had suggested or as Patterson (2013a) had indicated by stating that "Overall, the clearest conclusion from these and related studies is that the great majority of children with lesbian or gay parents grow up to identify as heterosexual" (p. 31).

Against his expectations, Sarantakos (2000; Schumm, 2015b, p.6) found higher rates of homosexuality among children of same-sex parents from Australia and New Zealand than among children of heterosexual parents from those two countries, although he did not provide exact percentages for either group of children.

Wainright, Russell, and Patterson (2004) used ADD HEALTH data to compare sexual attraction (heterosexual vs. nonheterosexual) among 44 children of same-sex female parents and 44 children of heterosexual parents. The children were between 12 and 18 years of age, with an average age of 15 years. Because there were fewer than ten children who reported same-sex sexual attraction, they did not report exact figures for the results but stated that the differences were not statistically significant. The results of their study are in question because most of the "same-sex" female parents were apparently not lesbians (Patterson, 2009b; Sullins, 2015b). However, if seven of the 44 children of the "same-sex" parents versus two of the children of the heterosexual parents had reported same-sex attraction, the results would not have been significant, even though the effect size would have been in the small-to-medium size range ($d =$ .38). Similar patterns of 7/1, 6/1, or 5/1 would not have been significant ($p > .05$, two-tailed) but would have nevertheless involved effect sizes of .49, .43, and .37, respectively, all in the small-to-medium range.

As noted by Ross and Dobinson (2013), Murray and McClintock (2005) found that 43% (3/7) of the adult children of bisexual parents were LGB while 38% (11/29) of the adult children of gay or lesbian parents were LGB, which would lead one to conclude that 39% (14/36) of the adult children of LGB parents were nonheterosexual in that study, compared to zero (0/63) percent of the adult children of heterosexual parents, a statistically significant difference ($p < .001$) as well as a substantial effect size ($r = 0.537, d = 1.27$).

Bos and Sandfort (2010) compared sons and daughters of lesbian (32 sons, 31 daughters) and heterosexual parents (34 sons, 34 daughters) on sexual questioning, where higher scores indicated less certainty about having heterosexual relationships as an adult. Effect sizes indicated that both sons of lesbians ($d = 0.12$, n.s.) and daughters of lesbians ($d = 0.53, p < .05$) were more likely to question their eventual heterosexual development. Biblarz and Stacey (2010a, p.15) indicated that Bos *et al.* (2006) had found an effect size of about 0.75 in which daughters of lesbian mothers were more likely to be involved with a lesbian or bisexual lifestyle ($d = 0.15$ for sons, see Schumm, 2010a, p. 725), which also predicted lower social competence for those daughters (Schumm, 2011a, p. 96).

Initially, Regnerus (2012a, p. 761) found that adult children of lesbian mothers and gay fathers (as he defined them) were more likely to report being nonheterosexual (39% and 29%, respectively, compared to 10-19% for all other family configurations). In his revised analysis (2012b) he reported 55% for adult children whose lesbian mother never lived with them and 32% for those whose mother did live with them; it is not clear why his new definition for gay fathers featured a reduced rate of only 20%. Even when Cheng and Powell (2015) deconstructed Regnerus's (2012a, b) research in several ways, statistically significant results remained for the sexual orientation outcome being associated with the adult child's report of the same-sex romantic behaviours of their parents, although effect sizes were not reported for those results by Cheng and Powell.

Gartrell, Bos, and Goldberg (2012) compared adolescent sexual behaviours in their longitudinal study of lesbian mothers and their children against adolescent sexual behaviours for children of presumably heterosexual parents, using national studies for the latter from 2002 and 2008. In the comparison with 2002 data, daughters of lesbian mothers had been three times (15.4% vs. 5.1%) as likely to have engaged in sex with other girls by age 17 (Gartrell, Bos, & Goldberg, 2011), but in the 2008 comparison that difference had decreased to 15.4% versus 10.7%, not statistically significant, though still 44% greater [(15.4 – 10.7)/10.7]. In the 2002 comparison, sons of lesbian mothers were less likely to have had sex with other boys than the sons of heterosexual parents (5.6% vs. 6.6%, n.s.) (Gartrell, Bos, and Goldberg, 2011). In the 2008 comparison, sons of lesbian mothers were slightly more likely (taking into account all youth, sexually active or not) to have had sex with other boys by age 17 (5.6% versus 1.4%), though the difference was not significant statistically. It was significant in both studies for fewer sons of lesbian mothers to have engaged in sex with girls by age 17 (37.8% versus 58.8 – 61.4% for sons of presumably heterosexual mothers). If the analysis is restricted to sexually active youth (using unweighted data), differences remain slight for daughters for whom one of the interesting things is how same-sex behaviour increased between 2002 and 2008 for the daughters of heterosexual parents ($p < .05$), but sons of lesbian mothers were more likely to be having sex with boys relative to girls (12.5%, 2/16) than were the sons of heterosexual parents (3.0%, 5/169) with an odds ratio of 5.47 (95% CI, 0.96 to 31.2, $p < .10$, two-tailed, $d = 0.32$). In that analysis the zero-order correlation ($r = .16$) was significant ($p < .05$) but the two-tailed Fisher's Exact Test was not significant ($p < .10$), so the results seemed to depend on which statistical test was chosen. Thus, among sexually active sons, the sons of lesbian mothers seem to have a somewhat higher rate of having sex with boys compared to girls, relative to the sons of heterosexual parents. Since there were only 39 sons and 39 daughters in the lesbian mother group of adolescents (of whom possibly only 16 sons and 27 daughters were sexually active) and only 235-237 in the other group (of whom only 135 and 169 were sexually active), the statistical power for the comparisons was not as great once the sexually inactive were excluded.

Swank, Woodford, and Lim (2013) assessed whether or not college students had an immediate family member or an extended family member who was LGBT. Of the students with an immediate LGBT family member, 31.0% (52/168) were LGBT compared to 15.5% (289/1870) of those without an immediate LGBT family members (odds ratio = 2.45, 95% CI, $1.73 - 3.48$; $d = 0.23$, $p < .001$). It should be noted that when researchers (Balsam, Beauchaine, Mickey, & Rothblum, 2005) studied same-sex couples who had obtained civil unions in Vermont (2000-2001) along with same-sex couples not in civil unions and siblings to the same-sex couples, they found that over 19% (p. 472) of the siblings were gay, lesbian, or bisexual, even though the objective of the study had been to recruit heterosexual couples for comparison purposes, further suggesting some genetic or social factors at work within families.

As noted in the previous paragraph, Richards, Rothblum, Beauchaine, and Balsam (2017) had surveyed a variety of same-sex and heterosexual couples between 2000 and 2001 and surveyed them again in 2005 and 2013. As of 2013, 8.8% of the adult children of lesbian parents (11/125?), 5.3% (1/19?) of the adult children of gay parents, and 12.0% (17/141?)

of the adult children of heterosexual parents had engaged in same-sex relationships (the question marks indicate that the authors did not specify the precise numbers that led to their reported percentages). While the differences between these groups were not significant statistically, the overall rate was over ten percent. Comparing the reported sample of 285 (29 with same-sex behaviour) participants against a simulated sample of 285 (14 or 4.9% of participants with same-sex behaviour), the result would be statistically significant ($p < .05$) by a two-tailed Fishers Exact Test ($d = .20$). My point is that I suspect that a 10% rate of same-sex behaviour is probably higher than what would be expected in the general U.S. population. The Richards *et al.* (2017) research is limited by their methodology, which did not assess sexual orientation as a function of the child's gender, the stability of the parental relationship, or the parents' marital status.

Studies without heterosexual comparison groups

There have also been some studies that reported nonheterosexual sexual orientation rates for adult children of same-sex parents, without having a heterosexual comparison group. Restricting studies to those that surveyed at least ten children one finds the following: (Bowling, Dodge, & Bartelt, 2017, between 9/23 (39.1%) and 9/52 (17.3%)[1]; Bozett, 1989, 16%, 3/19; Goldberg & Allen, 2013b, 27%, 3/11, two as queer, one as bisexual, p.341; Goldberg, Kinkler, Richardson, & Downing, 2012, 24% (10/42); Goldberg & Kuvalanka, 2012, 10%, 5/49; Gottlieb, 2003, 17% (2/12); Hays & Samuels, 1989, 12%, 3/26; Joos & Broad, 2007, 42.3%, 11/26, p. 282; Kuvalanka & Goldberg, 2009, 27% (21/78); LaVoie, Julien, & Fortier, 2006, 30-32%, 6/19 or 20; Lick, Schmidt, & Patterson, 2011, 40%, 36/91; Lick, Tornello, Riskind, Schmidt, & Patterson, 2012, 46% (32/69) and 23% (16/70); Gartrell, Bos, & Goldberg, 2011, 49% (18/37), daughters; 22% (8/37), sons, of lesbian mothers); O'Connell, 1993, 17%, 1/6 daughters, but 82% of 11 children had questioned their sexual orientation; Paul, 1986, 24% (8/34) identified as homosexual, with 35% having engaged in same-sex sexual behaviour and 53% having felt same-sex sexual attraction; Turner, Scadden, & Harris, 1986, 17%, 2/12 daughters). Barrett and Tasker (2001) in the Gay and Bisexual Parenting Study in Britain surveyed 101 gay/bisexual fathers about their children; it appears that about 35% of the children whom fathers thought were aware of the father's sexual orientation also were reported by the fathers as feeling confused about their own sexuality.[2]

Jedzinak (2004) interviewed seven daughters (ages 18-27) of lesbian mothers from the San Francisco Bay area and found that 43% identified as lesbian or bisexual, 57% had engaged in experimental same-sex sexual behaviour, and 71% had been open to exploring options other than heterosexuality while growing up while 71% reported that their mother's sexual orientation had been an influence on their own sexual orientation; 86% defined sexual orientation in fluid terms. Tornello and Patterson (2016) found that no more than 6.6% of the children of gay fathers were nonheterosexual, but they did not assess any influence of the gender of the children on that rate. Ball (2014) considered Gartrell *et al.* (2011) but only reported rates of bisexuality to exclusive homosexuality for which the percentages were 20% for daughters and 8% for sons, obscuring the much higher rates (49%, daughters; 22%, sons) of nonheterosexuality; Ball was correct in noting that in a later study sexual behaviours did not appear to differ for sons (Gartrell, Bos, & Goldberg, 2012).

Same-sex parents' preferences for their children

As discussed in more detail elsewhere (Schumm, 2011b), several studies suggest that lesbian mothers were more pleased, or at least more tolerant, with respect to the possibility of their children becoming LGB than were heterosexual mothers (Bryant, 1975, cited by Nungesser, 1980, p. 183; Flaks, 1993, p. 136; Gartrell, Banks, Reed, Hamilton, Rodas, and Deck, 2000; Gartrell, Deck, Rodas, Peyser, and Banks, 2005; Javaid, 1993; Kane, 2006). Javaid, for example, found that 54% (7/13) of his study's lesbian mothers would accept their children being LGBT compared to none of the heterosexual mothers ($d = 1.58, p < .05$). Furthermore, in one study, 43% (10/23) of the children of lesbian mothers versus none (0/19) of the children of heterosexual mothers felt their parent would prefer them to become gay or lesbian ($p = .001, d = 1.18$), with a stronger effect for daughters (56% (9/16) versus none (0/9, $p < .01$, $d = 1.36$) than for sons (14% versus none, not significant, $d = 0.63$)(Tasker & Golombok, 1997, p. 124). If the criterion was changed to whether the child thought their mother wanted them either to be gay or lesbian *or* had no preference, then the overall rate for those with lesbian mothers was 65.2% (15/23) versus 31.6% (6/19)(odds ratio = 4.06, 95% *CI*, 1.12 – 14.80, $p < .05$, $d = 0.71$), with stronger effects for daughters (75.0% (12/16) versus 22.2% (2/9)(odds ratio = 10.5, 95% *CI*, 1.51 – 72.81, $p < .05$, $d = 1.19$) than for sons (42.9% (3/7) versus 40.0% (4/10)($d = 0.06$). Golombok and Tasker (1996) found that the children of lesbian mothers were more likely to express interest in same-sex sexual relationships when their parent(s) had been more open to their children becoming LGB ($r = .38$, $d = .82$, $p < .05$, one-tailed),[3] had been involved in a larger number of lesbian relationships when the child was young ($r = .60$, $d = 1.50$, $p < .01$), and had been more physically affectionate in public with her female partners ($r = .74$, $d = 2.20$, $p < .001$). Flaks (1993, p. 136) found that 67% of his lesbian mothers expressed no preference for their child's eventual sexual orientation, compared to only 27% of heterosexual mothers (Two-sided Fisher's Exact Test, $p < .005$; $d = 0.88$). Golombok, Spencer, & Rutter (1983) found that 70% of their 27 lesbian mothers had no preference for their child's sexual orientation; compared to Flaks' 27% of heterosexual mothers, the result would be significant (two sided Fisher's Exact Test, $p = .001$, $d = 0.97$). Likewise, Costello (1997) found that, of 18 LGB parents she interviewed (Kuvalanka, 2013, p. 167), four preferred that their children grow up to be nonheterosexual while four preferred them to be heterosexual, implying that 77.8% of the LGB parents either preferred their children grow up to be LGB or were neutral about that development; compared to the 27% (4/15) of Flaks' heterosexual mothers, the difference would be statistically significant ($p = .005$, two-sided Fisher's Exact Test, $d = 1.19$, odds ratio = 9.63, 95% *CI*, 1.95 to 47.4, $p = .005$). Gartrell *et al.* (1999, 2000) reported that 50% (78/156) of their lesbian mothers had no eventual sexual orientation preference for their child as a toddler (only 28% expressed a preference for a heterosexual orientation, the remaining 22% was not specified), which increased to 65% (98/150, with only 21% favouring a heterosexual child) when the child was five years old ($p < .05$, $d = 0.35$;

$p < .001, d = 0.61$, respectively, compared to Flaks' data for heterosexual parents). Anecdotal reports have suggested that some lesbian mothers have told their daughters "to try girls" or "Why don't you try and see if you get on better with women?" (Schumm, 2010a, p.736). Bennett (2001) in her study of six lesbian mothers with teenagers found that all of the mothers expressed an acceptance of their children becoming LGBT even if some of them had worries about such an outcome. Kane (2006) found in her sample of lesbian, gay, and heterosexual parents from New England that only heterosexual parents seemed to worry about their children's eventual sexual orientation while heterosexual fathers, more than heterosexual mothers, worried about gender nonconformity in their sons. Even gay fathers, in Kane's study, worried (to a lesser extent) about gender nonconformity in their sons, mainly because of potential criticisms from outside the family (rather than being worried intrinsically about their sons becoming gay). Kane's results might partially explain why the association between parental sexual orientation and children's sexual orientation might be stronger for lesbian mothers and their daughters and weaker for gay fathers and their sons.

Anecdotal evidence

Elsewhere, I have presented further anecdotal evidence of same-sex parents encouraging their children to try same-sex romantic relationships, especially if they had difficulties with heterosexual ones (Schumm, 2013, pp. 421-426; also see Jedzinak, 2004). Some anecdotal comments (Schumm, 2010a, pp.735-736) have included: "It gives you more choice. I think my mother would have liked me to be gay. There are nice women out there and I've had my share of crushes on women" (daughter); "I guess I have choices about my sexuality" (daughter); "I think there were points for me when I questioned my sexuality, particularly because everything at home was open and I realized I had options" (daughter of gay father); "Because homosexuality was such a part of my upbringing, it's not something that was foreign or mysterious or forbidden so I was always able to see that that was an option" (daughter); "We grew up with an option about our sexuality that most people didn't have" (son of lesbian mother); "I have experimented sexually, and my parents have created a supportive environment for that" (daughter); "That's what my mother did" (daughter, when her mother turned to women after an unsatisfying heterosexual relationship, indicating she might follow in her mother's footsteps); and, "I think that my mother showed me that lesbianism is a possibility" (daughter). One researcher (Saffron, 1997) concurred, noting that "Some parents actively promoted homosexuality to their children" (p. 199) while others urged "their children to consider same-sex partners" (p. 201). Pennington (1987) indicated that her review of the literature found "Girls, more than boys, commonly fear that they, too, will be gay or that people will think they are gay" (p. 62, citing Berzon, 1978 and Lewis, 1980).

Let us review the effect sizes observed. In terms of lesbian mothers' preferences for their child's future sexual orientation (compared to the preferences of heterosexual mothers) the effect sizes ranged between 0.35 to 1.58 with an average (not weighted by sample size) of nearly 0.90; hence, it appears that lesbian mothers are more likely to prefer that their children become nonheterosexual and this effect is easily in the "large" range. In terms of whether children "pick up" on their mothers' preferences, we are dependent on one study but the effect sizes are between .71 and 1.18, averaging 0.95, again a large effect, but the effects seem greater for daughters (range of 1.19 to 1.36, very large effects) than for sons (0.06 to 0.63, weak to medium effects). However, Apostolou, (2016) with a sample of Cypriot parents (163 mothers, 166 fathers, whose oldest sons and daughters were between 15 and 16 years old), found that "parents, predominantly fathers, are less distressed if their daughters rather than their sons deviate from exclusive heterosexual orientation" (p. 387), although the effect sizes involved were small (approximately $d = 0.20$). If heterosexual parents are more favourable about having lesbian daughters than gay sons, it might logically be that lesbian mothers might be even more favourable about having lesbian daughters as well.

Turning to the sexual orientation of children, only one study considered fantasy about being homosexual with a medium effect for daughters (0.59) and probably a weak effect for sons. In terms of questioning one's sexual orientation, effect sizes ranged between .43 and .52 but with larger effects for daughters (0.53 to 1.32) than for sons (0.12). In terms of considering a same-sex romantic relationship or engaging in one, effect sizes ranged between 0.75 and 1.07 with stronger effects for daughters (0.75) than for sons (0.15). In terms of same-sex attractions, effect sizes were modest (0.36 to 0.49) but if same-sex attractions were experienced by children of lesbian mothers, a very large effect size (1.57) was associated with acting on those attractions and engaging in same-sex sexual behaviours.

In terms of adopting a LGBT identity, effects had a wide range from 0.20 to 1.55 with larger effects possibly associated with older children (e.g., college students) and having lesbian mothers as opposed to other LGBT relatives. There may be a trend for the children of same-sex parents to be more likely to engage in same-sex behaviour than to question their sexuality or adopt an LGBT identity, at least not until they are older. The strongest and most consistent effects may be in terms of lesbian mothers, relative to heterosexual mothers, being content with their children not becoming heterosexuals and with their children becoming aware of such preferences. Because of the numerous studies that appear to have found linkages between parental and adult child sexual orientation, with some research suggesting how that linkage occurs, it may be that this is an area for which the "no difference" hypothesis is at perhaps the greatest risk of any of those reviewed in this book.

Limitations

Some of the studies cited above were dissertation research that was not subsequently published in peer-reviewed journals. However, many dissertations have been accepted as legitimate evidence for supporting the "no difference" hypothesis (Schumm, 2008). Many studies have not featured heterosexual comparison groups. Most studies have not been based on large random samples, so it is difficult to generalise their results. Some studies may have deliberately oversampled LGB children of LGB parents, perhaps not mentioning this in their methodology sections; thus, some studies may over-represent the number of LGB children of same-sex parents. Few studies have assessed the association between child and parental sexual orientation as moderated by whether the child was adopted or genetically related to at least one of the same-sex parents. Some studies have not found a significant relationship between parental and child sexual orientation (e.g., MacAtee, 2005; Richards, Rothblum, Beauchaine, & Balsam, 2017). Some studies did not break down patterns by gender of the same-sex parent(s) or the gender of the child, which have often been important moderators (Schumm, 2010a). It is possible for a small study ($N = 8$) to find only one adult child of same-sex parents to be LGBT, which might seem to disprove any relationship between parent and child sexual orientation. However, although 1/8 versus 0/8 is not significant, the effect size is 0.53, a medium size effect, normally visible to the naked eye according to Cohen (1992). To spare the reader, I have limited the extent of my discussion of those who have favoured the "no difference" hypothesis in this area and selected only a few scholars who dared to disagree with it, but more details are available elsewhere (Schumm, 2013, which features 22 pages of quotes in support of the "no difference" hypothesis in this area, pp. 388-409; Schumm, 2015a, b; Schumm, 2016b).

A contrary hypothesis would be that not having a father figure in the home, having divorced parents, or having been raised by neither biological parent might all tend to influence children in a nonheterosexual direction (Francis, 2008; Frisch & Hviid, 2006; Udry & Chantala, 2005). I cannot disagree that those demographic issues might have some effect. However, I think the effects appear to be small compared to those seen with same-sex parenting. For example, Frisch and Hviid (2006) appeared to find that if a Danish boy knew his father, then 1771/414842 (0.43%) were later married to another man compared to when the boy had no idea of who his father had been 119/16229, 0.73%). Again for Danish boys, 1272/324055 (0.39%) had married men if they had come from intact parental families compared to 409/73139 (0.56%) from divorced or never married parental families.

Very few studies have tried to determine *why* or *how* there might be a linkage between parental and child sexual orientation; that is, few studies have considered mediating effects, a problem acknowledged recently (van Eeden-Moorefield, Few-Demo, Benson, Bible, & Lummer, 2018). If parental acceptance of a child becoming LGBT (as reported by the mother and perceived by the child) were a mediating factor, it might occur that parental sexual orientation was not a direct predictor of child sexual orientation – in other words, if heterosexual parents were more accepting of a child being LGBT, heterosexuality might be associated as well with a child's LGBT sexual orientation. Another angle on the mediation idea is that selection effects might involve more "gung ho" LGBT parents both volunteering more often to participate in research on same-sex parenting issues and also being more accepting of their children being LGBT, which could cause an artifactual relationship between parental and child sexual orientation.

Another concern is that sometimes children of same-sex parents are teased or bullied about their parents in terms of an expectation that they, the children, will become gay or lesbian themselves, due to heredity or socialisation; Robitaille and Saint-Jacques (2009) in their study of eleven adult children from same-sex parent families found that at least 27% of the children reported being told by their peers that they might become gay or lesbian because of their parents. Thus, it might not only be parental influence on a child but peer influences that might encourage exploration of a more diverse view of human sexuality. Might not an adolescent at some point think something like this: "Well, if I am going to be stereotyped as gay anyway, why not check it out? The teasing can't get any worse anyway." Because gender appears to be a moderator of intergenerational transfer of sexual orientation – mothers and daughters being more likely to share the other's sexual orientation – some research is more difficult to interpret because the parent or child's genders were not taken into account (Tornello & Patterson, 2016).

Future research

Few studies have considered how or why children of lesbigay parents might be more likely to experience same-sex attraction, develop a nonheterosexual sexual orientation identity, or become involved in same-sex sexual relationships, although Kuvalanka has discussed some possibilities (2013, pp. 166-167). However, it is interesting to us that Tasker and Golombok (1997) found that even daughters who were not same-sex attracted were more likely to engage in same-sex sexual relationships if they had lesbian parents (Schumm, 2004a). As mentioned above, anecdotal evidence may suggest that lesbian and gay parents may encourage their children to at least experiment with same-sex relationships, particularly if they have difficulties with heterosexual ones (Schumm, 2005, pp.443, 447; Schumm, 2013, pp.421-426). We think it is notable that an association between parental and child sexual orientation may exist even under conditions in which a high percentage of nonheterosexual parents had broken up (e.g., Cheng & Powell, 2015; Sirota, 1997, 2009; Zweig, 1999), though few scholars have hypothesised that divorce among heterosexuals would cause substantial differences in sexual orientation among adult children.

I would welcome scholars testing whether there were trends over time in terms of the strength of any association between parental sexual orientation and child sexual orientation; my own work suggested that the relationship was becoming stronger since the 1970s, perhaps as a result of greater social acceptance of homosexuality and same-sex parenting (Baunach, 2012; Schumm, 2013, p. 294; Smith, 2016). I would also encourage scholars to test more complex models in which, for example, parental sexual orientation might predict parental acceptance of their children becoming LGBT, which might predict the adolescent's sexual questioning or a greater acceptance or awareness of any same-sex sexual attractions, which might predict same-sex sexual experimentation and the development of same-sex romantic relationships, which might in turn predict sexual orientation identity development, so that direct and indirect effects could be assessed. Models should control for the genders of both parents and the children, especially in terms of any moderating influences (interaction effects) such as whether the children were adopted or genetically related to one of the same-sex parents. If genetics effects were predominant, there might be a stronger association between child and parental sexual orientation among biological children as opposed to adopted children, but the result might also vary by the genders of the parent and child. If I had to speculate, I would guess that male parents and children might experience more of a genetic linkage than female parents and children because female sexual orientation appears to be more fluid (Diamond, 2014) and perhaps more responsive to social environments. I think that cohort effects might be important as well; as acceptance of homosexuality has increased, parents, peers, and children may feel more comfortable with the development or acknowledgement of same-sex sexual orientation, same-sex romantic relationships, and/or same-sex sexual behaviours. Another research question might concern the extent to which a child's sexual orientation is more or less "fluid" (Diamond, 2014) depending on the sexual orientation of their parents and how variations in the development of the child's sexual orientation occur as a function of parental sexual orientation.

Conclusions

More scholarly ink has probably been spilled in this area of the potential effect of same-sex parents on children than in any other. Dozens, if not hundreds, of scholars have denied any role of parental sexual orientation. One scholar (Ronner, 2010) wrote that *anyone* who thought anything other was "delusional". But I think this has to be one of the better examples of how scientists can get their science or facts very wrong. There are now dozens of studies that appear to refute the "no difference" hypothesis with only a few that do not essentially (in terms of effect sizes, if not statistical significance) refute it. We need remember that Hunter and Schmidt (2004) demonstrated that even with substantial and genuine population effects, not all particular studies would yield significant results, so the mix of findings is still consistent with an overall positive association between parental and child sexual orientation. Not only are there studies, but most social science theories argue that parents do influence their children's choices and behaviours, so that it would not be surprising if parents had an effect on their children but that if they did *not* have any effect.

After decades of denial about the effects of same-sex parenting in this area, science may finally be getting around to the facts. It is possible that greater social acceptance of homosexuality over recent decades may be facilitating the extent to which same-sex parents may be able to influence their children's sexual orientation in terms of attraction, behaviour, or identity. At least one study (Zweig, 1999) found nearly 60% of the children of same-sex parents to report being other than exclusively heterosexual, compared to about 4% of the children of heterosexual parents. I think the burden of proof, as noted by Stacey and Biblarz (2001), has clearly shifted to those who would continue to argue for the "no difference" hypothesis in this area. There is also research suggesting genetic contributions to childhood gender typicality (CGT), adult gender identity (AGI), and sexual orientation, contributing to associations among all three of those factors (Burri, Cherkas, Spector, & Rahman, 2011). My calculations indicate that effect sizes among those three variables in Burri *et al.* range from 0.17 to 0.32 (all, $p > .05$, however). Thus, when scholars accept the "no difference" hypothesis in this area of gender identity, sexual orientation, and gender role nonconformity/ flexibility (as related to parental sexual orientation), they are not only denying any social connections among those variables but they may also be denying any genetic connections as well.

I think one could develop a plausible model with pathways (such as point A leading to point B leading to point C, etc.) in which having a same-sex parent would very often be associated (through genetics and/ or social/environmental influences, especially parental acceptance, as well as the acceptance of the parents' network of perhaps largely LGBT friends, of a child growing up to be LGBT) with a child learning an earlier awareness about and an acceptance of sexual diversity, including an option of growing up to be LGBT themselves. Having options in an LGBT direction that often would be supported, even if not encouraged, by an LGBT parent and LGBT friends, might lead to a greater questioning by the child of the child's own sexual orientation or experience of same-sex sexual attraction, which would increase the likelihood of sexual experimentation, especially if same-sex sexual attraction were present. Satisfaction with such sexual experimentation might confirm their sense of same-sex sexual attraction and encourage the further development of an LGBT personal identity. That is to say that there are probably some mediating variables between having an LGBT parent and developing an LGBT identity. It is possible that awareness of and greater acceptance of sexual diversity might be common among two-thirds of the children of LGBT parents even though engagement/ experimentation with same-sex sexual behaviour or the development of an LGBT identity might only occur in perhaps a third of the children of LGBT parents. The pathways are not deterministic in the sense that reaching point A automatically leads to point B, but I would estimate that the probabilities are greater if you reach point A, then you are more likely to reach point B and thereafter point C likewise. Recently, Diamond and Rosky (2016) agreed with this sort of assessment, stating that "girls raised by lesbian mothers experienced a family climate of acceptance regarding same-sex relationships and received less exposure (relative to the average female adolescent) to conventional societal pressures to pursue exclusively heterosexual relationships. As a result, they may have been more willing and able to consider – and to positively evaluate – their own propensity for same-sex sexuality. Of course, this is exactly what anti-gay activists have long warned about..." (p. 371). Bonander (2016) was told by a 40-year old lesbian mother how she talked to her 7-year old daughter Emma: "So I think a lot of our chats involve choice and how it's perfectly fine if she likes boys, girls, or both, if she has one sweetheart or many sweethearts" (p. 108). On the surface this might seem empowering, but without taking long-term consequences of sexual decisions into account, it could be setting one's child up for failure.

Notes
[1] Bowling *et al.*'s (2017) research was conservative in its estimates because all parents were restricted to bisexuals, and children were deemed nonheterosexual only if the parent knew about this (some parents may not have known and some children were too young to be aware of their sexual orientation) and if the child was over eight years of age.
[2] The 35% estimate was arrived at from Barrett and Tasker (2001, Table 3, p. 72). That table shows independent sample *t*-test comparisons between fathers' ratings of their eldest son or daughter's response to knowing they had a gay father. The degrees of freedom for "feels confused about their own sexuality" were 52, indicating N = 54. There were approximately the same number of sons and daughters, so I assumed N = 27 for each group until assuming N = 29 worked better for coming closer to the reported mean and standard deviation for sons. To obtain a mean score of 1.38-1.39 with SDs between 0.63 and 0.77, I started with each simulated respondent scoring 1 and adding scores of 2 until I reached a mean of 1.38. Then I added higher scores above 2 until I reached an SD near the indicated value. This yielded about 35% of the simulated respondents having scores above 1, indicating some confusion about sexuality. It must be noted that the narrative says that the items were coded (1 = very unlike my child, 5 = very like my child, p. 71) while the table shows the opposite coding (p. 72). I assumed the narrative was correct; otherwise, the percentage of children being rated as having sexual confusion

would have been much higher. The mean scores for daughters were similar, though the standard deviations were a bit higher.

[3] Blanchard and VanderLaan (2015, p. 1504) have discussed the usefulness of one-tailed statistical tests when theory or the preponderance of research suggest a direction to the expected effects of the test involved.

Chapter Nine

Gender Identity

What has been claimed?

In reviewing the research Golombok (2007) reported that there had been "no evidence of gender identity confusion for any of the children studied – all of the boys identified as boys and all of the girls identified as girls" (p. xvii). Lamb (2012) conceded that gender identity was an "aspect of psychological adjustment" (p. 105), but that same-sex parenting was not related to the gender identity development of children. Both Crowl *et al*. (2008) and Fedewa *et al*. (2015) reported no evidence of gender identity problems for children of same-sex parents. Patterson (2013b) summarised the literature in this area by noting that, with respect to gender identity, "No evidence has been reported in any of the studies to suggest difficulties among children of lesbian mothers" (p. 669). Golombok (2015) addressed the issue of gender identity by stating that "in all the studies conducted so far, not one child with gender identity disorder has been identified" (p. 68), an alleged finding argued earlier before the Massachusetts Supreme Court in *Goodridge vs. Massachusetts* (Schumm, 2016b, p. 693). Most recently, Trub *et al*. (2017, p. 3) have denied any relationship between having same-sex parents and their children's gender identity.

What do we know?

Yet some studies have found that same-sex parents often have wished to be of a different gender (Sarantakos, 1996a, 1998) while other studies have found that persons who identified as LGB in adulthood often reported gender atypical behaviours in their childhoods (e.g., VanderLaan, Gothreau, Bartlett, & Vasey, 2011). Sarantakos (1996b) reported that teachers described the children of gay and lesbian parents as "more confused about their gender" (p. 26), which may not have been surprising in that Sarantakos (1998) found that 55% of the gay men in his study reported they were a woman in a man's body while 45% of the lesbians reported being a man in a woman's body (Schumm, 2015b, p. 7). A few studies have reported anecdotal evidence that rarely an offspring of same-sex parents will identify as gender-queer or a different gender than their biological gender. Such rare conditions are more difficult to study, even more difficult to assess with respect to mediating factors.

But the literature has identified some cases of gender identity disturbances that were possibly associated with same-sex parenting. Golombok *et al.* (2003, pp. 28, 30) indicated that at least one son of a single (i.e., unpaired) lesbian mother (1/39 children from single-parent and two-parent lesbian families) had a very feminine score on the PSAI test – so feminine that it markedly reduced the overall PSAI scores for the children of all lesbian mothers. Jedzinak (2004) surveyed seven daughters of lesbian mothers from the San Francisco Bay area in 2003/2004 and found that over 71% reported diverse gender expression in childhood and in adulthood, although only one had identified herself as gender queer while in high school. Kuvalanka (2013, p. 168) studied 18 children of same-sex parents and found that three identified as genderqueer and one as gender ambiguous (22.2%); elsewhere she found 27% (8/30, p. 170) of adult children of LGBT parents had gender definitions other than male or female. Dundas and Kaufman (2000) reported that one son of a lesbian mother "thought it would be better to be a girl" (p. 76)(N = 27 families). Goldberg and Allen (2013b) reported that 9% (1/11) of their children described themselves as "gender queer". Bowling, Dodge, and Bartelt (2017) surveyed 33 bisexual parents and of those, four indicated that at least one of their children were "transgender or gender-questioning" (p. 91). There were a total of 52 children but in ten families none were above the age of eight. The denominator could be from 23 to 52 (7.7% to 17.4%, estimate 4/38 = 10.5%). From those six studies, one finds an 11% (18/163) rate of gender identity issues; compared to a 1.2% rate[1] for 163 children of heterosexual parents (simulated), a two-sided Fisher's

Exact Test would be significant ($p < .001$) with an odds ratio of 9.99 (95% *CI*, 2.28 to 43.8)($d = 0.42$). Dundas and Kaufman (2000) found that none of their lesbian mothers expressed a preference for a son, which might lead a son to want to be more like a daughter in order to please his mother in a pattern similar to that seen with respect to sexual orientation of mothers and their preferences for their own children.

Limitations

The evidence in this area remains largely anecdotal, enough to show that rarely the child of same-sex parents seems confused about their gender or at odds with it, but we have little on which to compare same-sex parents' children versus heterosexual parents' children other than rough estimates. The best that can be said is that it can be denied that same-sex parents never have children who report gender confusion or who self-identify as other than their gender identified at birth, such that even a 5% rate would statistically exceed a 1% rate given larger sample sizes. Another limitation that is especially valid given the mostly anecdotal evidence available so far is that what a person means when they describe themselves as "gender-queer" may vary from one person to another. For some it might mean transgender; for others, being indifferent to their physical gender. For some it might reflect being bisexual or asexual. At least some authors (Green & Friedman, 2013) believe that parents can influence their children to delay developing a definitive gender identity and that such delay would be a good thing. Whether that is true remains to be seen.

Future research

Although I have limited experience with transgender research, I assume that there has been relatively little systematic research on transgenderism as an outcome of parenting relationships through either heredity or socialisation, compared to the research that we have on lesbian parenting and child outcomes. Thus, the field is wide open for more research on any associations between parental sexual orientation and child transgender outcomes. It would be important to assess parental acceptance of a child's being transgender as a possible mediating variable between other parental variables and child outcomes. Given the low incidence rates in the general population, it may be difficult to find sufficient samples of transgender adult children, at least in the heterosexual parent population, if not among same-sex parents as well.

Conclusions

A recent book (Green & Friedman, 2013) has encouraged parents to engage in gender fluid parenting practices, which might increase the rate of children identifying with a gender other than their apparent biological gender. While research in this area is complex due to the low incidence rates, there seems to be an ideology within part of the LGBT community that sees gender itself as a personal choice rather than a biological given. If social learning theory is correct that parental modelling and instruction can make a difference in the life of a child, then perhaps parents might be able to teach their children that gender is more a psychological construct than a biological fact. But that appears to be a seldom researched question, as noted above. At the same time, from what limited evidence that could be gathered, it would seem that rates of non-binary gender labels among the children of same-sex parents were higher than what might have been expected in the population in general. Once again, contrary to proclamations to the opposite, there is some evidence, though far from conclusive, that the children of same-sex parents may be at a greater risk for gender identity differences compared to the children of heterosexual parents. I also think there is some evidence that gender identity differences or gender role nonconformity may be associated with later adult same-sex sexual orientation.

As to the question of harm, there are at least two issues. First, some youth who identify as transgender initially may change their identity later and revert to their biological sex; premature transitions might harm those who might have been among those who would have reverted. Second, some transgender persons will undergo radical surgery to complete their transformation. Any surgery involves risk of failure and of unforeseen damage to the patient.

Note
[1] Bockting (2014, p.746) cited Conron, Scott, Stowell, and Landers (2012) for an estimate of 0.5% transgenderism in the adult population. For my statistical comparisons I conservatively doubled (plus) that estimate to arrive at 1.2%. The rate of 11% would be contained within a 95% confidence interval of plus or minus 5% (6-16%) for N = 163.

Chapter Ten

Gender Roles

What has been claimed?

Hicks (2013) has discussed how even LGBT parents feel pressured to ensure that their children turn out "normal" in terms of stereotypical gender roles rather than feeling free to reject "gendered normativities" (p. 150). Mellish, Jennings, Tasker, Lamb, and Golombok (2013, p. 8) reported finding no differences in gender role behaviours across the children of gay, lesbian, and heterosexual adoptive parents. Patterson (2013b) concluded that "the overall findings suggest that children of lesbian mothers develop patterns of gender-role behavior that are much like those of other children" (p. 669). Many other scholars have rejected any idea of difference in children's gender roles as a function of parental sexual orientation (Armesto, 2002; Ball, 2012; Bos *et al.*, 2012; Ellis, 2015, p. 116; Fond, Franc, & Purper-Ouakil, 2012; Lev, 2010; Perrin, Siegel, *et al.*, 2013; Ritenhouse, 2011). If so, one might expect to find no patterns of association between having same-sex parents of either gender and gender role development. Golombok (2007) argued that "In terms of gender role behavior, no differences were found between children in lesbian and heterosexual families for either boys or girls. Daughters of lesbian mothers were no less feminine, and the sons no less masculine than the daughters and sons of heterosexual mothers" in spite of the lesbian mothers' preferences for "less sex-typed toys and activities for their daughters and sons" (p. xvii). More recently, with respect to lesbian mother families, Golombok (2015) stated that "research on this aspect of gender development has shown girls to be no less feminine, and boys to be no less masculine, than girls and boys from heterosexual homes (p. 68), a conclusion she also applied to children from gay father families (p. 191), which she reiterated recently (Golombok, 2017, p. 77).

Remarkably, in spite of such claims of "no difference" there are several social science theories that would predict that absence of both genders among two parents might have an influence on a child's gender role development (Biblarz & Stacey, 2010a; Bos *et al.*, 2012; Farr, Forssell, & Patterson, 2010; Goldberg, Moyer, Kinkler, & Richardson, 2012; MacCallum & Golombok, 2004; Patterson, Sutfin, & Fulcher, 2004). However, Goldberg, Gartrell, and Gates (2014), in their summary of research in this area, stated that "There is some evidence that the play behavior of girls and boys in same-sex parent families may be less gender-stereotyped than the play behavior of girls and boys in different-sex-parent families" (p. 3). Hicks (2013) argued that there was research evidence that same-sex parents were "careful not to impose rigid gender roles or expectations upon their children" (p. 155). Bosisio and Ronfani (2016) have also stated that "children with two mothers enact less gender-stereotyped behaviours, attitudes and preferences" (p. 455). Thus, while some scholars continue to claim support for the "no differences" hypothesis with respect to gender roles or gender role behaviour, a few scholars have cited some evidence of differences as a possible function of parental sexual orientation.

What do we know?

In terms of theory, some of the most explicit arguments have been made for children's gender roles being a function of parental sexual orientations. Goldberg, Kashy, and Smith (2012) have delineated these theories perhaps more clearly than many other scholars. They argue that both social construction and social learning theories would predict that children from heterosexual families would tend to adopt more traditional gender roles for their own gender than would children from lesbian or gay families; however, social learning theory would suggest such differences would be even greater when the child did not have a parent of the same gender to emulate (sons in lesbian families and daughters in gay father families would be even more feminine or masculine respectively than expected *ceteris paribus*). Since most research has been done with lesbian families, one might expect to see larger feminising effects on sons of lesbians relative to other parent/child gender combinations. However, the social learning effects could be countered by the more masculine tendencies of lesbian women and the more feminine tendencies of gay fathers, as discussed by Goldberg *et al*. (2012, p. 504), although gender effects might be expected to predominate.

Ball (2016) is careful to not suggest that "social science evidence shows an association between parental sexual orientation and the gender role development of children" (p. 97), but he acknowledges the existence of a minority of studies that could be used to make such an argument. Lamb (2012) cited a few studies between 30 and 40 years old in order to provide evidence that "children in nontraditional families sometimes have more flexible views of sex-roles" (p. 104), but results from such older studies might not still apply today. However, several studies have found significant differences in gender roles, as discussed elsewhere (Schumm, 2016b, pp. 689-692; 705-706). Notably, Biblarz and Stacey (2010a), Ball (2013), Crowl *et al*. (2008), and Schofield (2016) likewise reported significant findings in their reviews of the literature on gender roles of the children of same-sex parents. Golombok *et al*. (2014) recognised the possibility that children with same-sex parents might "show less sex-typed behaviour than children with heterosexual parents" (p. 456). Gianino (2008) reported that his study participants "expressed the hope that as a result of having gay parents, their children would grow up more socially tolerant and as a result of parental modelling would adopt less traditionally masculine and feminine gender roles" (p. 229; Schumm, 2013, p. 425).

Golombok, Spencer, and Rutter (1983) compared gender roles of children from lesbian and single parent heterosexual households and found no significant results; however, effect sizes were in the small to moderate range (mother's report, boys (.26) and girls (.38); child's report, boys (.21) and girls (.47)) in expected directions (boys more feminine and girls more masculine if raised in lesbian homes). Although Sarantakos (1996b) did not report statistics, he said that "Girls of gay fathers were reported to demonstrate more 'boyish' attitudes and behaviour than girls of heterosexual parents. Most young boys of lesbian mothers were reported to be more effeminate in their behavior and mannerisms than boys of heterosexual parents" (p. 26). Brewaeys *et al.* (1997) reported that sons of lesbian mothers had lower masculine gender role scores than did sons of heterosexual parents ($d = 0.78$) while daughters had lower feminine gender role scores ($d = 0.21$) than did daughters of heterosexual parents. Barrett and Tasker (2001) in the Gay and Bisexual Parenting Study in Britain surveyed 101 gay/bisexual fathers about their children; it appears that about 30-35% of the children whom fathers thought were aware of the father's sexual orientation also were reported by the fathers as feeling confused about their gender role. MacCallum and Golombok (2004) found that 12-year old sons of lesbian mothers scored much higher on scales of femininity ($d = 1.40, p < .05$) than did sons of heterosexual mothers.

Patterson, Sutfin, and Fulcher (2004) found that lesbian mothers held less traditional role expectations for their children than heterosexual mothers, with effect sizes from 0.92 to 0.97. Sutfin, Fulcher, Bowles, and Patterson (2008) reported that lesbian mothers (N = 58) held less traditional gender role attitudes than heterosexual parents (N = 56)($d = 0.75, p < .01$) and that children's (lesbian parents, 9 boys, 20 girls; heterosexual parents, 13 boys and 15 girls) gender role attitudes were less traditional if they had lesbian parents ($d = 0.72, p < .01$; .59 for daughters, .66 for sons); comparing boys' and girls' attitudes within each type of family, the boy/girl difference featured an effect size of .56 in lesbian families (N = 29) and .72 in heterosexual families (N = 28). Looking at differences in bedroom décor, boys ($d = .22$) and girls ($d = .80, p < .05$) of lesbian mothers had bedrooms with less gender role traditional décor than did boys and girls from traditional families; for the within family boy/girl differences, the differences between the bedrooms of boys and girls within lesbian families was large and significant ($d = 0.94, p < .05$) while the difference within heterosexual families was smaller ($d = 0.46$). Where high scores represent more gender typical bedroom decor for a child's gender, daughters of lesbian parents scored the lowest (Mean = 8.84) compared to sons of lesbian parents (10.65), and daughters (10.26) or sons (11.06) of heterosexual parents. That is to say that the daughters of lesbian mothers had the least traditional gender role décor.

It appears from the bedroom décor ratings, the scores were roughly equivalent except that bedroom décor for daughters of lesbians was far less traditional, which is why their bedroom ratings differed significantly from both boys in lesbian families and from girls in heterosexual families, as well as from boys in heterosexual families ($d = 1.25, p < .01$). Predicting children's attitudes about gender from bedroom décor ($b = .28, p < .05$) and parental gender role attitudes ($b = .30, p < .05$), both factors were significant, while parental gender role attitudes also predicted bedroom décor ($b = .28, p < .01$), indicating that parental gender role attitudes had both a direct and a significant indirect effect (through bedroom décor) on children's gender role attitudes.

Fulcher, Sutfin, and Patterson (2008) also found that lesbian mothers held less traditional gender role attitudes, with effect sizes between 0.58 and 1.08; they also found that parental gender role attitudes predicted children's gender role attitudes (with effects sizes of 0.72 and 0.80, although parental sexual orientation added little more after controlling for parental sex role attitudes, with effect sizes of .16 and .20, with lesbian parenthood predicting less traditional role attitudes in children after controlling for parental attitude). Such results suggest that parental sexual orientation may operate indirectly through the intervening variable of parental attitudes to influence a child's gender role development.

Bos and Sandfort (2010) found that children of heterosexual parents indicated significantly greater pressure from their parents to conform to traditional gender roles ($d = 0.39, p < .05$; .46 for sons, .34 for daughters). Goldberg, Kashy, and Smith (2012) looked at children's gender roles as reported by their parents, including 44 lesbian couples, 34 gay male couples, and 48 heterosexual couples. For parents with sons, lesbian parents credited their sons with less masculine gender roles ($d = 0.68, p < .05$) as did gay parents ($d = 0.34$); for parents with daughters, lesbian parents credited their daughters with more masculine gender roles ($d = 0.72, p < .05$) as did gay parents ($d = 0.23$). Comparing lesbian and gay parent differences, sons were somewhat less masculine from lesbian families ($d = 0.29$) while daughters were more feminine from gay father families ($d = 0.46$). Comparing boys versus girls for each type of family, there was a much larger gender difference reported from heterosexual families ($d = 2.94, p < .01$) than for gay ($d = 1.99, p < .01$) or lesbian ($d = 1.22, p < .05$) families. There was some gender differentiation going on in all three types of families, but the greatest distinctions were made in heterosexual families, more than twice as much as in lesbian families.

Unlike most other studies of children's gender roles, Goldberg, Kashy, and Smith (2012) provided ranges as well as means and standard deviations for their measure of gender role behaviours. For heterosexual parents' children, the most masculine tomboy girl scored (58.26) at only the 22nd percentile of masculinity ((63.75 − 58.26)/7.11 = -0.77, lowest 22% for sons of heterosexual parents); all the other daughters scored in a more feminine direction. The most feminine son of heterosexual parents (49.68) scored at the 85th percentile of masculinity ((49.68 − 41.10)/8.19 = 1.05) for the daughters of heterosexual parents. In other words, there was a clear distinction in gender role behaviour between sons and daughters of heterosexual parents even at the extremes with overlap only in the tails of the distributions closest to each other. In contrast, for children of lesbian parents the most extreme tomboy girl scored higher (64.34) than the average for sons of lesbians (58.67) and approximately equal to the average for sons (63.75) of heterosexual parents while the most feminine son of lesbian mothers scored (39.16) about a 0.24 of a standard deviation below the average for girls from heterosexual families (41.10) or more feminine than 60% of the girls from heterosexual families.

Another way of looking at the patterns is that the sons of lesbians and the sons of heterosexual parents maxed out at approximately the same high level of masculinity (79.25 and 81.26) but on the feminine side, 13% of the sons of lesbians scored lower on masculinity than any of the sons of heterosexual parents and the lowest scoring son of lesbian mothers scored at -3.45 standard deviations compared to the sons of heterosexual parents. For daughters, the lowest scores (least masculine, most feminine) were similar for children of lesbian mothers (18.76) and heterosexual parents (18.64) but the most masculine daughter of lesbian mothers scored at +2.84 standard deviations compared to the daughters of heterosexual parents and about 14% of the daughters of lesbian mothers scored higher on masculinity than any of the daughters of heterosexual parents. Given the small sample sizes, this means that two or three (13%) of the sons of the 20 lesbian mothers with boys scored lower than any of the sons of heterosexual parents on masculinity (were more feminine) and at least one son of a lesbian mother scored lower (39.16, more feminine) on masculinity than the average masculinity score (41.10) for the daughters of heterosexuals. Likewise, of the 24 lesbian mothers with daughters, about three (14%) scored higher on masculinity than any of the 25 daughters of heterosexual parents and at least one daughter of a lesbian mother scored higher (64.34) on masculinity than the average score (63.75) for the 23 sons of heterosexual parents. The question would be – do such scores represent gender flexibility or gender distortion? At the very least there seem to be some children of lesbian mothers who are being rated as more like the way the other gender children are being rated by heterosexual parents.

However, when Farr, Forssell, and Patterson (2010) assessed gender roles for adopted children between 13 and 72 months of age (parental reports), differences as a function of parent sexual orientation (lesbian, gay, heterosexual) and child gender were minimal (effect size differences between lesbian and heterosexual parents' children were < .15) and counterintuitive (e.g., sons of gay fathers were the most masculine; daughters of gay fathers were the most feminine; to date, the authors have not reported gender role scores at their second wave of the study when the children were between six and 10-11 years of age).

Goldberg, Kashy, and Smith (2012) looked at children's gender roles as reported by their parents, including 44 lesbian couples, 34 gay male couples and 48 heterosexual couples. For parents with sons, lesbian parents credited their sons with less masculine gender roles ($d = 0.68$, p < .05) as did gay parents ($d = 0.34$); for parents with daughters, lesbian parents credited their daughters with more masculine gender roles ($d = 0.72, p < .05$) as did gay parents ($d = 0.23$). Comparing lesbian and gay parent differences, sons were somewhat less masculine from lesbian families ($d = 0.29$) while daughters were more feminine from gay father families ($d = 0.46$). Comparing boys versus girls for each type of family, there was a much larger gender difference reported from heterosexual families ($d = 2.94, p < .01$) than for gay ($d = 1.99, p < .01$) or lesbian ($d = 1.22, p < .05$) families.

Most recently, Goldberg and Garcia (2016) studied adopted children of lesbian, gay, and heterosexual parents and found at least a trend for less traditional gender roles for those children who did not have an opposite parent in their household (i.e., sons of lesbian mothers and daughters of gay fathers). In particular, sons of lesbians scored lower on masculinity at three times points with effect sizes between approximately 0.60 and 0.90 while daughters of lesbians scored in a more masculine direction with effect sizes of approximately 0.30 to 0.40. Daughters of gay fathers tended to score in more of a masculine direction compared to daughters of heterosexual fathers, with approximate effect sizes of 0.10 to 0.45. While the results were mixed for sons of gay fathers compared to the sons of heterosexual fathers, the overall trend seemed to be less gender role differentiation by gender for children of same-sex parents compared to that for children of heterosexual parents.

Possibly reflecting such a gender interaction, Titlestad and Pooley (2014) reported that daughters of lesbian mothers often "felt having lesbian or bisexual mothers would be more difficult for boys" (p. 347). Dundas and Kaufman (2000) found that many of their lesbian mothers were worried about a son not having a male role model in a lesbian family. Likewise, in a study of adopted children, Golombok, Mellish, Tasker, Jennings, Casey, and Lamb (2014) stated that "Whereas the heterosexual families had an equal number of boys and girls, there was a preponderance of boys adopted by gay fathers and a preponderance of girls adopted by lesbian mothers" (p. 458), a result in accord with previous studies (p. 464). Golombok, Spencer, and Rutter (1983) found in their study of lesbian and single-parent heterosexual households that 63% of the children of the lesbian mothers were girls compared to 39% of the children of the heterosexual mothers. Golombok (2015, p. 191) observed that there was a trend, similar to that noted by Biblarz and Stacey (2010a), for lesbian mothers to adopt girls and for gay fathers to adopt boys, though she attributed that pattern to influences from adoption agencies.

Goldberg, Kashy, and Smith (2012) found that 55% of the adopted children of lesbian mothers were girls while 56% of the adopted children of gay fathers were boys, although that difference was not significant statistically. Farr, Forssell, & Patterson (2010) in their study of adopting families found that 59% of lesbian couples had adopted girls compared to 36% of gay adoptive fathers. Tornello, Sonnenberg, and Patterson (2015) studied over 300 gay fathers and found that more than 70% of their children were boys. Bos, Kuyper, and Gartrell (2017) did not break down their results by adoption status, but in a population sample from the Netherlands found that 75% of the children of gay fathers were boys while 74.4% of the children of lesbian mothers were girls (p. 7). On the other hand, some studies have found mixed results (Bos, Goldberg, van Gelderen, & Gartrell, 2012; see Schumm, 2016b, p. 691). There also seem to be at least some situations in which lesbian mothers with boys are deemed by other LGBT persons to be an outcast minority for the sin of "mothering a son" (Chrisp, 2001, p. 205). On the other hand, some studies have used samples of lesbian mothers with equal numbers of boys and girls (e.g., Shechner, Slone, Lobel, & Shechter, 2013).

If same-sex attracted persons have different views of their own gender role traits in terms of masculinity or femininity, they might well parent differently. If nonheterosexuals and heterosexuals differ in their self-perceptions of their masculinity and femininity, that might influence their children. For example, Martin-Storey and August (2016) surveyed 251 college students; comparing self-ratings on masculinity versus femininity, heterosexual men ($d = 3.12$) and heterosexual women ($d = 3.28$) had quite different outcomes than did nonheterosexual men ($d = 1.25$) or nonheterosexual women ($d = 0.98$). In that same study, heterosexual men rated themselves as more masculine than did nonheterosexual men ($d = 0.76$) and lower on femininity as well ($d = 0.83$); heterosexual women rated themselves as less masculine than did lesbians ($d = 1.10$) but more feminine ($d = 0.89$). Dundas and Kaufman (2000) likewise found that many of their lesbian mothers (52%, 14/27) had wished to be a man at some time. As noted earlier, Sarantakos (1998) found that 55% of the gay men in his study reported they were a woman in a man's body while 45% of the lesbians reported being a man in a woman's body (Schumm, 2015b, p. 7). These traits might well be passed along to children in terms of gender roles, gender identity and sexual orientation, unless same-sex parents self-select for fewer differences compared to heterosexuals on masculine/femininity traits.

Perhaps the jury is still out, but trends seem to be growing in the direction that same-sex parents may raise children whose gender role orientations are not as clearly defined by biological gender as such roles may be for children of heterosexual parents, which might be related to differences in how the parents perceive their own gender roles or relative levels of masculinity and femininity. Same-sex parents may also intentionally teach less traditional gender roles to their children (Gianino, 2008) and adjust their home environments likewise. The general pattern seems to be for boys to be more feminine and girls more masculine relative to children from heterosexual homes while there seems to be a trend for same-sex parents to adopt children of their same gender when possible.

Limitations

Research is not consistent in showing differences in gender role development; some studies seem to suggest differences for the children of same-sex parents while other studies do not. The lack of equivalence among studies and between heterosexual parent and same-sex parent groups within studies makes assessment of this area more difficult. The use of statistical controls in some studies (e.g. Goldberg & Garcia, 2016) has sometimes reduced the apparent degree of gender role differences between the children of same-sex and heterosexual parents. Furthermore, it appears that the social contacts of children of same-sex parents often do not involve very many heterosexual males or the observation of many heterosexual romantic relationships, which might influence gender role expression among the children of same-sex parents, but there has been little research connecting social contacts with gender role behaviour for the children of same-sex parents (Schumm, 2015c, p. 17).

Future research

There has been relatively little research available to explain why children from same-sex families might adopt less traditional gender roles. Would it be because their parents were less satisfied with traditional gender roles (Gianino, 2008)? Do their parents change the home environment to reflect less traditional roles (Sutfin *et al.*, 2004; Fulcher *et al.*, 2008)? Do same-sex parents expose their children to less traditional roles of friends outside the home? We need more complex theories and more detailed research to investigate if and how such differences may come about. It is also possible that parents who have only one child might socialise that child differently than if they have two children of different genders. Parent gender might interact with child gender(s) so that lesbian mothers might influence sons and daughters differently than gay fathers in terms of gender role behaviour.

Conclusions

While there is considerable variance in study results in this area, at least some studies do indicate trends for the children of same-sex parents to adopt less rigid gender roles, with sons being more feminine and daughters being more masculine. Effect sizes for sons with lesbian mothers range between .60 and 1.40; one study found an effect size of 0.34 for sons of gay fathers. Effect sizes for daughters of lesbian mothers run from .21 to .72, while effect sizes for daughters of gay fathers ran from .10 to .72. It seems that the largest effects tend to occur in more studies for the sons of lesbian mothers, although at least one study found the largest effect for daughters of lesbian mothers. At least one or two studies seemed to find that parental sex role attitudes predicted the sex role attitudes of children, largely independently of parental sexual orientation, although lesbian mothers appeared to have less gender stereotyped gender role attitudes, with effect sizes from 0.34 to 1.08. At least one study involving very young children did not seem to find much difference in children's gender role attitudes as a function of parental sexual orientation.

Although Biblarz and Stacey (2010a) laud this gender role flexibility, some of the effect sizes are large enough (> .50) that it is doubtful that mere "flexibility" is always what is at play here, recalling that Cuijpers (2017) found an effect size of .24 or greater to have clinical relevance. We have seen earlier that even gender itself can seem to be influenced by same-sex parenting, so influence over gender *roles* should be less difficult than that. Those children whose gender is influenced might well show gender role behaviour differences while other children may not see their gender differently than their biological gender but still adopt gender roles that are less traditional than children of heterosexual parents. Some of these gender role differences have been observed in relatively young children and do seem to be related to the parental and home environment.

Summary for Part Three

Contrary to most scholarly commentary, there do appear to be some differences in all three aspects of sexual identity – gender identity, gender-role behaviour, and sexual orientation (Patterson, 2013b, p. 668) as a function of same-sex parenting. How can errors in this area be detected? I would suggest that a paucity of citations might be one clue. Another clue might be any claim that "no" studies have ever found any contrary information, a claim that might suggest the author had not done a thorough job of reviewing a large number of studies, for surely if the number of studies was large, at least one or two might have found some difference merely by chance. Using Patterson (2013b) as an example is useful because her chapter was published in perhaps the major handbook of family studies in the past five years. Many scholars will refer to this handbook because of its large size, comprehensive coverage of the family research area, and its distinguished editors.

Before Patterson discusses each area of sexual identity, she states clearly that "Research relevant to each of these three major areas of concern is summarized below" (p. 668). Readers would surely get an impression that her summaries would contain all the relevant information and would be complete and comprehensive. However, in the three areas of gender identity, gender-role behavior, and sexual orientation she cited 6, 13, and 12 studies. Readers may compare for themselves how many studies have been cited in the preceding three chapters with respect to each of these topics.

As far as the age of the studies cited, respectively, the ranges were 1978-2010, 1981-2009, and 1980-1997. In each case, older studies were cited while the most recent studies cited were from three to seventeen years old, as if nothing had been done in recent years, even though one might presume that research has been increasingly prevalent in more recent years. Readers are free to compare the age ranges cited in the previous three chapters as compared to the ranges used by Patterson (2013b). Patterson could argue that she did not have as much space to review this literature but that should not have restricted her use of the most recent studies – if anything, one might have expected the older studies to be slighted in favour of much more recent studies.

Lastly, one might look at the author's "certainty" imposed upon the reviews. For gender identity, Patterson argues that "No evidence has been reported in any of the studies to suggest difficulties among children of lesbian mothers" (p. 669). The use of "No" would seem to imply certainty in her conclusions but it actually rests upon an assumption that she has reviewed all relevant studies, including ones that might have differed from her overall conclusions.

For gender-role behaviour, Patterson concludes that "the overall findings suggest that children of lesbian mothers develop patterns of gender-role behavior that are much like those of other children" (p. 669), although she cites one review of the literature that differed from her conclusion (Stacey & Biblarz, 2001) as an indication of "some controversy" (p. 669). It is surprising to me that Patterson did not cite Biblarz and Stacey (2010a), who also reviewed the literature on gender-role behaviour and found some possible differences, especially as one might think a more recent review of the literature would supersede a much older review of the same literature. Patterson did not cite a number of research reports that either found that lesbian mothers had less traditional gender-role attitudes and/or that their children also tended to have less traditional gender-role attitudes (Goldberg, Kashy, & Smith, 2012; Bos & Sandfort, 2010; MacCallum & Golombok, 2004; Brewaeys et al., 1997; Sarantakos, 1996b), as well as not citing some of Patterson's own similar research findings on gender roles (Fulcher, Sutfin, & Patterson, 2008; Patterson, Sutfin, & Fulcher, 2004; Sutfin, Fulcher, Bowles, & Patterson, 2008). Rather, Patterson cited some of her research as evidence in favour of "no differences" in the area of gender roles (Patterson et al., 2004; Sutfin et al., 2008), as well as MacCallum and Golombok (2004).

With respect to sexual orientation, Patterson (2013b) concluded that "rates of homosexuality are similar among the offspring of lesbian, gay, and heterosexual parents" (p.669). Patterson noted some studies that featured 8-9% rates of homosexuality among children of same-sex parents without seeming to realise that such rates would be higher than typically found among the children of heterosexual parents at the time these studies were done. Thus, overall, one might well be skeptical of research reviews in which only a few studies are cited, almost no contrary evidence is cited, and there are few recent citations while there are quite a few much older studies reported. Patterson's review did not mention numerous research reports that found higher rates of same-sex sexual attraction, dating, sexual behaviour, or same-sex sexual identity among children of same-sex parents (Sirota, 1997, as reported in Schumm, 2008; Kunin, 1998; Zweig, 1999; Murray & McClintock, 2005; Bos & Sandfort, 2010; Gartrell, Bos, & Goldberg, 2011, 2012; Biblarz & Stacey, 2010a; Balsam, Beauchaine, Mickey, & Rothblum, 2005; Joos & Broad, 2007; Kuvalanka & Goldberg, 2009, among several others cited previously), including some of her own research that featured very high rates (40% or so) of same-sex romantic involvement among children of same-sex parents (Lick, Schmidt, & Patterson, 2011; Lick, Tornello, Riskind, Schmidt, & Patterson, 2012). In her defence, it could be argued that she missed a trend for increasing rates of same-sex romantic involvement, basing her conclusions on reliance on earlier studies or that perhaps she had to submit her chapter long before the actual handbook was published.

In a larger sense, Patterson's (2013b) review of the literature has many limitations that in an overall sense make it at least somewhat incomplete, if not outright inaccurate. This type of situation should serve as a warning to the public, to the courts, to scholars, and to students everywhere that just because a famous author publishes a literature review in a major, comprehensive handbook does not imply that it should be automatically accepted as accurate or comprehensive. Such reviews may not even contain some of the most interesting and recent research results from the field. Patterson's review is not alone in having such limitations; many other reviews of the literature have the same issues, but her review is of greater interest to me because of its inclusion in what is deemed by many to be one of the major handbooks on marriage and family in the world today.

PART FOUR

WHAT DO WE KNOW ABOUT THE CHILDREN OF SAME-SEX PARENTS IN TERMS OF MENTAL HEALTH AND RELATED ISSUES?

Introduction to Part Four

Other Child Outcomes

While a few scholars have recognised the possibility of some differences as were discussed in Part Three, even fewer have recognised differences as will be discussed in Part Four of this book. Sometimes a scholar here or there might have said there were differences but those differences were an artifact of higher rates of instability among same-sex parents (see chapter three). I suspect that because many of these other outcomes came closer to what might be defined as "harm", there was even more opposition to finding mere differences in these areas. One could argue that being gay is no disadvantage, so what is the harm if same-sex parents are more likely to raise children who become LGBT? But when the topic is mental health or drug abuse, it is harder to dismiss findings of difference as not mattering in terms of harm as well as difference. As I noted previously in chapter one, even if differences were found in some aspect of mental health, I would expect critics to redefine any difference as harmless, even if, at the street level, parents were losing their children because of such "differences".

Chapter Eleven

Mental Health

What has been claimed?

Stacey and Biblarz (2001) reviewed 21 studies on same-sex parenting outcomes and concluded that those studies "almost uniformly claim[ed] to find no differences in measures of parenting or child outcomes" (p. 167). In terms of children's mental health, Stacey and Biblarz (2001) concluded that "these studies find no significant differences between children of lesbian mothers and children of heterosexual mothers in anxiety, depression, self-esteem, and numerous other measures of social and psychological adjustment" (p. 171) and that "every relevant study to date shows that parental sexual orientation *per se* has no measurable effect on the quality of parent-child relationships or on children's mental health or social adjustment" (p. 176). Cooper and Cates (2006) included a quote by Bilchik to the effect that "It has now been established by the research that their children [the children of gay and lesbian parents] are just as likely to be healthy and well adjusted" (p. vi). Like many others, Harder (2016a, b) concluded that "children raised by same-sex parents are no more likely to suffer from the many health and behavioural outcomes that are of concern" (pp. 900, 1295), a conclusion echoed by Compton (2013, p. 260); Ellis (2015, p. 116), Golombok (2015, 2017), Ruspini (2016), and many others (Schumm, 2016b, pp. 665-668). Golombok in particular stated that "With respect to psychological adjustment, not a single study has shown that children raised by lesbian mothers are more at risk for emotional or behavioural problems than are peers from heterosexual homes" (2015, p. 66). Ball (2016) has affirmed that "studies show no association between parental sexual orientation and children's psychological adjustment and social functioning" (p. 94). Patterson and

Goldberg (2016) concluded that not only were children of lesbian or gay parents doing as well as the children of heterosexual parents (with "no differences in sexual, social, or psychological adjustment", p. 2) but the work of the "few investigators" who might have reached different conclusions had "been discredited by reputable scholars and by major scientific organisations" (p. 2).

Judge Vaughn Walker in *Perry v. Schwarzennegger* stated that "Children raised by gay or lesbian parents are as likely as children raised by heterosexual parents to be healthy, successful and well-adjusted. The research supporting this conclusion is accepted beyond serious debate in the field of developmental psychology" (Allen, 2013, p. 635; Allen, 2015, p. 154; cited in Schumm, 2015b, p. 1). Biblarz and Stacey (2010a) likewise stated that "scholars have achieved a rare degree of consensus that unmarried lesbian parents are raising children who develop at least as well as their counterparts with married heterosexual parents" (p. 5). Note that their comparison did not excuse differences on the basis of a lack of marriage rights but implied that lesbian mothers (and presumably gay fathers) did not need marriage to meet or exceed the child outcomes typically experienced by married heterosexual parents.

Perlesz, Brown, Lindsay, McNair, deVaus, and Pitts (2006) stated that "Critical reviews and direct research on the outcomes of children raised in lesbian-parented families worldwide demonstrate convincingly that children's psychosocial adjustment and intellectual development is influenced more by family processes such as conflict between parents than it is by family structure, such as the number of parents or their sexual orientation, and that children with lesbian parents differ little from their heterosexually parented peers" (p. 177). Folgero (2008) argued that "children of homosexual parents turn out to have the same personal development as children of heterosexual parents" (p. 139) and that "There is, however, little evidence of significant differences between children growing up with homosexual parents and children growing up with heterosexual parents" (p. 138). Malmquist, Mollerstrand, Wikstrom, and Nelson (2013) stated that with respect to social and psychological development of children from lesbian and heterosexual families, "child outcome research... has shown no or trivial differences between the groups" (p. 120). Goldberg, Gartrell, and Gates (2014) concluded that research had found "few differences between children raised by lesbian and heterosexual parents in terms of self-esteem, quality of life, psychological adjustment, or social functioning" (p. 3). Harris (2016, p. 123) reviewed the literature and claimed that the children of same-sex parents were doing well in school and were not troubled emotionally or psychologically. Mezey (2015) argued that the children of LGBT parents "fare better in terms of mental health than children with heterosexual parents" (p. 64), while Bosisio and Ronfani (2016) recently claimed that children of same-sex parents "show fewer social and behavioural problems than their peers who have grown up in heterosexual parent families" (p. 455). The American Psychological Association argued that this was not an area "where credible scientific researchers disagree" (*Obergefell v. Hodges*, 2015, slip opinion, p. 26). In other words, disagreement is not permissible unless you want to be discredited as a legitimate scientist. Furthermore, Farr (2017a) has claimed that, if you examine the mental health of adopted children over a five-year longitudinal study, there were no differences among parental or teacher reports of outcomes for the children.

Last but not least, one U.S. court concluded that "the quality and breadth of research available, as well as the results of the studies performed about gay parenting and the children of gay parents, is robust and has provided the basis for a consensus in the field" and "these reports and studies find that there are no differences in the parenting of homosexuals or the adjustment of their children... the issue is so far beyond dispute that it would be irrational to hold otherwise" (Brodzinsky, Green, & Katusny, 2012, p. 240; Schumm, 2016b, p. 667). In other words, anyone who might dare disagree was essentially declared "irrational" not merely by other scholars, progressive social science organisations or newspaper editorials (Morgan, 2014, p. 17) but by the U.S. legal system itself! Ball (2013) from his own extensive review of the social science literature argued that "The social science evidence showing a lack of an association between parental sexual orientation and the psychological and social functioning of children is so conclusive and so uniform, that efforts to impose marriage and parenting restrictions on lesbians and gay men based on concerns about such functioning are irrational (and therefore unconstitutional) because they lack a defensible factual foundation" (p.698) and that "The clear absence of empirical findings showing differences in the psychological and social functioning of children of lesbians and gay men, when compared to the children of heterosexual parents, means that the contention that parental sexual orientation is associated with such functioning cannot be defended factually, and thus fails to satisfy the rational basis test" (p.699). Not only have lesbian mothers been given credit for being better parents than heterosexual parents by some scholars, a recent Dutch study found that lesbian mothers rated their own parental competency substantially higher than did heterosexual mothers (Bos, Kuyper, & Gartrell, 2017, p. 9, $d = 0.72, p < .01$; also higher than heterosexual fathers, $d = 0.64, p < .05$; gay fathers rated themselves less competent than heterosexual fathers, $d = 0.41, p < .05$ and less competent than did heterosexual mothers, $d = 0.29$; the variable was coded so that higher scores indicated less reported competency). Bos, Kuyper, and Gartrell (2017) concluded that "There were no significant differences found on any assessment of children's psychological well being in female same-sex and male same-sex parent households versus different-sex parents" (p.12). Given the apparent *total* scientific consensus (Adams & Light, 2015), the *conclusive* imprimatur of the U.S. legal system, and the apparent lack of *any* contrary evidence, how could it be possible that anyone might disagree and be able to support that disagreement with valid social science research?

What do we know?

Goldberg and Allen (2013a) called for "wading into these deeper waters" (p.364) with respect to possible differences between same-sex and heterosexual parents and/or their children. Perhaps we can dare to look "behind the research curtain" as one reviewer of Schumm (2016b) put it. It seems clear that if assessments of mental health are based on the reports of lesbian mothers or gay fathers about their children, there is little evidence with which to dispute the "no difference" hypothesis (e.g., Shechner *et al.*, 2013). For example, Bos, Kuyper, and Gartrell (2017), using national data from the Netherlands, have reported no differences in child well-being, as described by parents, as a function of parental sexual orientation, with similar results from similar U.S. national data (Bos, Knox, van Rihn-van Gelderen, & Gartrell, 2016).

Social desirability/selection effect biases

However, very few studies have measured, much less controlled for, appropriate forms of social desirability (Schumm, 2015a, p. 40; Stober, 2001), even though this has been recognised as a potential issue by other scholars (e.g., Anderssen, Amilie, & Ytteroy, 2002, p. 348; Bos & Sandfort, 2010, p. 123; Farr, 2017b, p. 100; Frank, 2016, pp. 246-247; Gartrell, Hamilton, Banks, Mosbacher, Reed, Sparks, & Bishop, 1996, p. 279; Golombok, 2015, p. 65; Raley, 2010, p. 188; Shechner, Slone, Lobel, & Shechter, 2011, p. 183; Tan and Baggerly, 2009, p. 183; Tasker & Golombok, 1997, p. 146; Tasker & Golombok, 1998, p. 64; Telingator & Patterson, 2008, p. 1365; Van Rijn-van Gelderen *et al.*, 2015, p. 72). For example, Gartrell *et al.* (1996) stated that "Some may have volunteered for this project because they were motivated to demonstrate that lesbians were capable of producing healthy, happy children. To the extent that these subjects might wish to present themselves and their families in the best possible light, the study findings may be shaped by self-justification and self-presentation bias" (p. 279). Erich, *et al.* (2009) stated similarly, "Responses of this sort are subject to the effects of social desirability and impression management" (p. 403). Golombok, MacCallum, Goodman, and Rutter (2002) similarly stated that "With any investigation that uses parental reports, one must be aware of the social desirability bias whereby parents try to present themselves and their children in the best possible light" (p. 965). Goldberg (2010, p. 169) also acknowledged this problem. It should be easily apparent that if parents are "in charge" of rating their own competence as parents and they have motivations to rate themselves as highly as possible, then such ratings would have relatively little validity from a scientific point of view without controls for such motivations or social desirability.

Because most studies of same-sex parenting have not been blinded and are usually convenience samples, it is possible that selection effects have occurred so that either parents with better-off children have been more likely to volunteer or that parents, being aware of the potential political or legal uses of their answers, may have tilted their responses in directions favourable to the apparent well-being of their children (Bos, Gartrell, van Balen, Peyser, & Sandfort, 2008, p. 218).[1] It is also possible that more conflicted lesbian families would be more likely to drop out of research, tilting the results in favour of the remaining lesbian families appearing better off than heterosexual comparisons, as has occurred in at least one study (Tasker & Golombok, 1995, p. 207, $p = .001$, with $d \geq 1.50$, based on a t-test value of 3.87 with 19 degrees of freedom). LGBT families may feel a greater need to justify their parenthood and therefore may be inclined to provide more socially desirable responses (or they may work harder at parenting and achieve more success).

Mental health

At least one study (Tan & Baggerly, 2009), of 733 adopted children, found that preschool children of lesbian mothers scored higher (less well off) on internalising problems ($d = 0.37$) and externalising problems ($d = 0.33$), including subscales for (more) aggressive behaviours ($d = 0.80$), being withdrawn ($d = 0.80$), and emotional reactivity ($d = 0.47$) than children of heterosexual parents. For their sample of older adopted children, results were less favourable for the children of lesbian mothers in terms of internalising problems ($d = 0.44$), externalising problems ($d = 0.66$), social problems ($d = 0.37$), thought problems ($d = 0.72$, p < .05$), attention problems ($d = 0.39$), and combined problems ($d = 0.49$). Some studies featured mixed results; Goldberg and Smith (2013) found three of four problem scale ratings better for children of heterosexual couples (d's between .01 and 0.16) but gay fathers rated their children lower on internalising problems than did heterosexual parents ($d = 0.25$). Other studies have found small effects in favour of the children of lesbian parents (Farr et al., 2010). Shechner et al. (2013) found that lesbian mothers in two-parent households rated their children higher on internalising problems ($d = 0.14$) but lower on externalising problems ($d = 0.19$) than did mothers from two-parent heterosexual families, a mixed but non-significant result. If coping well (assuming the child stays calm and in control when faced with a challenge) can be considered an aspect of mental health, even though Bos, Knox, van Rijn-van Gelderen, and Gartrell (2016) claimed that they had found no significant differences in mental health across the children of same-sex and heterosexual families in U.S. data, the children of heterosexual parents were rated by their parents better than were the children of same-sex parents ($d = 0.34, p < .05$), an effect that was stronger for daughters ($d = 0.57, p < .05$) than for sons ($d = 0.11$).

Sullins (2016b, c) in an analysis of ADD HEALTH data (albeit with only 20 adolescents from same-sex families) found that at wave IV of that study, adolescents with same-sex parents had higher rates of depression ($d = .85, p = .001$), suicidal ideation ($d = .97, p = .04$), obesity ($d = .84, p = .009$), and greater distance from one or both parents, usually the parent outside of the same-sex family ($d = .71, p = .01$), with the results for suicidal ideation, anxiety, and distance from parents persisting from wave I. Perceived stigma was much higher for the adolescents from same-sex families ($d = 1.17, p = .01$), which could account for some of the differences. When Sullins controlled for 12 variables (wave I depression, suicidal ideation, anxiety; parental child abuse, parental distance, and stigma; age, sex, race, education of adolescent; parent education, parent income) the effect of same-sex parenthood was reported in Table 3 (p. 5) to be nearly statistically significant ($p < .10$), but when he added obesity at wave IV as a 13th control variable, the results declined to non-significance. Later Sullins (2016c) included controls for parental stability and found that they did not change his results in any notable way. I remain skeptical about using nearly as many variables as you have participants in one of your two groups, so I think Sullins' results (2016b, c) need to be treated with due caution, as he recognised himself.

Drug and alcohol abuse

While there have been mixed results in many other areas, especially in terms of parental ratings of children's problem behaviours (Schumm, 2015b, 2016b), one of the most consistent adverse result appears to have been in the use of illegal drugs, where the six studies of which

I am aware that were done in the United States have found higher, though not always significantly so, rates of drug use among the children of same-sex parents (Schumm, 2015b, p. 12; 2016b, p. 672), a result that parallels higher levels of illegal drug use among sexual minority youth in general (e.g., Donahue, Langstrom, Lundstrom, Lichtenstein, & Forsman, 2017, p. 326, $d = 0.29$, $p < .001$). However, studies done recently in Britain and the Netherlands have *not* found a higher use of illegal drugs among the children of same-sex parents (Bos, van Gelderen, & Gartrell, 2015; Golombok & Badger, 2010). The most notable study done in the USA found a 60% rate of illegal drug use versus 21% ($d = 0.89$, $p < .05$) for children of lesbian mothers versus heterosexual mothers (Goldberg, Bos, & Gartrell, 2011); critics downplayed that result (for the U.S. Supreme Court) because the rates were only for "occasional" use of marijuana or hashish (Manning, Fettro, & Lamidi, 2014, p. 494). However, Goldberg *et al.* (2011) also found higher rates of alcohol use (80% vs. 50%, $d = 0.67$, $p < .05$), tobacco use (27% vs. 14%, $d = 0.32$, $p = .051$), cocaine (13% vs. 6%, $d = 0.22$; for daughters only, 15% vs. 3%, $d = 0.46$, $p < .10$); and LSD or other hallucinogens (21% vs. 8%, $d = 0.38$, $p < .05$). Likewise, Sirota (1997) found a 44% versus 15% ($d = 0.68$, $p < .05$) rate of drug use among the daughters of gay fathers, a result *not* explained entirely by previous parental divorces (Schumm, 2008). Sarantakos (2000, pp. 131-132) reported higher alcohol and drug use among the children of same-sex parents but did not provide statistics. Other studies have found effect sizes from .00 to 0.63 (Marquardt, Glenn, & Clark, 2010; Regnerus, 2012a; Sarantakos, 2000; Schumm, Landess, & Williams, 2014; Wainright & Patterson, 2006). For example, Wainright and Patterson (2006) looked at several different types of drug use (tobacco use, alcohol use, frequency of getting drunk, frequency of binge drinking, marijuana use, risky use of alcohol and drugs, problems related to alcohol use, sex under influence of alcohol or drugs, number of best friends who smoke) finding effect sizes from .00 to 0.27, none significant; however, to have 8 of 9 possible outcomes turn out in the direction of greater use for children from same-sex parent families is relatively unlikely ($p < .05$, one sample binomial test); if in fact there were no difference in any of the nine items, chance should have left some results in one direction, and other results in the opposite direction. In other words, if a coin is unbiased, you should seldom succeed in getting eight heads and one coin on its edge out of nine tries. In business applications, control charts are used on the same assumption, that having nine results on the same side of the long-term average or mean would be unlikely from a statistical perspective (Brase & Brase, 2015, p. 277). In sum, most studies in the United States have found higher rates of drug use among the children of same-sex parents, though the differences have not always been statistically significant.

Greenan and Tunnell (2006) identified recreational drug use as "destructive to individuals and very destabilizing to families" (p. 230), but that such usage was a behavioural norm within the gay community, thus potentially affecting same-sex parents and their children. Drug abuse appears to be higher in general among LGBT persons and anti-discrimination policies in different States may not be helping reduce such rates. While Schumm (2013) cited a number of other studies on drug abuse among LGBT persons, one of the more interesting findings is that LGB participants in the U.S. National NESARC study were more likely to report a drug abuse disorder in the past year compared to heterosexuals (odds ratio = 4.21, $p < .05$, after adjusting for gender, age, race/ethnicity, education, marital status, and income). In States with no protective policies, the odds ratio was only 2.19 ($p < .05$); with the same controls but in States with protective policies the odds ratio was 4.56 ($p < .05$) with the interaction effect being nearly significant ($p < .07$). If protective policies reduced the need for LGB persons to self-medicate by reducing discrimination or stigma, one would have expected the relative use of drugs to be lower in States with more LGBT protective policies. However, we do not know how LGB parents use drugs compared to heterosexual parents, much less how State anti-discrimination policies influence relative drug use by parents of any sexual orientation.

Educational attainment

Biblarz and Stacey's (2010a) review of the literature claimed that lesbian parents seemed to encourage greater "interest, effort, success in school" (p.8, citing MacCallum & Golombok, 2004; Wainright, Russell, & Patterson, 2004). Some studies have found problems with educational progress but the problems seemed to be greatly reduced when the stability of the same-sex parental relationships were controlled statistically (Schumm, 2016b). If the rates of instability were similar for same-sex parents and heterosexual parents, that approach might make sense, but if the rates were different then it would be more appropriate to use instability as a mediating factor and testing for any significant indirect effect of same-sex parenting through instability on educational progress, a type of theory testing that has seldom been used in research with LGBT families (van Eeden-Moorefield et $al.$, 2018). Golombok et $al.$ (1997), using the Pictorial Scale of Perceived Competence (i.e., cognitive and physical, separately) and Social Acceptance (e.g., from mother and peers)(Harter & Pike, 1984) found that the children of heterosexual parents rated themselves higher on cognitive competence $(d = 0.94, p < .001)$ and physical competence $(d = 0.55, p < .01)$ than did the children of lesbian mothers, even though the lesbian families were far better off in socioeconomic resources and had parents with better mental health. Similarly, Golombok et $al.$ (2003) found that children from two-parent heterosexual families rated their own cognitive competence $(d = 0.14)$ and physical competence $(d = 0.38)$ higher than did children from two-parent lesbian families despite substantial advantages for the latter families.

In a third study of the cognitive and physical competence of children, as rated by the children themselves, Shechner, Slone, Lobel, and Shechter (2013) found effect sizes of .16 for cognitive competence and .25 for physical competence in favour of the children of two-parent heterosexual households compared to children from two-parent lesbian households (peer relations were rated better by children from the heterosexual families as well, $d = 0.18$), even though the heterosexual families had more children ($d = 0.90, p < .05$). Shechner *et al.* (2013) concluded that they had found no differences; however, one of their effect sizes (child's internalising reported for single heterosexual versus single lesbian mothers), an effect size of 0.58, was not significant statistically, suggesting their study had very low statistical power (76 families split into four groups). Bos, Knox, van Rijn-van Gelderen, and Gartrell (2016), though they reported no such differences, did find that daughters of heterosexual parents were rated by their parents better on learning behaviour than were daughters of lesbian mothers ($d = 0.42, p < .06$; differences for sons were in the other direction, $d = -0.15$).

Sarantakos (2000) reported higher rates of truancy for children of same-sex parents and also noted that "Low performance at school was also mentioned by many adult children who, looking back at their school years, felt that they did not perform up to capacity" (p. 132), partly perhaps because some same-sex parents seemed to Sarantakos to have had less firm expectations regarding their children's education (Sarantakos, 1996b, p. 27). Sarantakos (1996b) found effect sizes as large as 3.75 in ratings by teachers of how well children of heterosexuals were doing in school subjects compared to the children of same-sex parents (see Schumm, 2016b, p. 676 for more details); however, despite claims of bias as the cause (Herek, 2014), the children of same-sex parents were rated *better* by the teachers in some subject areas with effect sizes of 0.32 and 0.54. In other words, was that presumed bias also working to make the teachers give the children of same-sex parents some *better* ratings?

MacCallum and Golombok (2004) found that when independent interviewers met with the children of heterosexual and lesbian mothers, they found higher school functioning among the former ($d = 0.79, p < .05$), even though the children of the lesbian mothers rated their own interest in school higher ($d = 0.54, p < .05$). Fedewa and Clark (2009) found that, even though socioeconomic status favoured same-sex parents, the children of heterosexual parents were doing better in school (d's of 0.07 and 0.17); their results were further complicated because lesbians rated their own parenting behaviours more favourably than did heterosexual mothers ($d = 0.23$) while gay fathers rated themselves far worse than did heterosexual fathers ($d = -1.30, p < .01$). Rosenfeld (2010) noted an interesting reversal of trends in that "Among children

175

raised by highly educated parents, the children of heterosexual married couples made better progress in school than the children of same-sex couples" (p. 768); much research has featured highly educated same-sex parents, yet here Rosenfeld, otherwise often cited for claiming that same-sex parenting did not cause delays in a child's education, says that children of same-sex parents were disadvantaged educationally when their parents were highly educated, which seems counterintuitive to what one might have expected (if children copy their parents' emphasis on education in their own lives and career development). An interesting study would be to compare how many times Rosenfeld's (2010) results have been cited to show no educational differences versus how many times his footnote has been cited.

Allen (2013) looked into Canadian census data and found that the children of heterosexual parents had greater chances of graduating from high school, but his results can be disputed because some children of same-sex parents might have moved out of their homes early and not been captured in the census data. Richards *et al.* (2017) claimed that the adult children of same-sex couples were "thriving" but, in terms of educational attainment, even though the adult children (N = 147) of heterosexual parents were younger on average and had less time to obtain more education, they tended to have more education than adult children raised by lesbian mothers (N = 134, $d = 0.20, p < .10$) or gay fathers (N = only 25, $d = 0.05$), though the effect sizes were small.

On the other hand, some studies found the children of same-sex parents doing better in school (MacCallum & Golombok, 2004). Rosenfeld (2013) and Allen *et al.* (2013) argued about whether Rosenfeld's (2010) results showed that there were no educational differences in the children of same-sex parents once you controlled for parental instability. Potter (2012), Potter and Potter (2017), and Schumm *et al.* (2014; Schumm, 2016b, p. 679) found few differences in educational outcomes for the children of same-sex and heterosexual parents after controlling for parental instability. However, in such cases, parental instability should be used as a mediating/intervening variable between parental sexual orientation and educational outcomes to permit an assessment of the indirect effect of parental sexual orientation on educational outcomes, which might be significant statistically even if the direct effect of sexual orientation was not significant. Again, it is worth remembering van Eeden-Moorefield *et al.*'s (2018) acknowledgement that mediation effects have seldom been studied in this area of research.

Crime and conduct problems

While most studies that have asked lesbian mothers to rate their children's problem behaviours have found few differences compared to ratings by heterosexual mothers, there have been a few exceptions. Hawkins (2011) asked same-sex and heterosexual parents about their own relationships, their relationships with their adolescents, and problems with their adolescents. Even though same-sex parents reported more satisfactory relationships with their partners, though not with their children ($d = 0.14$, mothers; 0.29, fathers), they reported greater conduct problems on the part of their adolescents (mothers, $d = 0.50, p < .01$; fathers, $d = 0.33$, $p = 0.18$, two-tailed tests). Sullins (2015c), using random, nationally representative data, found that children from same-sex parent families had higher rates of conduct problems ($d = 0.53, p < .001$). Regnerus (2012a, b) found higher rates of having been arrested or having pleaded guilty to non-minor offences for children from his definition of same-sex families. Schumm *et al.* (2014) re-evaluated Regnerus's data and combined three measures of criminal activity into one binary measure, as well as redefining more and less stable same-sex families differently. Rates were lower for adult offspring from intact biological parents (13.6%) compared to heterosexual stepfamilies (25.2%, $p < .001$), less stable same-sex families (39.6%, $p < .01$), and more stable same-sex families (40.0%, $p < .002$). As noted elsewhere (Schumm, 2016b, p.674), the difference between heterosexual stepfamilies and same-sex families was not significant ($p < .12$). However, possibly the most interesting result was that within the same-sex families, the higher crime rate did not come from nonheterosexual children (0% rate) but from their heterosexual children (35% arrested, 25% convicted, 16% jailed). Thus, we found some more possible evidence for a "congruence" hypothesis in which having parents and children of the *same* sexual orientation might be associated with better child outcomes (Schumm, Landess, & Williams,

2014); other scholars have also hinted at the possible existence of such a situation (Rouse, 2002, p. 196; Kuvalanka, 2013, pp. 168-169; Manning *et al.*, 2014; Stacey & Biblarz, 2001). On the other hand, Crouch, Waters, McNair, Power, and Davis (2014) did not find any differences in conduct problems as a function of parental sexual orientation.

In a rare case of the use of mediating/intervening variables, Bos and Sandfort (2010) reported that the greater the sexual questioning of their participants (which was greater for children of same-sex parents) the lower were global self-worth ($d = .39, p < .05$) and social competence ($d = 0.49, p < .01$). In other words, though not examined often, this one study suggested that predispositions towards homosexuality were adversely related to self-worth and personal social competence.

Sexuality

For daughters of lesbian mothers compared to daughters of single parent heterosexual mothers, Tasker and Golombok (1997) found a greater rate of multiple cohabitations (71% versus 22%, $d = 1.04, p < .105$, p. 131), multiple sexual partners (88% versus 56%, $d = 0.78, p < .05$, p. 127), earlier initiation of cohabitation (71% versus 17%, $d = 1.17, p < .05$, p. 131) in terms of starting cohabitation after knowing the partner for less than six months, and a greater rate of having five or more sexual partners in early adulthood among children (62.5% versus 22.2%, $d = 0.84, p < .10$, p. 127)(Schumm, 2011a, p. 110-111; Schumm, 2015c, p. 20). While Udry and Chantala (2005) found that adolescent girls who had lost fathers were more likely to act out sexually (with either boys or girls or both), the Tasker and Golombok (1997) study attempted to control for father absence, with most of their daughters having been raised without fathers. While these results have not been replicated, they might suggest greater sexual diversity or tolerance among children of same-sex parents, even when the children have developed a heterosexual sexual identity. However, Sullins (2015b) similarly found a high rate of early divorce and cohabitation among the children (ages 19 to 25) of same-sex couples, especially married same-sex couples (58% versus 35% to 48% for all other parental categories, p. 16). Another explanation might be that if a daughter's father hurts or abandons both her mother and herself, the attachment injury, the trauma may be enough to convince both mother and daughter that men are not to be trusted or granted deep acceptance sexually, which might predispose both mother and daughter to more casual sexual relationships with men and/or women, but probably more in depth with women.

Self-control/Delayed gratification

Bos, van Balen, and van den Boom (2004, p. 758; 2007, p. 40) compared 100 lesbian and 100 heterosexual families and found that the heterosexual parents rated self-control and related items as more important goals for their children than did lesbian mothers, with effect sizes between .40 and .55. They also found effect sizes of 0.37 to 0.46 with respect to greater structure and limit setting among heterosexual parents compared to same-sex parents (Schumm, 2016b, p. 685). One must ask, if parents don't value self-control or self-regulation as an important goal for their children, will children be less likely to develop self-regulation as they grow up? (Schumm, 2015b, p. 17). Three recent studies used national U.S. data to investigate differences in child outcomes in terms of behavioural control or emotional control. Sullins (2015a) found higher rates of serious emotional problems (17% vs. 7%, $d = 0.31$) for children of same-sex parents, even after controlling for a number of other variables.[2]

Reczek, Spiker, Liu, and Crosnoe (2016) used data from the National Health Interview Survey (NHIS) to compare child outcomes for cohabiting and married same-sex and opposite-sex couples (same-sex couples may not have identified as LGBT persons, sexual orientation identity questions were not asked in the NHIS). Raw data results indicated that the children of married opposite-sex families had better health (14% poor to good, versus 19-21% for the other three groups), fewer severe to definite emotional difficulties (4% versus 8-15%), and fewer said their child was not well-behaved (2% versus 5-13%). They found that children of cohabiting same-sex parents were reported by parents to have more emotional difficulties compared to children of cohabiting different-sex parents (odds ratio = 1.75, p < .05) while children of married same-sex parents were reported to have greater behavioural problems compared to children of married different-sex parents (odds ratio = 2.16, p < .05), patterns that remained even after controlling for socioeconomic differences and even biological relatedness between the parents and their children. An interesting finding in Reczek *et al.* is that for all of their outcome variables, biological relatedness was an advantage for children, regardless of marital status of the parents or numerous other control variables, a result parallel to what Sullins (2015a) had found. Later, they (2017), in response to Sullins (2017), redid their analyses and found that same-sex parents reported more emotional difficulties with their children (32-39%) compared to heterosexual couples (15-25%). In terms of severe to definite emotional difficulties, the rates were 11-24% for children of same-sex couples compared to 4-8% for heterosexual couples. In terms of odds ratios, now the children of same-sex married appeared to have even greater chances of having emotional difficulties (OR = 3.44, p < .05) as did the children of same-sex cohabiting couples (OR = 2.07, p < .01) compared to children from heterosexual married couples (the odds ratio for heterosexual cohabiting couples' children was 1.62, p < .01). Even so, there were only 32 same-sex married couples in the National Health Interview Surveys from 2008 to 2015, making most comparisons of very low statistical power. In their analyses, Reczek *et al.* (2017) controlled for as many as 29 variables, nearly as many as their number of same-sex married families.

Since same-sex parenting inherently involves a lower degree of biological relatedness, it is likely that their study (Reczek *et al.*, 2016) should have assessed the mediating effect of biological relatedness. Their raw data are worth consideration. The children of same-sex married parents rated 13% of their children as not well-behaved compared to 2% for married heterosexual parents ($d = 0.41, p < .001$, using N = 216 for each group); including "somewhat true" with "true" as responses to that question yielded 32% versus 21%. Among the cohabiting families, ratings were between 33% and 34%. In terms of emotional difficulties, ratings (definite or severe emotional difficulties) were 8.5% for same-sex married parents compared to 4% for married heterosexual parents ($d = 0.17, p < .10$, using N = 216 for each group) and 8% for heterosexual cohabiting parents and 15% for same-sex cohabiting parents. After controlling for numerous factors, including biological relatedness, some of the differences were reduced to non-significance. However, in all cases children appeared to be doing better, the greater the biological relatedness to their parents. Bos, Knox, van Rijn-van Gelderen, and Gartrell (2016) used national data from the U.S. National Survey of Children's Health Data, matching 95 female same-sex (not necessarily lesbians because sexual orientation was not measured directly) and 95 opposite-sex families. Although Bos *et al.* concluded that there were no significant differences across the two groups, daughters from same-sex families scored higher on emotional difficulties ($d = 0.14$) and worse on coping behaviour ($d = 0.57$, p < .05) while sons scored worse on coping behaviour ($d = 0.11$).

Family engagement

Richards *et al.* (2017) also compared the adult children of same-sex parents with those of heterosexual parents on frequency of contact with those parents. Presumably a higher rate of contact would suggest greater family cohesion and better mental health (these were not measured in the study). The effect sizes favoured more contact for the adult children of heterosexual parents compared to the adult children of lesbian mothers ($d = .85$, $p < .05$) or gay fathers ($d = .49$, $p < .05$). The other notable issue is that the standard deviations (being a measure of greater risk if they are larger, Schumm, Bosch, & Doolittle, 2009) were much smaller for the adult children of heterosexuals' scores (0.85) than for the adult children of lesbian mothers (1.38) or gay fathers (1.87) in spite of the fact that gay fathers were, on average, earning much more ($97k) per year than either the lesbian ($74k) or the heterosexual parents ($83k). Richards *et al.* (2017) also found less congruence on religion between the same-sex parents and their children (i.e. parent and child religion did not match: 45% for adult children of heterosexual parents compared to 67% for adult children of same-sex male couples, 54% for adult children of female same-sex couples) as well as lower levels of endorsement of formal religion (64%, 65%, and 45%, respectively), which might mean less support from formal religious groups for higher levels of self-control or self-regulation.

Additional child outcomes

While results are limited, some research has found issues with the emotional atmosphere of or emotional outcomes from same-sex parenting. Brewaeys *et al.* (1997) found effect sizes (though not significant statistically) indicating more problems as measured by the CBCL scale among the children of lesbian mothers than among the children conceived by their biological heterosexual parents (boys, $d = 0.48$, girls, $d = 0.07$). Puryear's (1983) research found only 20% of the children of lesbian mothers drawing pictures of their mother cooperating with them compared to 67% ($d = 1.07$, $p < .01$) of the children with single-parent heterosexual mothers; with respect to drawing pictures of cooperation with another adult the rates were 10% versus 78% ($d = 1.90, p < .01$). Miller, Mucklow, Jacobsen, and Bigner (1980) reported that 38% of lesbians (N = 34) versus 3% of heterosexual women (N = 31) in their study indicated that they did not respect their own father ($d = 0.94$, $p < .001$) or their mother (29% vs. 10%, $d = 0.51$) suggesting attachment problems in their families of origin. Sirota (1997) found that 78% of the daughters of gay fathers versus 44% of the daughters of heterosexual fathers reported problems with insecure attachment ($d = 0.72$, $p < .001$) while the results for feeling uncomfortable with close relationships were similar, 44% vs. 12% ($d = 0.75$, $p < .001$). MacCallum and Golombok (2004), despite many advantages for their lesbian households, including less bullying against their children as reported by the child ($d = 0.09$), found that the global self-esteem of children, from interviews by independent researchers, was higher for children from heterosexual two-parent families than from children with lesbian mothers ($d = 0.47, p < .10$).

Perrin, Pinderhughes, Mattern, Hurley, and Newman (2016) generally found few differences between how fathers rated their children as a function of sexual orientation, but with respect to the child being unhappy/depressed/tearful the relative percentages were 17.9% for the 56 gay fathers who apparently responded to that question compared to 11.3% from the National Health Inventory Survey (NHIS, N = 10,

195), a result that involved an odds ratio of 1.71 but was not significant (one-sided Fisher's Exact Test, $p < .10$). An interesting point is that had Perrin *et al.* (2016) collected data from twice as many gay fathers (but retaining the 17.9% rate), the results would have been significant ($p < .05$) with a two-tailed Fisher's Exact Test – an example of how small sample sizes of same-sex parents can resist determinations of statistical significance, no matter how large the comparison sample might be of heterosexual parents. To be fair, one should compare apples with apples; a hidden issue with the Perrin *et al.* (2016) study is that the gay fathers had very high incomes (up to more than $200,000 annually) and 92% had at least a college degree, that is, they had much higher socioeconomic levels than a typical heterosexual sample would have. Golombok, Blake, Slutsky, Raffanello, Roman, and Ehrhardt (2017) studied same-sex parents from 95 families (with no heterosexual comparison group), but the generalisability of their results must be questioned because nearly 50% of their families had annual incomes exceeding $150,000, with nearly 19% exceeding $500,000.

Regnerus (2012a, b) reported higher rates of depression and suicidal thoughts among adult offspring of same-sex parents compared to those from stable, heterosexual families. Investigating this further, Schumm *et al.* (2014) found further support for a "congruence" hypothesis. For example, in terms of suicidal thinking, the rates for the adult children of the most stable lesbian families (3.7%) did not differ much from the rates for children from intact heterosexual families (5.4%). However, rates for nonheterosexual children from lesbian families (0%) and heterosexual children from heterosexual families (4.6%-8.4%) were lower than rates for heterosexual children from lesbian families (5.0%) or nonheterosexual children from heterosexual families (12% to 27.8%). Family instability seemed to predict higher rates of suicidal thinking as did a lack of congruence in sexual orientation between parents and their children. Sullins (2015c) found greater social problems ($d = 0.43, p < .01$) and total problems ($d = 0.41, p < .001$) for children of same-sex families compared to heterosexual families, though other differences were smaller (e.g., emotional problems, $d = 0.09$; peer difficulties, $d = 0.24$).

Marital status of same-sex parents

Will same-sex marriage improve same-sex parenting? Implicit in much of the same-sex marriage argument was that marriage would improve the mental health of the children of same-sex couples by providing for more parental stability and granting higher social status to the children of same-sex married parents. However, Sullins (2015b) found that the data from Wainright and Patterson (2006) indicated that children of unmarried same-sex parents were often doing better than children of married same-sex parents (Schumm, 2015c, p. 16). The married same-sex parents did appear to have more stable relationships than did unmarried same-sex parents, as expected, although selection effects might have led more stable same-sex couples to get married. Readers may also wish to refer back to the discussion of the apparent effects of legal marriage on the mental health of same-sex couples, on page 41.

Changes over time

Another way of assessing the mental health of the children of same-sex parents would be to study how the children may have changed over time. While such studies are rare, there are at least two such studies. Farr, Forssell, and Patterson (2010) reported on wave one of such a study and reported on wave two later (Farr, 2017a) with a sample of families who had adopted children. How did the children change over time as reported by parents or teachers? Parents reported on their children's problem behaviours as did their teachers or child care providers. At wave one, both lesbian ($d = .33$) and gay ($d = .17$) parents reported fewer problem behaviours than did heterosexual parents, as did teachers ($d = .21, .07$, respectively). Over time though, parental reports of child problems increased for all parents but more for lesbian ($d = 0.72, p < .05$) and gay ($d = 0.29$) than heterosexual parents ($d = 0.17$) as also occurred for teacher reports for lesbian ($d = 0.35$) and gay ($d = .41$) parents but not for heterosexual parents (-.05, a slight reduction in problems). At wave two, heterosexual parents were reporting fewer problem behaviours than lesbian parents ($d = 0.24$) and were tied with gay parents ($d = -0.01$). At wave two, teachers reported fewer problems for children of heterosexual parents than for children of gay ($d = 0.41$) or lesbian ($d = 0.20$) parents. Thus, at wave one, same-sex parents started off with an advantage over the heterosexual parents but by wave two that advantage had disappeared or switched the other way around, now favouring the children of the heterosexual parents. In other words, the trend lines were more or less opposite of each other, with the children of same-sex parents starting off better but ending up with more problems in general and compared to the children of heterosexual parents no better off or worse off, a reversal from the situation at wave one. It is not clear if that trend was nothing but "regression toward the mean" or an indication of long-term trends favouring outcomes for the children of heterosexual parents over those for same-sex parents. It is all the more interesting because the average household incomes for the families was $188,000 (p. 255) at wave two, $166,000 at wave one, so the families represented some of the most highly resourced families in the United States. At the same time, more heterosexual families dropped out between waves one and two, which might have advantaged them, if the heterosexual drop-outs had been among the parents with children with more behaviour problems.

Lavner, Waterman and Peplau (2012) also, like Farr (2017a), examined changes over time for adopted children, from two months after adoption to two years later for 60 heterosexual, 15 gay, and 7 lesbian families. Children of both same-sex and heterosexual adoptive parents made similar gains in cognitive development ($d = 0.51, 0.59$, respectively) over two years. While in terms of internalising and externalising problems the two groups of children were similar two years after adoption, they reached that similarity as small increases occurred for children in same-sex adoptive families ($d = .06$ and $.07$ for externalising and internalising problems, respectively) while medium declines ($d = 0.42, 0.48$) occurred for the children of heterosexual parents over the same two years. As with Farr (2017a), the trend lines appeared to be heading in opposite directions, which could reflect nothing but a "regression to the mean" or the start of a far longer trend, not favouring the children of same-sex parents.

Van Rijn-van Gelderen, Bos, and Gartrell (2015) conducted a follow-up study (wave three) to earlier studies at waves two (Bos, Gartrell, van Balen, Peyser, & Sandfort, 2008) and one (Bos, van Balen, & van den Boom, 2007). In principle, one should have been able to compare the children's internalising and externalising problem scores across all three times, but it is not clear that they used the same scaling at all three times and they did not use the same heterosexual comparison groups nor always have a heterosexual parent comparison group across the three waves. However, in general it appeared that the children of lesbian parents were reported by parents to have fewer problems with effect sizes between 0.09 and 0.19.

Limitations

Because of the issue of selection effects and social desirability, I think it is unlikely that asking parents about the mental health of their children will yield much in the way of valid information. It would be more valid to seek the opinions of teachers (e.g., Vanfraussen, Ponjaert-Kristoffersen, & Brewaeys, 2002, whose teachers rated the adjustment of lesbians' children lower, $d = 0.52, p < .05$ (see Schumm, 2016b, p. 688 for more details) than the adjustment of the children of heterosexual parents) or other professionals or that of the children themselves, in my opinion.

Another issue of increasing concern is the use of population studies in which sexual orientation has not been measured, leading researchers to use the presence of two adults of the same-sex in the household as a proxy for lesbian or gay parents (e.g., Bos *et al.*, 2016; Reczek, *et al.*, 2016). For example, Reczek et al. noted that "nor could we make claims about whether same-sex parents in this study identified as gay and lesbian" (p. 1626) and that their "approach to identifying same-sex couples risked misclassification bias because of miscoded parent sex" (p. 1625). In some cases, it is difficult to check such data because the data may be restricted by the government.[3] The concern is that you might have a 30-year-old mother and her 50-year-old mother (grandmother) raising a foster child together who would be deemed a "same-sex" or lesbian couple. Unless age differences are taken into account, this could easily happen, with other combinations as well (older son and his father; two uncles, two aunts, two sisters, two brothers, all raising adopted or foster children or the biological child of one parent of the pair). It is also possible that a heterosexual couple might have brought a bisexual wife's lesbian lover into the family, leading researchers to count the household as a "lesbian" family, when it is something more complicated. Recall that Wainright and Patterson's (2006, 2008) research appeared to involve matched samples of 44 heterosexual and 44 lesbian parent couples but actually as many as 61% of their "same-sex" families were apparently heterosexual families (Patterson, 2009b; Sullins, 2015b).

Equivalence issues

Many studies have not dealt with the initial lack of equivalence between their same-sex parent and heterosexual parent families. As I showed some time ago (Schumm, 2005), any negative influences of same-sex parenting (if they exist) might be cancelled out by other differences (e.g., if the same-sex parents had higher annual household incomes, fewer children to support, more personal education in general or in parenting skills in particular compared to heterosexual families). As discussed in more detail elsewhere (Schumm, 2016b), studies of adoptive children often involve parents, regardless of sexual orientation, of extraordinarily high levels of socioeconomic success, making it difficult to generalise any results to adoptive children involved with poor to lower-middle class parents. Assessing a child's mental health as a function of parental sexual orientation is difficult if the parents' economic and mental health conditions are not similar to begin with.

For example, Golombok *et al.* (2014) found advantages for the children of same-sex parents, but that might not be a surprise once one considers that the same-sex parents had much higher levels of socioeconomic status (gay parent A, 86.7% [26/30] professional/managerial class; heterosexual parent A, 66.7% [22/33], two sided Fisher's Exact Test, $p = .08$; gay parent B, 89.7% [35/39], heterosexual parent B, 70.2% [33/47], two-sided Fisher's Exact Test, $p < .05$), along with lower levels of anxiety ($p = .13$, $d = .29$), depression ($p < .01$, $d = .40$), and stress (p

< .01, d = .49). For example, in a different report on the same study as Golombok *et al.* (2014), Mellish *et al.* (2013) reported that there were no differences in child outcomes across gay, lesbian, and heterosexual adoptive families. However, they indicated some interesting differences as shown below (p. 4):

	Gay Father A/B	Lesbian Mother A/B	Heterosexual Father/Mother
Depression	7%/3%	17%/15%	19%/25%
Anxiety	10%/0%	17%/8%	11%/18%
Parenting Stress	10%/3%	16%/16%	18%/24%
Relationship Problems	3%/3%	8%/6%	12%/13%

The point is that to show there are no differences between two groups in an outcome, the groups should be equivalent to start with. It is not scientifically sound to compare children from two groups of parents when one group of parents has higher levels of depression, higher levels of anxiety, greater levels of parenting stress, and more relationship problems. At the very least, statistical controls should be used to try to render the two groups more equivalent in underlying conditions before comparing child outcomes.

One minor limitation is that Schumm (2015b, p. 12) listed the differences in drug use in Regnerus (2012a) in the wrong direction by mistake, showing lower rates among children of same-sex parents, when the rates were actually higher except for alcohol use. Sullins' (2015b) study was characterised by a very small sample of only 17 to 20 same-sex families (17 lesbian, 3 gay men), split into two parts to compare married and unmarried same-sex parents.

Future research

There has been, in my opinion, a surprising dearth of research on same-sex parenting in terms of time preference and delayed gratification. Generally, research has found higher rates of alcohol and tobacco use among homosexuals, though such research has seldom made distinctions in use between parents and non-parents. It is possible that same-sex parents may restrict their use of risky substances for the sake of their children. It would be useful to assess parental beliefs in teaching delayed gratification or self-regulation (Baumeister & Tierney, 2011; Vohs & Baumeister, 2016) and the extent to which children seem to have achieved varying levels of self-control. It would also be helpful to investigate how parent and child gender and sexual orientation might interact in influencing the child's mental health. For example, if a parent and child are of the same gender or the same sexual orientation, is that situation associated with improved mental health? When comparing parental reports of child outcomes, various forms of social desirability need to be measured and controlled statistically to reduce the chances of selection effects or various response biases suppressing or masking actual differences among children (regardless of the direction of the effects).

Another area in which there has been less research is how the acquisition of a child influences the child's mental health later in life. It is often considered that having a child from a previous heterosexual relationship is a concern because the mother or father have often divorced their previous partner(s) at least once, so that the child becomes a child of divorce. Jennings, Mellish, Tasker, Lamb, and Golombok (2014) reported that "For heterosexual couples, genetic kinship may be perceived as stabilizing; however, for many same-sex adopters the reverse was true" (p. 221). The concern was that gaining a child without any biological linkage to either parent allowed the parents to "have equal, non-genetic relationships to their children" (p. 220). Would such "equality" of non-genetic relationship promote better mental health outcomes for children or not? We do not know.

The concern about asymmetrical biological linkage is real; some research has found that the nonbiological co-mother may feel jealousy towards the biological mother, whose biological link to the child may help create a stronger emotional bond to that biological mother (Goldberg & Allen, 2013a, p. 364; Goldberg *et al.*, 2008; O'Leary, 2010; Pelka, 2009; Schumm, 2015c, p. 19; Sullivan, 2004). For example, Gartrell, Rodas, Deck, Peyser, and Banks (2006) reported that among lesbian couples with ten-year-old children, 49% (18/37) of the co-mothers in still intact relationships had experienced issues of jealousy or competitiveness with the child's biological mother. Thus, it appears that having a child that has a biological relationship to one parent but not the other may be a concern as well for some same-sex parents. Some children have been conceived from unknown donors in order to protect the lesbian mothers from later claims by the biological father. In one of the few studies on this process, Gartrell, Bos, Goldberg, Deck, and van Rijn-van Gelderen (2015) compared mothers who had used known versus unknown sperm donors; 43% of the latter were dissatisfied with what they had done compared to 11% of the former ($p < .05, d = 0.78$).

When gay men use a surrogate woman to bear them a child, there are a number of issues, including the potential for the woman to be exploited. To what extent do these different processes put the convenience of the potential parents ahead of the future welfare of the child? I am not saying all of the possible avenues are a potential problem for a child, but some may pose greater risks to that child's future mental health than others – and I am not sure that we know which processes present more or less such risk. Trying to promote parental equality by deliberately having children with no biological relationship to either parent runs counter to research that suggests that children with no biological ties to either parent generally perform more poorly than children who do have at least some biological tie to one or both parents (Reczek *et al.*, 2016; Sullins, 2015a).

Conclusions

One of the clearest findings in this area is that if you ask same-sex parents how their children are doing, they will generally tell you they are doing well. At the same time, social desirability response bias, though known to be a risk, has not been measured or controlled in most studies. Furthermore, studies have often compared children from very different socioeconomic worlds. Some studies have compared "same-sex" families without knowing if "same-sex" actually meant LGBT families. Notwithstanding the claims that same-sex parents are superior in skills and attitudes versus heterosexual parents (despite lack of access to marriage and despite discrimination), in some studies in which children were assessed directly in terms of physical and social competence, the children of heterosexual parents, contrary to what you might expect for all of their limitations in life and parenting, rated themselves *better* than did children of same-sex parents. When issues of family cohesion and child self-control have been studied (less often than parental self-reports) some evidence has been found to suggest that the children of same-sex parents are doing a bit more poorly than children of different-sex parents with a wide range of effect sizes.

Until studies routinely control for pre-existing differences between the two groups of parents and control for social desirability, I doubt that we will get to the bottom of this issue. It is not correct scientifically to take a group of highly educated, wealthy, mentally healthy same-sex parents and compare their children to the children of uneducated, poor, mentally ill heterosexual parents and think you have set up a fair comparison. Yet this sort of comparison has been popular in the scientific literature. If you think about it, it should be surprising that no differences have been found, given the remarkable advantages often availed by the same-sex parents. It is a bit like putting a professional sports team up against a team of adolescents and watching them play to a tie and then proclaiming that this is absolute proof of how great the professional team was that day! It is more likely a credit to the much younger team rather than to the professional team.

Notes

[1] Wilkinson and the APA Task Force on Statistical Inference (1999) clearly state that "An author's self-awareness, experience, or resolve does not eliminate experimenter bias. In short, there are no valid excuses, financial or otherwise, for avoiding an opportunity to double-blind" (p.596). The lack of controls for appropriate forms of social desirability and the frequent use of researcher identity to recruit participants (i.e., "as a lesbian mother" or "as a heterosexual mother of three children", "I know where you are coming from") may threaten the validity of many self-report based studies on parenting, regardless of parental sexual orientations.

[2] Sullins (2015a) report may have underestimated the impact of same-sex parenting (https://papers.ssrn.com/abstract=2500537).

[3] I was interested in attempting to replicate the work of Bos, Knox, van Rijn-van Gelderen, and Gartrell (2016) but the U.S. government has restricted access to the data that allowed Bos *et al.* (2016) to determine which parents were "same-sex". I could be granted that access but only at the cost of a $20,000 fee at the Kansas City Restricted Data Center. Anyone lacking such funds cannot check published results for accuracy.

Summary for Part Four

To illustrate some of the problems of "bad science" in the area of same-sex parenting, let us return to Patterson's (2013b, pp.670-671) summary chapter in the *Handbook of Marriage and the Family* (Peterson & Bush, 2013), in which she also considered a variety of aspects of personal development of the children of same-sex parents. Included in her review of the characteristics of personal development of children were separation-individuation, psychiatric evaluations, behaviour problems, personality, self-concept, locus of control, moral judgement, school adjustment, and intelligence. Notably, time preference or delayed gratification were not mentioned at all. While Patterson cited Puryear (1983), she did not indicate that Puryear had found adverse results for the families of same-sex parents, as described by their own children. She did not cite Biblarz and Stacey (2010a), who reviewed the literature and found some areas of differences. Of the 23 citations for the nine areas, 65% (15/23) were more than 13 years old, with 30% (7/23) being more than 23 years old. No contrary findings were mentioned. Nevertheless, Patterson (2013b) concluded that "The research findings suggest that concerns about difficulties in these areas among children of lesbian mothers are unwarranted" and that "As was the case for sexual identity and for social development, studies of these aspects of personal development have revealed no major differences between children of lesbian vs. heterosexual mothers" (p.671). There were no mentions of the limitations of the studies, such as pre-existing lack of equivalence or lack of controls for social desirability. Findings with respect to cognitive competence, use of illegal drugs, and several other child outcomes were overlooked. However, my belief is that the average reader would "take away" the idea that there were few relevant limitations in the research and that the results uniformly and consistently supported the effectiveness of same-sex parenting. Possibly we have what some have called a preordained conclusion in search of scientific support. Sure, some might accuse me of the same, but which authors (myself or others) routinely cite research that might support more than one side of the argument? Which authors have cited the largest number of research sources (i.e., have done their homework)? Which authors have deconstructed the research in the most detail, with an emphasis on effect sizes rather than only levels of statistical significance?

PART 5

CONSEQUENCES OF SAME-SEX MARRIAGE

Introduction to Part Five

In addition to concerns about same-sex parents as couples or outcomes for their children, a major issue has been whether or not same-sex marriage had led to any negative externalities for heterosexuals. The concept is that if there are no negative consequences (externalities) for heterosexuals from the legalisation of same-sex marriage, then there should be no complaints about or objections to the legalisation of same-sex marriage. Several studies have been published on this issue but one of the primary studies done with U.S. data was by Langbein and Yost (2009), which will be the focus of this section of the book.

Langbein and Yost (2009) claimed that their results with data from 50 U.S. States had indicated that there were no negative externalities with respect to same-sex marriage. Among their study's limitations, it did not (1) have long-term data on the effects of same-sex marriage and (2) it did not consider fertility rates as a possible negative externality. In the following chapter, using data from 50 U.S. States, fertility rates for 2014 are predicted from median age at marriage for women, median household income for 2014, percent of each State's population living in urban areas, percent of women with at least a bachelor's degree, and years since same-sex marriage had been legalised in each State as of 2014. Years since legalisation of same-sex marriage predicted later age at marriage (effect size of 0.65) and fertility rates (effect size of 0.40). The primary conclusion is that it remains rational to consider the potential for there to be negative externalities associated with legalisation of same-sex marriage in States, but such effects may only be detectable statistically over longer periods of time.

Chapter Twelve

Are there really no negative consequences
of same-sex marriage in the U.S.?

Langbein and Yost (2009) analysed data from the United States (50 States and the District of Columbia) from three time periods. Instead of treating their data as three time points for 51 cases, they combined the data into the equivalent of 153 cases at one time, although in some of their analyses the number of cases used fell to 141. Then they predicted several outcome measures from over 70 variables and concluded, despite the acknowledged limitations of their data and methodology, that "The argument that same-sex marriages poses a negative externality on society cannot be rationally held" (p. 292). Aside from the fact that it would be remarkable for data from any one article (Hunter & Schmidt, 2004, p. 18) to make any other argument irrational, the Langbein and Yost (2009) report had a variety of serious limitations, some noted by Allen and Price (2015), limitations of which some are shared by similar, later analyses of State data (Dillender, 2014; Dinno & Whitney, 2013). First, they used a rather weak measure of same-sex marriage law, only whether or not a State had such laws, or bans on same-sex marriage (at three time points). Here, a new measure was used, the number of years since a State has either legalised same-sex marriage or that has been done for the State by court order, an approach Langbein and Yost (2015, p. 162) recommended themselves. Indeed, some recent research suggests that it may take some time for the effects of same-sex marriage law to take effect within a society (Trandafir, 2014). Second, they did not assess fertility rates as an externality, and it remains possible that *other* important externalities, not considered here, remain to be investigated by others above and beyond this report. Thus, it is agreed that "a more conclusive answer than the one we have collectively provided is still needed" (Langbein & Yost, 2015, p. 162).

Their research can be criticised from a number of other perspectives (Allen & Price, 2015), but those are beyond the scope of this book (e.g., they tripled their cases to over 150 by using the three time points for each State as if they were independent observations, inflating the degrees of freedom; they used over 70 predictive variables, which seems high compared to the traditional statistical standard of having at least five cases (preferably ten to fifteen cases) per variable used in regression analyses, which may have accounted for their R^2s of 0.92 to 0.97 (p. 301); (see Green, 1991; Maxwell, 2000; Schumm & Crawford, 2015; Schumm, Southerly, & Figley, 1980; Stevens, 1992, p. 125; Vittinghoff & McCulloch, 2007); and they used a dummy variable to represent each State but also had a dummy variable for same-sex marriage that only occurred for one to four States, hence possibly having, in effect, duplicate variable(s)). In general, scientists prefer parsimony – if a less complex model works well, why use a far more complicated model? Here, a much less complex model was tested, with far fewer variables than used by Langbein and Yost (2009). That, of course, may increase the chances of omitted variable bias, but adding more variables than used here would lower the desired ratio (10 or 15 to one) of cases to variables.

Issue of fertility rates

Fertility rates are one area of outcomes for same-sex marriage that do not appear to have been investigated to date, although Allen (1996) had raised the issue. Cherlin (2010) regards fertility as an underappreciated demographic in the United States but did not tie it to changes in same-sex marriage law. My search of the literature for intersections of "same-sex marriage" and "fertility rates" yielded no research on this topic in the United States and only a few opinion pieces, some in law reviews. I did not find any scientist other than Allen (1996) predicting an association, positive or negative, between legalisation of same-sex marriage and changes in fertility rates in the United States.

Theory and the Second Demographic Transition

The Second Demographic Transition (SDT, Lesthaeghe, 2010, 2014; also see discussion in Tanturri, 2014) theory postulates that Western society is increasingly characterised by a complex of demographic trends, including declining fertility, increased age at marriage, parenthood outside marriage (out-of-wedlock births), more efficient contraception and access to abortion, increased childlessness among women, more frequent divorce, increasing cohabitation, and an increasing variety of socially accepted family arrangements. Langbein and Yost (2009) studied some of these matters, notably excepting fertility and average age at marriage. SDT changes may be financed by higher median incomes in different States and sustained by higher levels of education for women, but opposed by rural, more conservative citizens in each State. Thus, the model becomes one with fertility rates as the dependent variables, age at marriage as an mediating or intervening variable serving as a proxy for the SDT transformation as well as a measure of reducing marriage (i.e., later age at marriage means lower rates of marriage for those in their 20s and 30s, during periods of greater fertility), with median household income, percent urban population in each State, and the percent of women (age 25 or more) in each State with at least a bachelor's degree serving as exogenous variables. State fertility rates for 2000 were also used, in a second model, when predicting 2014 fertility rates, to help determine how the independent variables might have influenced changes in fertility rates compared to a baseline of year of 2000. While some may feel that lower fertility rates are a good trend, such rates portend (aside from immigration into a nation) fewer adults to pay for social security and fewer workers in general to supply consumer goods and services for the whole society. If extensive immigration is encouraged to offset fertility rates below replacement levels, then the supply of workers may be gained at the expense of national culture (e.g., France might become less recognisably French), especially if the immigrants have much higher birth rates than the traditional ethnic populations and tend to refuse to accept the unique values or laws of that particular culture (e.g., if large percentages of the immigrants were against free speech or religious freedom and were in favour of honour killings).

Hypotheses

Our predictions were that higher income and higher 2000 birth rates would predict higher 2014 fertility rates on the theory that people will have more children if they can afford to do so and on the theory that fertility rates over time would be positively correlated due to presumably at least somewhat stable underlying factors predictive of fertility. Our predictions were also that greater urbanicity and greater education for women would predict lower fertility rates on the theory that women with higher levels of education and all persons living in urban areas would have more opportunities, other than fertility, for their lifestyle patterns. Urbanicity might serve as a proxy for social capital provided for adults by each State. We also expected that later age at marriage would predict lower fertility levels because of shorter time periods of fertility prior to menopause for women who married later in life. We expected that the more years since the legalisation of same-sex marriage, the greater the delay in age at marriage and the lower the fertility level in general. Fertility levels might be lower given greater availability of same-sex marriage because some gay, lesbian or bisexual persons might avoid entering into a mixed-orientation marriage (Power, Perlesz, Brown, Schofield, Pitts, McNair, & Bickerdike, 2012) in which they would have had children in favour of entering into a same-sex marriage. That is to say, some gay, lesbian or bisexual persons might not feel as constrained in their relationship choices in States that offered them legal same-sex marriages. Furthermore, same-sex marriage may produce an inequality of marriage that indirectly discourages heterosexuals from early marriage or marriage at all, as well as reducing their incentives for fertility (Schumm, 2015c).

Measurement

Fertility rates (births per 1,000 women aged 15-44) for 2014 were obtained from Hamilton, Martin, Ostermann, Curtin, & Mathews (2015, p.38, Table 12). Fertility rates for each State in 2000 were obtained from Martin, Hamilton, Ventura, Menacker, and Park (2002, p.40). Median age at marriage (years) for women for each State was obtained from a five year (2009-2013) average of American Community Survey data reported by the Population Reference Bureau (http://www.prb.org/DataFinder/Topic/Rankings.aspx?ind=133). Median household income (in dollars) for each State as of 2014 was downloaded as an excel file from the U.S. Census Bureau (https://www.census.gov/hhes/www/income/data/statemedian, Table H-8, Median Household Income by State: 1984 to 2014). The percentage of the population of each State living in urban areas (as of 2010) was taken from U.S. Census Data from (http://priceonomics.com/the-most-urbanized-states-in-america) and (https://www.census.gov/newsroom/releases/archives/2010_census/cb-12.50.html). The percentage of women (age 25 and older) in each State as of 2013 that had a bachelor's degree or higher was obtained from Hess, Milli, Hayes, & Hegewisch (2015), Table 4-1 on page 125. The number of years since same-sex marriage had been legalised in each State was used as an independent variable. If same-sex marriage had been legalised in 2015 (or not legalised as of the end of 2014), then the code for this variable was zero; otherwise the code was the number of years that same-sex marriage had been legal in each State, using a code of "1" for legalisation in 2014, "2" for legalisation in 2013, etc.

Analysis

Ordinary least squares (OLS) regression was used to predict fertility rates from age at marriage, percent urban, median household income, percent of women with bachelor's degrees or higher, and years since same-sex marriage had been legalised in each State, using 2014 as the baseline year (years since marriage was coded as zero for those States that did not legalise same-sex marriage until 2015 after the *Obergefell v. Hodges* decision). Fertility rates were predicted with (second model) and without (first model) fertility rates for 2000 included in the regression model. Age at marriage was predicted from years since same-sex marriage, percent urban, median income, women's education, and years since same-sex marriage had been legalised. Results were not weighted by State population because each State was treated as a separate legal entity, but results did not appear to differ when weighted by State populations except that virtually all variables were statistically significant after being weighted.

Results

Results are presented in Table 1 (on p. 208 below). With respect to predicting fertility rates, our predictions were supported. The strongest predictor of fertility rates was later age at marriage ($p < .001$), whether or not fertility rates in 2000 were used as a predictor variable. Years since legalisation of same-sex marriage significantly predicted age at marriage (effect size of $d = 0.65, p < .05$) while it showed a trend towards significance for predicting fertility (effect size of $d = 0.40, p < .10$). Our results also suggest that the use of data from 50 States may limit any ability to find significant results for effect sizes that are below 0.50, limiting our ability to detect even low to medium effect sizes. Without fertility rate for 2000 in the model, a two-tailed Sobel test for the mediating effect of age at marriage was significant ($-2.21, p < .05$), but with the 2000 fertility rate in the model, the Sobel (Warner, 2008, p. 456; www.quantpsy.org/sobel/sobel.htm) effect was not quite significant ($p < .08$) by a two-tailed test. Thus, it appears that legalisation of same-sex marriage might predict fertility rates both directly and indirectly; while some of the levels of significance are marginal, the effect sizes are in the small to medium range.

Conclusions

It is remarkable that so few studies have looked at fertility rates as they might be associated with same-sex marriage. It appears that perhaps even the Family Research Council (FRC) had overlooked fertility as a possible negative externality, as Langbein and Yost (2009) based their selection of outcomes on known FRC concerns. The legalisation of same-sex marriage appears in our model to operate both directly on fertility rates and indirectly through median age at marriage for women. These results indicate that fertility rates may be influenced by changes in same-sex marriage law *over time*. This is to say that merely because a State has legalised same-sex marriage does not mean that fertility rates will change immediately; such changes may take several years to be detectable statistically. The legalisation of same-sex marriage would also appear to be associated with the Second Demographic Transition through our proxy variable of median age at marriage for women. If one accepts median age at marriage as a proxy for the SDT, our results would imply that legalisation of same-sex marriage is both a part of the SDT (as evidenced by its ties to median age at marriage) and has an independent effect on fertility rates, possibly over and above any social trends connected in general to the SDT.

An argument can be made that our model reverses the causality – that fertility predicts changes in law or earlier age at marriage. Social life is complex; thus, it is challenging to rule out a number of alternative hypotheses. However, most of the legalisation of same-sex marriage came about via court decisions rather than public votes and one might question how fertility rates would influence judicial decision-making even if they influenced public voting behaviour. Changing norms about marriage (i.e., who is eligible) might well change attitudes toward marriage or about the relative value of marriage (Schumm, 2015a). As far as fertility predicting age at marriage, I would think that some early fertility (e.g., teenage out-of-wedlock birth) might delay marriage. Furthermore, wanting a child soon might be one factor that influenced the timing of marriage, but surely there are many other factors. But once married, I think the natural process of sexual interaction might greatly increase the odds of higher fertility rates. Thus, I would argue that the predominant effect runs from age at marriage to fertility rather than in the opposite direction.

I think this study highlights the importance of one's selection of dependent variables. Just because one outcome is not related to a predictor does not mean that another outcome would not be related, if examined. I do not think it is good science to test five outcomes and, finding all presumably unrelated to something, to go further and appear to assume that there could not possibly be any other outcomes that might be related to the predictor. The study also demonstrates the importance of using strong rather than weak measures of predictor variables. There are many ways to "water down" one's predictors to enhance the chances of not rejecting the null hypothesis. One way is to recode a time dependent variable into a binary (did/did not occur) variable. If things take time to have an impact, such recoding will likely reduce the chances of detecting things over time.[1]

This author has never been fond of thinking that one research report by itself should change history; nor have other scholars (Herek, 2006; Henson & Roberts, 2006; Hunter & Schmidt, 2004, p. 18). Thus, I question whether it was proper for Langbein and Yost (2009)'s study to have wielded so much apparent power in court decisions regarding same-sex marriage (Schumm, 2015c). Langbein and Yost did note that their research might not even have been needed in the opinions of some observers because "many might believe that this conclusion [i.e., no negative effects of same-sex marriage] is so obvious that it does not warrant testing" (p. 292). Again, I question that sort of claim. Is there *anything* in social science that does not need testing from time to time? After all, societies change over time, so what we might have found to be valid in one decade might not remain valid in another. While I make no claim that this chapter settles any question for all time, I do think it refutes the idea that one cannot *rationally* hold the view that same-sex marriage might impose some negative externalities on U.S. society, at least at the present time. The results here also tend to support the claim by Ioannidis (2005) that quite often preliminary research on new topics is going to be incorrect, which he asserts is particularly likely when the topics are tied to prejudices in a scientific field and there are few studies, and those that exist feature small sample sizes and small effects. I remain concerned that courts may make decisions often based on incomplete or inaccurate, at least premature, social science. Larger studies based on random, nationally representative data may help to provide more accurate results with regard to many controversial issues (e.g., Sullins, 2015a) and may prove more useful for judicial authorities.

Table 1

REGRESSION MODEL FOR FERTILITY RATE PREDICTED BY AGE AT MARRIAGE, MEDIAN INCOME, PERCENT URBAN, WOMEN'S EDUCATION, FERTILITY RATE IN 2000, AND YEARS SINCE SAME-SEX MARRIAGE LEGALIZED FOR 50 U.S. STATES

Dependent Variables:	Age at Marriage (2009-2013)	Fertility Rate (2014)	
		In General	Controlling for Fertility Rate, 2000
Age at Marriage	-----	-.79***	-.50*
Percent Urban	.27*	.17+	-.12
Median Income	-.59**	.17	.32+
Women's Education	.78***	.01	-.09
Years since SSM	.31*	-.20+	-.20+
Fertility Rate, 2000	-----	----	.35*
Adjusted R^2	.489	.644	.668
F	12.72	18.74	17.42
df	4, 45	5, 44	6, 43
p	< .001	< .001	< .001

+ $p < .10$
* $p < ..05$
** $p < .01$
*** $p < .001$

Note

[1] There are many other ways to deploy weak predictor variables (Schumm, 2015a; Schumm & Crawford, 2015). If you want to compare two groups, you can weaken the effect by having one group contain members of the second group. Along these lines, Wainright and Patterson (2006) compared 44 children of heterosexual parents with 44 children of allegedly lesbian parents; however, later, using the same data, Patterson (2009b) was more restrictive and limited the comparison to 18 children of allegedly lesbian parents, suggesting that there were doubts about the "same-sex" qualifications of 26 (59%) of the allegedly lesbian parents, as later supported by Sullins (2015b), although Sullins narrowed the count to 17. You can also weaken predictors by counting dead people as (stable) dyadic couples; Rosenfeld (2014) appears to have treated 96 widows or widowers as part of his "couple data" for predicting subsequent relationship or marital stability. You can also insert intervening variables into your model to hide any mediating effects of independent variables (which occurs when direct effects are reduced to non-significance, making it appear that the independent variables have no role in the model at all when they may have significant mediating effects). Yet another way to weaken a predictor variable is to control for a variable that is virtually the same as the predictor variable, such as using gender and the presence (or not) of a Y chromosome in your model or using race and skin colour together; Sullins (2017) wisely notes how using parental sexual orientation and parental biological relatedness to their child is a confounding situation since it is nearly impossible for a child to be biologically related to two parents of the same gender. In other words, using biological relatedness as a control variable will weaken the apparent effects of parental sexual orientation in most situations.

PART SIX

HOW IT ALL FITS TOGETHER

Introduction to Part Six

How can all of this information be integrated or put together? What we have seen so far is that same-sex parents may have lower rates of stability, especially lesbian mothers. Same-sex parents may be less likely to emphasise traditional gender roles, traditional views of gender as a binary factor, and traditional views of sexual expression (e.g., restricting sex to legal marriage). They may value self-control less in their children than heterosexual parents. The children of same-sex parents may be more likely to question their sexual orientation or sexuality while growing up and more likely to try same-sex sexuality, even if not sexually attracted to same-sex persons. The children are less likely to adopt traditional gender roles and perhaps be more likely to reject traditional definitions of gender. In the USA, the children of same-sex parents appear more likely to engage in substance abuse, at least occasionally. The children's mental health from their mothers' perspectives appears fine, but as rated in terms of drug abuse or by other observers seems more questionable. How do we make sense of all this information?

Chapter Thirteen

Putting it Together

I think the primary "take-away" is that, despite many declarations to the contrary for decades by many scholars, children do learn from their parents – not just reading or mathematics, but personal values as they relate to sexuality, sexual expression, gender roles, the meaning of gender itself, and possibly even the importance of self-control or emotional self-regulation. Same-sex parents appear to hold more progressive values with respect to such issues and those values would seem to have been adopted in many cases by at least some of their children (Bos, Gartrell, Roeleveld, & Ledoux, 2016). This is pretty much common sense, in agreement with most social science theories, except that it has been denied for decades in the interests of promoting or protecting the civil rights of LGBT persons. While the rights of LGBT persons may have been advanced, it is not clear that the integrity of social science in general has been protected nearly as much.

The value of having more progressive or diverse sexual expression, gender roles, or even gender itself can be debated; that is, some will argue that being homosexual or having more androgynous gender roles or more fluid gender are neutral outcomes that should have no bearing on civil rights or social stigmatisation. Indeed, Rosky (2013a, b) had gone so far as to suggest that the federal government should promote homosexuality as a way of reducing unwanted or teenage pregnancies among vulnerable women. That might be an interesting opinion, but I see it as no reason to have jilted science in the name of political progress.

Where the crunch comes, I think, is in the area of time preference and delayed gratification or self-control. The higher rates of drug abuse and the earlier expression of sexuality would seem to reflect a lower degree of self-regulation or self-control. If true, those outcomes could be disputed, since most psychologists appear to think that self-regulation is a critical personal trait. Research clearly suggests that having better self-regulation is associated with numerous better outcomes for adults, even if the self-regulation trait was developed early in childhood (Laird, Marks, & Marrero, 2011). Alongside the issue of same-sex parenting and children's self-regulation should be the issue of the extent to which church organisations and/or personal religiosity promote self-regulation of the children of same-sex and/or heterosexual parents. Baumeister and Tierney (2011) believe that religion, in general, seems to promote better self-control. I am again reminded of Luntz's (2009) paragraph on a chasm in American values as he said "two-thirds (66 percent) of non-religious Americans agree with the statement 'If it feels good, do it,' despite its selfish, dangerous undertones. By comparison, fully 71% of religious Americans disagree with the concept of instant gratification. What we have here is a chasm between the value systems of these two American camps" (p. 261). That effect is at the "large" level ($d = 0.79, p < .001$, if N = 200) (Schumm, 2011b, p. 68). I think the point ultimately will be the extent to which self-control and delayed gratification values allow us to make more A and C types of decisions in life versus B or D types of decisions. How that works out as a function of parental sexual orientation (or even personal sexual orientation) has never been decisively tested, but I think it would be a promising avenue of investigation. Where I think there is a possibility for the churches and science to come together is on the issue of self-regulation, which really amounts to learning how to make more A and C decisions than B and D decisions. If framed in that background, we might come to a better understanding of same-sex parenting than through an almost exclusive focus on sexual orientation and gender roles. Furthermore, my belief is that a commitment to casual sex (belief that premarital cohabitation is OK, that it is OK for unmarried couples to get together only for sex, and using pornography is OK, sometimes defined as sociosexual orientation) reflects values that likely support Type B decisions.

Thus, it is notable that when I predicted support for same-sex marriage and parenting from age, education, being bullied as a child, quality of family life as a child, political orientation (progressive/conservative), type of family of origin, and commitment to casual sex, the best predictor of support for same-sex marriage was commitment to casual sex, not any of the other predictors, although commitment to casual sex did also predict political orientation (Schumm, 2015a, p. 14). But one might well object and say, so what? What is harmful about being committed to casual sex? For belief in casual sex to be a Type B decision, you would need to show it being related to adverse consequences, would you not?

When I correlated commitment to casual sex with other consequences (Schumm, 2015a) using the NFSS data, commitment to casual sex was negatively related to religious variables, a loving atmosphere in the family of origin, life happiness, current physical health, current relationship happiness, and to believing that children need both a mother and a father. It was positively related to actually using pornography often, drinking alcohol often, drinking to get drunk, using marijuana, using other illegal drugs more often, smoking tobacco more often, gambling for money more often, having legal problems from drinking, having close relationship problems due to drinking, having been arrested, having been convicted of a crime, having spent time in jail, feeling depressed in the past week, being an impulsive person, getting angry easily, getting stressed out easily, doing things without thinking about the consequences, trying new things even if you have to break rules to do them, having suicidal thoughts in the past year, ever having had a sexually transmitted infection, having had more abortions, thinking that marriage is an outdated institution, worry that your partner does not really love you, having thought about leaving your current partner, having cohabited outside of marriage, and having cheated sexually on your partner (Schumm, 2015a, p. 15).

That is a lot of factors to consider, but does it really seem that believing in casual sex is a harmless value? But there has been very little research in this latter area. Most of my conclusions in that area are based on almost incidental parts of larger research reports. Yet one may wonder, are type B decisions related at all to homosexual sex? Elsewhere (Schumm, 2013, p. 334) I noted that in response to a question "What do you know about sexual minority youth?" one LGB youth replied, "We have all the fun" (Russell, 2003, p. 1253), which Russell noted "beautifully illustrates the resilience that characterizes the lives of most sexual minority youth" (p. 1253).

Some research supports the idea that LGB youth may be having more "fun" – Ueno (2010) and Blake *et al.* (2001) found that youth with same-sex contact or LGB identity reported a higher fun-seeking orientation ($d = 0.39$, $p < .001$) or were more likely than heterosexual youth to have ever had sexual intercourse (86% vs. 48%, $p < .001$), within the past three months (69% vs. 34%, $p < .001$), to have had more sexual partners ever (average of 3.6 vs. 2.7, $p < .001$), and more partners within the past three months (2.1 vs. 1.1, $p < .001$), to have started having sex earlier (13.7 vs. 14.3 years of age, $p < .001$), and to have been or got someone pregnant (30% vs. 11%, $p < .001$). For similar patterns in other studies, refer to Schumm (2013, pp.335-336). Being overbenefitted refers to getting more benefits than you might deserve compared to others, which is, in theory, associated with feeling guilty. Being underbenefitted is associated with getting less and associated with feeling angry. If having more "fun" (than heterosexual youth sexually) translates into feeling overbenefitted, we should recall that "those who are over-benefitted also feel discontent, likely due to feelings of guilt" (Dainton & Zelley, 2006, p.247). Thus, feelings of guilt might be due as much to being overbenefitted sexually as to experiences of stigma or discrimination, which some have argued are not related to mental health in any event (Schumm, 2013, p.333). In other words, it may not be minority stress from being stigmatised or discriminated against that leads to problems, but feelings of guilt derived from an awareness that by being gay, one is getting "more sex (boys) or better sex (girls)" than the average heterosexual peer. As far as I know, that contrary theory has not been tested directly yet with reference to sexual orientation.

Legal implications

I am disappointed that many U.S. courts were misled into accepting as valid research, research that was biased, incomplete, and focused on significance levels rather than effect sizes. Numerous studies whose results would have been inconvenient for the "no difference" hypothesis were overlooked or ignored. Research on same-sex parenting has often been cited because it came to the politically correct conclusions, not because it was of the highest quality (Schumm & Crawford, 2018b). In one sense, this book is an attempt to redress that imbalance. In another sense, it is a call for scientists to be more careful in the future and not deceive courts about scientific evidence, regardless of what third parties may want scientists to expound upon as "experts". I am not necessarily saying that courts have made bad decisions but that they were certainly fed "bad" science, no matter how correct their decisions might have been in the end.

Going backwards in time, I think it should be clear to the reader that U.S. courts were often informed that the "no difference" hypothesis was correct with respect to same-sex parenting, when there was actually considerable evidence against that hypothesis. At the very least, courts deserved better research than that to which they were often exposed. If a judge were to see that side A has six expert witnesses and side B has one or two, perhaps "why?" should have been asked. I am not sure, but I suspect that in one case an expert witness withdrew because he feared for the lives of his wife and children if he were to testify against the "no difference" viewpoint. A court should be concerned with such things. If side A says that research is clearly definitive and totally supports side A with no exceptions, I would hope the court would realise that science does not actually work that way. If I were a judge, I think it would be a good exercise to ask side A (and/or side B) to produce at least three studies that did not support their view of things – after all, statistical variation means that there should be one or two at least out there, even if they did not mean much. If side A (or B) cannot do that, something is probably amiss with their science or at least their ability to review the literature. But my hope is that this book persuades courts and the lay public that science is far from perfect and is capable of making major mistakes that are not discovered for decades, especially when there are financial or political pressures pushing the process more than scientific curiosity by itself.

Also, I have noticed a "mission creep" in which polyamorists are wanting to claim the same rights as LGBT groups (also see Morgan, 2014, p. 150). Chauveron, Alvarez, and van Eeden-Moorefield (2017) noted that "As other members of the queer community, such as transgender parents or polyamorous families, gain visibility in the larger society, the law will need to adjust to include their parenting rights" (p. 131). Chauveron *et al.* (2017) want a future in which courts treat "the same-sex couple as any other couple" (p. 130). Presumably, this line of reasoning would also extend to transgender couples and polyamorous families. I see a potential for the same sort of incomplete and biased research to be used to promote a polyamorist agenda to courts around the world. I also anticipate a future in which homosexuality in youth, especially young women, may be seen by federal governments and federal courts as advantageous for society (Rosky, 2013a, b) rather than merely a neutral issue.

Chapter Fourteen

Discussion

It is remarkable how *resistant* social science appears to be to acknowledging, much less accepting, apparent facts about same-sex parenting, even when numerous studies back up at least some of these findings. Many of these discoveries would appear to support the early fears of the courts that were discussed by Patterson and Redding (1996) or the fears of some conservative scholars which were criticised as largely unfounded by Stacey and Biblarz (2001). Part of the issue is that politically incorrect research is often dramatically stigmatised (Redding, 2013) or simply ignored (e.g., many reviews have seldom cited conservative scholars, except perhaps rarely only for the purpose of discrediting their research). I have detailed elsewhere some of the problems faced by conservative researchers (Schumm, 2016b; Appendix C here).

It is possible that some scholars might argue that I have imputed my own conservative values into this review of the literature, and they view it as an example of confirmation bias. While most philosophers would probably not accept any idea that scholars are value-free in their work, the "no difference" hypothesis represents a unique situation. If the "no difference" hypothesis was actually correct, in the hyperbolic way it has been presented by many scholars, there should have been *no* findings that could be found in a literature search, aside from 2.5% random errors, that contradicted the "no difference" theory in a direction unfavourable to same-sex parents (2.5% could have contradicted that theory in a favourable direction). That is to say, if the "no difference" dogma were really correct then no matter what my values or biases might be, I should not have been able to find any contradictory research beyond the 2.5% level due to random chance.

The "dogma" of "no difference"

My assessment is that the research presented in this book has shredded any pretence that the dogma of "no difference" is factually correct. I say dogma because so many scholars seem clueless about so much of the research that does not support their values with respect to LGBT family issues. If dozens of scholarly results won't convince you otherwise, will anything? That is why I have called it a "dogma" of "no difference" rather than mere theory of "no difference". The issue of harm is more ambiguous. It can be argued that differences in sexual orientation, gender identity, or gender role behaviour, are not matters of harm, only matters of diversity. I dispute that characterisation only because of the many associations between sexual orientation and various adverse outcomes, which to me seem to be related to type B decisions (Schumm, 2013). In terms of mental health outcomes, once you get past maternal ratings of children, there seem to be quite a number of adverse associations between same-sex parenting and child outcomes. However, there are so few studies in some of these specific outcomes that they could be anomalies. Taken together, I think they do raise concerns about the welfare of children of many same-sex parents.

Weak use of social science theory

In addition to social science research issues, I think that social science theory has been unfairly discounted in this area of study. Earlier we mentioned how Stacey and Biblarz (2001) indicated that nearly every theory of socialisation would suggest that children imitate, model after, or learn from their parents. Yet such theory was discounted by some scholars because it did not fit the "no difference" hypothesis. Thus, one role that theory can play is to help us avoid falling into traps laid by bias in how research is done or in how it might be interpreted. Sexual minority stress theory (Martin-Storey, 2015) makes the case that many symptoms manifested by LGBT persons can be accounted for, possibly entirely, by stigma against sexual orientation. Some research claims to have supported sexual minority stress theory, at least in part (e.g., McLaughlin *et al.*, 2012;Toomey, Ryan, Diaz, Card, & Russell, 2010). We think a number of other possibilities have been overlooked. It is not good science to accept one explanation, test it, and then assume all has been solved for all time.

Alternatives to sexual minority stress theory

I think that alternative explanations to sexual minority stress theory need to be developed and tested. People can be stigmatised for many things, for example being overweight, being underweight, using illegal drugs, engaging in sex with multiple casual partners, for gender nonconformity, for dyeing their hair or having a nontraditional haircut, etc. Unless a variety of factors are measured, sexual orientation stigma might be picking up other types of stigma, not necessarily related to sexual orientation. In other words, since you may not be able to tell what a person's sexual orientation is, but you might be able to observe gender non-conformity or other correlates of sexual orientation, those types of observables should be measured and controlled statistically before attributing stigma to sexual orientation *per se*.

One might ask whether there are differences in the ways gender nonconforming high school students are treated depending on their identity in terms of sexual orientation; perhaps, LGBT gender non-conforming students internalise stigma more than non-LGBT gender nonconforming students. Furthermore, some research has found that adolescent reports of stigma were not correlated significantly with as many as 15 psychological outcomes (Bos & Gartrell, 2010; Gartrell & Bos, 2010); Wald (2006) also discounted the impact of stigma on child outcomes, stating that "While the present of stigma is clear, the research does not find that it has a significant harmful impact on the children's mental health" (p.399). Sullins (2015a) found that in a nationally representative U.S. sample, children of same-sex parents were less likely to be bullied (15%) than were the children of heterosexual parents (19%). Even internalised homophobia might represent guilt from being overbenefitted (Nye, 1979, p. 7) rather than guilt or stigma imposed by outsiders. Research should take into account such theoretical possibilities rather than assuming constructs are determined by only one or a few factors.

Theory construction

A final issue with theory pertains to theory construction. Theory construction, one might assume, would proceed along the lines of consensus building in social science; as consensus is formed, theory is built around that consensus. But what if the consensus is incorrect? Then theory construction may mislead current and future researchers. Adams and Light (2015) demonstrated that there was consensus in social science in favour of the "no difference" hypothesis (which we have confirmed in part; Schumm & Crawford, 2018a), but we believe that a careful examination of data suggests otherwise, suggesting that consensus is not always a helpful guide to theory construction. Furthermore, if consensus can fail in this area, why not in other areas of social science or science in general?

Chapter Fifteen

Conclusions

I am suggesting there is an alternative way to evaluate evidence ever since Patterson and Redding's (1996) and other classic reviews of the literature on same-sex parenting. Phrases such as "no evidence" or "not a single study" or "Uncontroverted scientific evidence" may reflect merely "socilese" – social science over-simplifying itself to suit the demands of lawyers who, regardless of their side in a dispute, finding themselves in a binary win/lose world, wanting *definitive* statements from sociologists, not "mixed-results" findings.

In contrast, I am suggesting that the real world of social science involves a mixture of greys. Scholars must resist any temptation to accept simplistic solutions, especially if those solutions contradict well-established, common sense social science theory. Such resistance may not come without a cost. If you are hired as an expert witness and deviate from the view that one side and only one side has all the right answers you might lose your job and fees. If you try to present both sides of an issue in court, one or both sides may deem you a traitor to their cause. Stacey (2004) has discussed such issues in more detail. However, science should not be "thrown under the bus" for the sake of any political agenda, left or right. Regardless of the merits of the facts with respect to political or legal implications, it appears that substantial amounts of "fact" have been ignored or suppressed in the process of moving forward the civil rights agenda of LGBT persons.

Scholars might have said things like these:

Children of same-sex parents, in some studies but not all, are more likely to become heterosexual than homosexual.

225

Same-sex parents, though not same-sex childfree couples, are somewhat less likely to have stable relationships.

While European studies disagree, most U.S. studies indicate that children of same-sex parents are more likely to use, at least occasionally, illegal drugs or substances.

The children of same-sex parents appear, from maternal descriptions, to be similar in psychological health to children of heterosexual parents, but virtually no studies have controlled for appropriate forms of parental social desirability and many have not controlled for pre-existing differences between the two groups of parents.

... then, those sorts of statements would have been defensible from a scholarly point of view, even though the following more detailed statements would also have been valid:

Children of same-sex parents, in some studies, have been ten to twenty times more likely to grow up to experience same-sex sexual attractions, explore same-sex romantic relationships, or to identify as LGBT and the differences have probably been increasing in recent years, in some part due to parental encouragement or acceptance, as well as growing societal acceptance.

Same-sex parents, though not same-sex couples, are up to two or three times as likely to have unstable relationships as heterosexual parents in first marriages (the jury may still be out on comparisons with heterosexual stepfamily couples).

While studies are inconsistent, studies from the U.S. indicate something between trends and significant differences in the use of illegal substances by older children or adult children of same-sex parents compared to those of heterosexual parents.

CONCLUSIONS

While reports about children's psychological health differ little between lesbian and heterosexual mothers, it is not known how those comparisons might change if pre-existing differences had been controlled by design or by statistics, as well as controls for social desirability and selection effects. Since the lesbian mothers studied usually had higher education, better mental health, and fewer children than the heterosexual mothers, as well as perhaps a greater felt need to "justify" themselves as parents, it is entirely possible that with controls in place, their children's mental health might have appeared to be worse than that of the children of heterosexual mothers. There are virtually no studies of how the children of mentally ill, poor, uneducated lesbian mothers are doing compared to the children of similarly situated heterosexual mothers.

Yet what we have seen in many cases have been statements like these:

Parental sexual orientation has no effect whatsoever on and no association with the sexual orientation of their children.

All lesbian and gay relationships are just as stable as heterosexual relationships.

The children of same-sex parents are in no way different from or disadvantaged with respect to the children of heterosexual parents regardless of any economic or psychological differences between the two groups of parents.

While the first two groups of statements have some degree of scientific plausibility, the last group of statements simply do not reflect the best science, as I hope you have detected after reading this book. There do appear to be significant and substantial differences between same-sex and heterosexual parents and in the long-term outcomes for their children, contrary to many, many allegations by numerous social scientists over the past decades. Even so, one of the most important outcome areas – time preferences or delayed gratification, especially with respect to human sexuality – has almost entirely been overlooked in such comparisons and further, more detailed and complex research continues to be needed. Some may suggest that this book was written because the author "hates" gay people, but it is rather than I care about how science is done and how it is used in the public square, especially before courts of law. My fondest hope is not that same-sex marriage be declared illegal or same-sex adoption be banned (after all, new laws are seldom reversed or negated), but that perhaps a few persons here and there will have been challenged to think more carefully about scientific research in areas of political controversy and be a little less eager to jump to conclusions that may not in fact be warranted after a careful, detailed, systematic review of the research literature. Perhaps a few graduate students here and there will read this book and gain some insight into how to review the literature in other areas of social science that may be in need of similar intensive analyses. I am not optimistic that courts will revise their procedures to avoid the sorts of problems that I hope this book has exposed.

Epilogue

Yes, "scientific consensus" can be wrong. I might even tend to be *more* skeptical when "scientific consensus" is claimed; after all, if it was so obvious, *why* would you need to go so far out of your way to proclaim it? There have been many claims that all honest scientists "agree" about all aspects of research regarding same-sex parenting, as well as other areas (e.g., military training) involving LGBT persons (Belkin, quoted by Shane, 2017; also see Schumm, 2004d, 2015a, pp.22-24 and Belkin, Ender, Frank, Furia, Lucas, Packard, Samuels, Schultz, & Segal, 2013), but the facts on the ground do not support many of the so-called "consensus" claims or as I have called it, the "dogma" of "no differences". If such claims of "no difference" were actually correct in an absolute sense, then it should be impossible for anyone to find *any* evidence to the contrary. However, refuting such claims (as with the monk Telemachus, who died protesting the gladiatorial killings in the Roman Colosseum, 1 January 404 AD) means wading into a messy (research, in my case) arena, into which many scholars have not wished to go. Like that monk Telemachus, I am saying "Stop this butchering (of science)!" no matter how much the crowds or politicians may revel in the killing of science for political purposes.

While I am delighted that many progressives claim to value truth, like Senator Schumer, as well as *Time* magazine, I am concerned about a lack of energy directed to getting at that truth by many progressive scholars when there was a possibility that such truth might not agree with politically or legally desirable outcomes. It is remarkable that one could find 90% of over 70 literature reviews having drawn incorrect conclusions about some aspects of same-sex parenting or that the politically correct results of studies might do nearly as effective a job of predicting academic citations as did the quality of those research reports. Unlike perhaps *Time*, I do not think that truth is quite dead yet, but in terms of science it seems to have been battered quite a bit in at least some areas. It was not so much that scholars had not read the literature to some degree, but that they thought they knew what was true, yet what they thought they knew, was not true. Unexamined, unquestioned research may seem and even feel like reliable, solid science, but careful, detailed examination may reveal something entirely different. Research such as what you have read in this book has been ignored, ridiculed, even attacked, but my guess is that at least some of it will be deemed "self-evident" after more time passes, and it is no longer seen as a political threat to LGBT civil rights. Social science researchers and I have had access to the same published research; recalling Doherty's (2006) quote, perhaps few have been as willing to follow where the evidence might lead, even if it was unpopular politically. I will leave it to other scholars to pursue any possible situations in other fields of study where science may have been sacrificed in the name of politics or religion or other ideals.

BIBLIOGRAPHY

Abbott, D. A. (2012). Do lesbian couples make better parents than heterosexual couples? *International Journal of Humanities and Social Sciences, 2*(13), 30-46.

Adams, J., & Light, R. (2015). Scientific consensus, the law, and same sex parenting outcomes. *Social Science Research, 53*, 300-310.

Alanko, K., Santtila, P., Harlaar, N., Witting, K., Varjonen, M., Jern, P., Johansson, A., von der Pahlen, & Sandnabba, N. K. (2010). Common genetic effects of gender atypical behavior in childhood and sexual orientation in adulthood: A study of Finnish twins. *Archives of Sexual Behavior, 39*, 81-92.

Allen, D. W. (1996) An economic assessment of same-sex marriage laws. *Harvard Journal of Law and Public Policy*, 29, 949-980.

Allen, D. W. (2013). High school graduation rates among children of same-sex households. *Review of Economics of the Household, 11*, 635-658.

Allen, D. W. (2015). More heat than light: A critical assessment of the same-sex parenting literature, 1995-2013. *Marriage & Family Review, 51*, 154-182.

Allen, D. W., Pakaluk, C., & Price, J. (2013). Nontraditional families and childhood progress through school: A comment on Rosenfeld. *Demography, 50*, 955-961.

Allen, D. W., & Price, J. (2015) Same-sex marriage and negative externalities: A critique, replication, and correction of Langbein and Yost. *Econ Watch Journal, 12*, 142-160.

Allen, M., & Burrell, N. (1996). Comparing the impact of homosexual and heterosexual parents on children: Meta-analysis of existing research. *Journal of Homosexuality, 32*, 19-35.

Alderson, P. (2004). Absence of evidence is not evidence of absence: We need to report uncertain results and do it clearly. *BMJ, 328*, 476-477.

Altman, D. G., & Bland, J. M. (1995). Absence of evidence is not evidence of absence. *BMJ, 311*, 485.

Amato, P. R. (2010). Research on divorce: Continuing trends and new developments. *Journal of Marriage and Family, 72*, 650-666.

Amato, P. R. (2012). The well-being of children with gay and lesbian parents. *Social Science Research, 41*, 771-774.

Amato, P. R., & Anthony, C. J. (2014). Estimating the effects of parental divorce and death with fixed effects models. *Journal of Marriage and Family, 76*, 370-386.

American Psychological Association. (1994). *Publication manual of the American Psychological Association* (4th Ed.). Washington, DC: Author.

American Psychological Association. (2001). *Publication manual of the American Psychological Association* (5th Ed.). Washington, DC: Author.

American Psychological Association. (2004). *Sexual orientation, parents, & children: Research summary*. Washington, DC.: Author.

American Psychological Association. (2005). *Lesbian & gay parenting*. Washington, DC: Author.

American Psychological Association. (2010). *Publication manual of the American Psychological Association* (6th Ed.). Washington, DC: Author.

Anderssen, N., Amilie, C., & Ytteroy, E. A. (2002). Outcomes for children with lesbian or gay parents: A review of studies from 1978 to 2000. *Scandinavian Journal of Psychology, 43*, 335-351.

Anderson, E. (2013). The need to review peer review: The Regnerus scandal as a call to action. *Journal of Gay & Lesbian Mental Health, 17*, 337-351.

Apostolou, M. (2016). The evolution of same-sex attractions: Parental and intimate partners' reactions to deviations from exclusive heterosexual orientation. *Personality and Individual Differences, 101*, 380-389.

Armenia, A., & Troia, B. (2017). Evolving opinions: Evidence on marriage equality attitudes from panel data. *Social Science Quarterly, 98*, 185-195.

Armesto, J. C. (2002). Developmental and contextual factors that influence gay fathers' parental competence: a review of the literature. *Psychology of Men & Masculinity, 3*, 67-78.

Averett, P., Nalavany, B., & Ryan, S. (2009). An evaluation of gay/lesbian and heterosexual adoption. *Adoption Quarterly, 12*, 129-151.

Badgett, M. V. L., & Herman, J. L. (2013). Patterns of relationship recognition by same-sex couples in the United States. (2013). In A. K. Baumle (Ed.), *International handbook on the demography of sexuality* (pp. 331-362). New York: Springer Dordrecht.

Baetens, P., & Brewaeys, A. (2001). Lesbian couples requesting donor insemination: An update of the knowledge with regard to lesbian mother families. *Human Reproduction Update, 7*, 512-519.

Bailey, D. H., Ellingson, J. M., & Bailey, J. M. (2014). Genetic confounds in the study of sexual orientation: Comment on Roberts, Glymour, and Koenen (2014). *Archives of Sexual Behavior, 43*, 1675-1677.

Bailey, J., Bobrow, D., Wolfe, M., & Mikach, S. (1995). Sexual orientation of adult sons of gay fathers. *Developmental Psychology, 31*, 124-129.

Bailey, J. M., Dunne, M. P., & Martin, N. G. (2000). Genetic and environmental influences sexual orienting and its correlates in an Australian twin sample. *Journal of Personality and Social Psychology, 78*, 524-536.

Bailey, J. M., Vasey, P. L., Diamond, L. M., Breedlove, S. M., Vilain, E., & Epprecht, M. (2016). Sexual orientation, controversy, and science. *Psychological Science in the Public Interest, 17*, 45-101.

Baiocco, R., Santamaria, F., Ioverno, S., Fontanesi, L., Baumgartner, E., Laghi, F., & Lingiardi, V. (2015). Lesbian mother families and gay father families in Italy: Family functioning, dyadic satisfaction, and child well-being. *Sexuality Research & Social Policy, 12*, 202-212.

Ball, C. A. (2003). Lesbian and gay families: Gender nonconformity and the implications of difference. *Capital University Law Review, 31*, 691-749.

Ball, C. A. (2012). *The right to be parents: LGBT families and the transformation of parenthood*. New York: New York University Press.

Ball, C. A. (2013). Social science studies and the children of lesbians and gay men: The rational basis perspective. *William & Mary Bill of Rights Journal, 21*, 691-764.

Ball, C. A. (2014). *Same-sex marriage and children: A tale of history, social science, and law*. New York: Oxford University Press.

Ball, C. A. (2016). *Same-sex marriage and children: A tale of history, social science, and the law*. New York, NY: Oxford University Press.

Balsam, K. F., Beauchaine, T. P., Mickey, R. M., & Rothblum, E. D. (2005). Mental health of lesbian, gay, bisexual, and heterosexual siblings: Effects of gender, sexual orientation, and family. *Journal of Abnormal Psychology, 114*, 471-476.

Balsam, K. F., Beauchaine, T. P., Rothblum, E. D., & Solomon, S. E. (2008). Three-year follow-up of same-sex couples who had civil unions in Vermont, same-sex couples not in civil unions, and heterosexual married couples. *Developmental Psychology, 44*, 102-116.

BIBLIOGRAPHY

Balsam, K. F., Rothblum, E. D., & Beauchaine, T. P. (2005). Victimization over the life span: A comparison of lesbian, gay, bisexual, and heterosexual siblings. *Journal of Consulting and Clinical Psychology*, *73*, 477-487.

Balter, M. (2008). Why we're different: Probing the gap between apes and humans. *Science*, *319*, 404-405.

Baptiste, D. A., Jr. (1987). The gay and lesbian stepparent family. In. F. W. Bozett (Ed.), *Gay and lesbian parents* (pp. 112-137). New York: Praeger.

Barber, M. E., & Schwartz, A. (2013). Growing the research base. *Journal of Gay & Lesbian Mental Health*, *17*, 253-255.

Barrett, H., & Tasker, F. (2001) Growing up with a gay parent: views of 101 gay fathers on their sons' and daughters' experiences. *Educational and Child Psychology*, *18*, 62-77.

Baumeister, R. F., Catanese, K. R., & Vohs, K. D. (2001). Is there a gender difference in strength of sex drive? Theoretical views, conceptual distinctions, and a review of relevant evidence. *Personality and Social Psychology Review*, *5*, 242-273.

Baumeister, R. F., & Tierney, J. (2011). *Willpower: Rediscovering the greatest human strength*. New York, NY: Penguin Press.

Baumrind, D. (1995). Commentary on sexual orientation: Research and social policy implications. *Developmental Psychology*, *31*, 130-136.

Baunach, D. M. (2012). Changing same-sex marriage attitudes in America from 1988 through 2010. *Public Opinion Quarterly*, *76*, 364-378.

Becker, A. B., & Todd, M. E. (2013). A new American family? Public opinion toward family status and perceptions of the challenges faced by children of same-sex parents. *Journal of GLBT Family Studies*, *9*, 425-448.

Belcastro, P. A., Gramlich, T., Nicholson, T., Price, J., & Wilson, R. (1993). A review of data based studies addressing the affects of homosexual parenting on children's sexual and social functioning. *Journal of Divorce & Remarriage*, *20*, 105-122.

Belkin, A., Ender, M. G., Frank, N., Furia, S. R., Lucas, G., Packard, G., Samuels, S. M., Schultz, T., & Segal, D. R. (2013). Readiness and DADT repeal: Has the new policy of open service undermined the military? *Armed Forces & Society*, *39*, 587-601.

Bennett, C. S. (2001) *The psychology of parenthood for the midlife lesbian mother of teens*. (Unpublished Doctoral dissertation, California School of Professional Psychology, Berkeley/Alameda, California). *Dissertation Abstracts International*, 62(03), 1612B. UMI No. 3009210.

Bernstein, M. (2015). Same-sex marriage and the future of the LGBT movement: SWS presidential address. *Gender & Society*, *29*, 321-337.

Berkowitz, D., & Ryan, M. (2011). Bathrooms, baseball, and bra shopping: Lesbian and gay parents talk about engendering their children. *Sociological Perspectives*, *54*, 329-350.

Bernard, J. (1972). *The future of marriage*. New Haven, CT: Yale University Press.

Berzon, B. (1978). Sharing your lesbian identity with your children: A case for openness. In G. Vida (Ed.), *Our right to love*. Englewood Cliffs, NJ: Prentice-Hall.

Biblarz, T., & Savci, E. (2010). Lesbian, gay, bisexual, and transgender families. *Journal of Marriage and Family*, *72*, 480-497.

Biblarz, T., & Stacey, J. (2010a). How does the gender of parents matter? *Journal of Marriage and Family*, *72*, 3-22.

Biblarz, T., & Stacey, J. (2010b). Ideal families and social science ideals. *Journal of Marriage and Family*, *72*, 41-44.

Bickel, W. K., & Marsch, L. A. (2001). Toward a behavioral economic understanding of drug dependence: Delay discounting processes. *Addiction, 96*, 73-86.

Blake, S. M., Ledsky, R., Lehman, T., Goodenow, C., Sawyer, R., & Hack, T. (2001). Preventing sexual risk behaviors among gay, lesbian, and bisexual adolescents: The benefits of gay-sensitive HIV instruction in schools. *American Journal of Public Health, 91*, 940-946.

Blanchard, R., & VanderLaan, D. P. (2015). Commentary on Kishida and Rahman (2015), including a meta-analysis of relevant studies on fraternal birth order and sexual orientation in men. *Archives of Sexual Behavior, 44*, 1503-1509.

Blee, K. M. (2015). Methods, interpretation, and ethics in the study of White supremacist perpetrators. *Conflict and Society: Advances in Research, 1*, 9-22.

Bockting, W. O. (2014). Transgender identity development. In D. L. Tolman & L. M. Diamond (Eds.), *APA handbook of sexuality and psychology* (Vol. 1, pp. 597-628). Washington, DC: American Psychological Association.

Bonander, A. R. (2016). *Family communication about sex: A qualitative analysis of gay and lesbian parents' parent-child sex communication.* Unpublished doctoral dissertation, University of Nebraska-Lincoln.

Boon, S. L., & Alderson, K. G. (2009). A phenomenological study of women in same-sex relationships who were previously married to men. *Canadian Journal of Human Sexuality, 18*, 149-168.

Borenstein, M., Hedges, L. V., Higgins, J. P. T., & Rothstein, H. R. (2009). *Introduction to meta-analysis.* Chicester, UK: Wiley & Sons.

Bos, H. M. W., Gartrell, N. K., Peyser, H., & van Balen, F. (2008). The USA National Longitudinal Lesbian Family Study (NLLFS): Homophobia, psychological adjustment, and protective factors. *Journal of Lesbian Studies, 12*, 455-471.

Bos, H. M. W., & Gartrell, N. (2010). Adolescents of the USA National Longitudinal Lesbian Family Study: Can family characteristics counteract the negative effects of stigmatization? *Family Process, 49*, 559-572.

Bos, H. M. W., Gartrell, N., Roeleveld, J., & Ledoux, G. (2016). Civic competence of Dutch children in female same-sex parent families: A comparison with children of opposite-sex parents. *Youth & Society, 48*, 628-648.

Bos, H. M. W., Goldberg, N., van Gelderen, L., & Gartrell, N. (2012). Adolescents of the U.S. National Longitudinal Lesbian Family Study: Male role models, gender role traits, and psychological adjustment. *Gender & Society, 26*, 603-638.

Bos, H. M. W., Knox, J. R., van Rijn-van Gelderen, L., & Gartrell, N. K. (2016). Same-sex and different-sex parent households and child health outcomes: Findings from the National Survey of Children's Health. *Journal of Developmental and Behavioral Pediatrics, 37*, 179-187.

Bos, H. M. W., Kuyper, L., & Gartrell, N. K. (2017). A population-based comparison of female and male same-sex parent and different-sex parent households. *Family Process*, online first.

Bos, H. M. W., & Sandfort, T. G. M. (2010). Children's gender identity in lesbian and heterosexual two-parent families. *Sex Roles, 62*, 114-126.

Bos, H. M. W., van Balen, F., & van den Boom, D. C. (2004). Experience of parenthood, couple relationship, social support, and child-rearing goals in planned lesbian mother families. *Journal of Child Psychology and Psychiatry, 45*, 755-764.

BIBLIOGRAPHY

Bos, H. M. W., van Balen, F., & van den Boom, D. C. (2005). Lesbian families and family functioning: An overview. *Patient Education and Counseling*, *59*, 263-275.

Bos, H. M. W., van Balen, F., & van den Boom, D. C. (2007). Child adjustment and parenting in planned lesbian-parent families. *American Journal of Orthopsychiatry*, *77*, 38-48.

Bos, H. M., van Balen, F., Sandfort, T. G., & van den Boom, D. C. (2006). *Children's psychosocial adjustment and gender development in planned lesbian families.* Amsterdam, Netherland: University of Amsterdam, Social and Behavioral Sciences Department of Education.

Bos, H., van Gelderen, L., & Gartrell, N. (2015). Lesbian and heterosexual two-parent families: Adolescent-parent relationship quality and adolescent well-being. *Journal of Child & Family Studies*, *24*, 1031-1046.

Bosisio, R., & Ronfani, P. (2016). 'Who is in your family?' Italian children with non-heterosexual parents talk about growing up in a non-conventional household. *Children & Society*, *30*, 455-466.

Bozett, F. W. (1985). Gay men as fathers. In S. M. H. Hanson & F. W. Bozett (Eds.), *Dimensions of fatherhood* (pp. 327-352). Beverly Hills, CA: Sage.

Bozett, F. W. (1987). Children of gay fathers. In F. W. Bozett (Ed.), *Gay and lesbian parents* (pp. 39-57). New York: Praeger.

Bozett, F. W. (1989). Gay fathers: A review of the literature. *Journal of Homosexuality*, *18*, 137-162.

Bowling, J., Dodge, B., & Bartelt, E. (2017). Sexuality-related communication within the family context: Experiences of bisexual parents with their children in the United States of America. *Sex Education*, *17*, 86-102.

Brase, C. H., & Brace, C. P. (2015). *Understanding statistics: Concepts and methods.* (11th Ed.). Stamford, CT.: Cengage Learning.

Brewaeys, A., Ponjaert, I., Van Hall, E. V., & Golombok, S. (1997). Donor insemination: Child development and family functioning in lesbian mother families. *Human Reproduction*, *12*, 1349-1359.

Brodzinsky, D. M., Green, R. J., & Katuzny, K. (2012). Adoption by lesbians and gay men: What we know, need to know, and ought to do. In D. M. Brodzinsky & A. Pertman (Eds.), *Adoption by lesbians and gay men: A new dimension in family diversity* (pp. 233-253). New York, NY: Oxford University Press.

Brown, R., & Perlesz, A. (2007). Not the other mother: How language constructs lesbian co-parenting relationships. *Journal of GLBT Family Studies*, *3*, 267-308.

Bryant, B. S. (1975). *Lesbian mothers.* (Unpublished master's thesis, California State University, Sacramento).

Burri, A., Cherkas, L., Spector, T., & Rahman, Q. (2011). Genetic and environmental influences on female sexual orientation, childhood gender typicality, and adult gender identity. *PLoS ONE*, *6*(7), e21982.

Cameron, P. (2004). Numbers of homosexual parents living with their children. *Psychological Reports*, *94*, 179-188.

Cameron, P. (2005). Child molestations by homosexual foster parents: Illinois, 1997-2002. *Psychological Reports*, *96*, 227-230.

Cameron, P. (2009). Gay fathers' effects on children: A review. *Psychological Reports*, *104*, 649-659.

Cameron, P., Cameron, K., & Proctor, K. (2017). Children of homosexuals more apt to become homosexual and experience parental molestation: Surveys over three decades. *Marriage & Family Review*, *53*, 429-433.

Canning, T. T. (2005). Gay and heterosexual fathers: A comparative analysis of child behavior and well-being. *Dissertation Abstracts International: Section B. Science and Engineering*, *66* (07), 3995.

Chamorro, J., Bernardi, S., Potenza, M. N., Grant, J. E., Marsh, R., Wang, S., & Blanco, C. (2012). Impulsivity in the general population: A national study. *Journal of Psychiatric Research*, *46*, 994-1001.

Chan, R. W., Brooks, R. C., Raboy, B., & Patterson, C. J. (1998). Divison of labor among lesbian and heterosexual parents: Associations with children's adjustment. *Journal of Family Psychology*, *12*, 409-419.

Chauveron, L. M., Alvarez, A., & van Eeden-Moorefield, B. (2017). The co-evolution of marriage and parental rights of gays and lesbians. *Journal of GLBT Family Studies*, *13*, 114-136.

Chen, P., & Vazsonyi, A. T. (2013). Future orientation, school contexts, and problem behaviors: A multilevel study. *Journal of Youth and Adolescence*, *42*, 67-81.

Cheng, S., & Powell, B. (2015). Measurement, methods, and divergent patterns: Reassessing the effects of same-sex parents. *Social Science Research*, *52*, 615-626.

Cherlin, A. J. (2010) Demographic trends in the United States: A review of research in the 2000s. *Journal of Marriage and Family*, *72*, 403-419.

Child Welfare Information Gateway, U.S. Department of Health and Human Services. (2011). *Working with lesbian, gay, bisexual, and transgender (LGBT) families in adoption*. (Bulletins for Professionals). Washington, D.C.: Author.

Chrisp, J. (2001). That four letter word – sons: Lesbian mothers and adolescent sons. *Journal of Lesbian Studies*, *5*, 195-209.

Ciano-Boyce, C., & Shelley-Sireci, L. (2002). Who is mommy tonight? Lesbian parenting issues. *Journal of Homosexuality*, *43*, 1-13.

Clark, J. B., Riggle, E. D. B., Rostosky, S. S., Rothblum, E. D., & Balsam, K. F. (2015). Windsor and Perry: Reactions of siblings in same-sex and heterosexual couples. *Journal of Homosexuality*, *62*, 993-1008.

Clark, V. (2001). What about the children? Arguments against lesbian and gay parenting. *Women's Studies International Forum*, *24*, 555-570.

Cohen, J. (1988). *Statistical power analysis for the behavioral sciences* (2nd Ed.). Hillsdale, NJ: Lawrence Erlbaum.

Cohen, J. (1992). A power primer. *Psychological Bulletin*, *112*, 155-159.

Cohen, J. (1990). Things I have learned (so far). *American Psychologist*, *45*, 1304-1312.

Collier, K. L., Bos, H. M. W., & Sandfort, T. G. M. (2013). Homophobic name-calling among secondary school students and its implications for mental health. *Journal of Youth and Adolescence*, *42*, 363-375.

Columbia Law School. (2017). *What does the scholarly research say about the wellbeing of children with gay or lesbian parents?* [whatweknownow.law.columbia.edu/topics/lgbt-equality/what-does-the-scholarly-research-say-about-the-wellbeing-of-children-with-gay-or-lesbian-parents/].

Compton, D. R. (2013) The family and gay men and lesbians. In A. K. Baumle (Ed.), *International handbook on the demography of sexuality* (pp. 257-273). New York: Springer Dordrecht.

BIBLIOGRAPHY

Conley, T. D., Ziegler, A., Moors, A. C., Matsick, J. L., & Valentine, B. (2012). A critical examination of popular assumptions about the benefits and outcomes of monogamous relationships. *Personality and Social Psychology Review*, *17*, 124-141.

Conron, K. J., Scott, G., Stowell, G. S., & Landers, S. J. (2012). Transgender health in Massachusetts: Results from a household probability sample of adults. *American Journal of Public Health*, *102*, 118-122.

Cooper, L., & Cates, P. (2006). *Too high a price: The case against restricting gay parenting* (Updated 2nd Ed.). New York, NY: American Civil Liberties Union (ACLU) Foundation.

Cornish, R. (2005). *5 minute church historian*. Colorado Springs, CO: NavPress.

Costello, C. Y. (1997). Conceiving identity: Bisexual, lesbian, and gay parents consider their children's sexual orientations. *Journal of Sociology and Social Welfare*, *24*(3), 63-89.

Crouch, S. R., McNair, R., & Waters, E. (2017). Parent perspectives on child health and well-being in same-sex families: Heteronormative conflict and resilience building. *Journal of Child and Family Studies*, *26*, 2202-2214.

Crouch, S. R., Waters, E., McNair, R., & Power, J. (2014). The health perspectives of Australian adolescents from same-sex parented families: A mixed methods study. *Child: Care, Health, and Development*, *41*(3), 1-9.

Crowl, A., Ahn, S., & Baker, J. (2008). A meta-analysis of developmental outcomes for children of same-sex and heterosexual parents. *Journal of GLBT Family Studies*, *4*, 385-407.

Cuijpers, P. (2017). Four decades of outcome research on psychotherapies for adult depression: An overview of a series of meta-analyses. *Canadian Psychology*, *58*, 7-19.

Dainton, M., & Zelley, E. D. (2006). Social exchange theories: Interdependence and equity. In D. O. Braitwaite & L. A. Baxter (Eds.), *Engaging theories in family communication: Multiple perspectives* (pp. 243-259). Thousand Oaks, CA: Sage.

Davies, R. (1979). Representing the lesbian mother. *Family Advocate*, *1*, 21-23, 36.

Davis, M. A. (2013). Demographics of gay and lesbian adoption and family policies. In A. K. Baumle (Ed.), *International handbook on the demography of sexuality* (pp. 383-401). New York: Springer Dordrecht.

Destro, R. A. (2012). "You have the right to remain silent": Does the U.S. Constitution require public affirmation of same-sex marriage? *BYU Journal of Public Law*, *27*, 397-440.

Dewaele, A., Van Houtte, M., Symons, K., & Buysse, A. (2017). Exploring first sexual intercourse, sexual orientation, and sexual health in men. *Journal of Homosexuality*, *64*, 1832-1849.

Diamond, L. M. (2013). Sexuality in relationships. In J. A. Simpson & L. Campbell (Eds.), *The Oxford handbook of close relationships* (pp. 589-614). New York, NY: Oxford University Press.

Diamond, L. M. (2014). Gender and same-sex sexuality. In D. L. Tolman & L. M. Diamond (Eds.), *APA handbook of sexuality and psychology* (Vol. 1, pp. 629-652). Washington, DC: American Psychological Association.

Diamond, L. M., & Butterworth, M. (2009). The close relationships of sexual minorities. In M. C. Smith & N. DeFrates-Densch (Eds.), *Handbook of research on adult learning and development* (pp. 350-377). New York, NY: Routledge.

Diamond, L. M., & Rosky, C. J. (2016). Scrutinizing immutability: Research on sexual orientation and U.S. legal advocacy for sexual minorities. *Journal of Sex Research*, *53*, 363-391.

DiBennardo, R., & Gates, G. J. (2014). Research note: US Census same-sex couple data: adjustments to reduce measurement error and empirical implications. *Population Research and Policy Review*, *33*, 603-614.

DiLapi, E. M. (1989). Lesbian mothers and the motherhood hierarchy. *Journal of Homosexuality*, *18*, 101-121.

Dillender, M. (2014) The death of marriage? The effects of new forms of legal recognition on marriage rates in the United States. *Demography*, 51, 563-585.

Dinno, A., & Whitney, C. (2013). Same-sex marriage and the perceived assault on opposite sex marriage. *PLoS ONE*, 8(6), e65730.

Doherty, W. J. (2006). Foreword. In J. J. Bigner (Ed.), *An introduction to GLBT family studies* (pp. xvii-xxiii). New York, NY: Haworth Press.

Donahue, K., Langstrom, N., Lundstrom, S., Lichtenstein, P., & Forsman, M. (2017). Familial factors, victimization, and psychological health among sexual minority adolescents in Sweden. *American Journal of Public Health*, *107*, 322-328.

Doolittle, K. L. (1999). Don't ask, you may not want to know: Custody preferences of children of gay and lesbian parents. *Southern California Law Review*, *73*, 677-704.

Duncan, M. L. (2016). Adoption, GLBT. In C. Shehan (Ed.), *The Wiley Blackwell encyclopedia of family studies* (Vol. 1, pp. 44-49). Malden, MA: Wiley Blackwell.

Dundas, S., & Kaufman, M. (2000). The Toronto Lesbian Family Study. *Journal of Homosexuality*, *40*(2), 65-79.

Durso, L. E., & Gates, G. J. (2013). Best practices: Collecting and analyzing data on sexual minorities. In A. K. Baumle (Ed.), *International handbook on the demography of sexuality* (pp. 21-42). New York: Springer Dordrecht.

Editors of the Harvard Law Review. (1989). Developments in the law: Sexual orientation and the law. *Harvard Law Review*, *102*, 1508-1671.

Edwards, K. M., & Sylaska, K. M. (2013). The perpetration of intimate partner violence among LGBTQ youth: The role of minority stress. *Journal of Youth and Adolescence*, *42*, 1721-1731.

Erich, S., Kanenberg, H., Case, K., Allen, T., & Bogdanos, T. (2009). An empirical analysis of factors affecting adolescent attachment in adoptive families with homosexual and straight parents. *Children and Youth Services Review*, *31*, 398-404.

Erich, S., Leung, P., & Kindle, P. (2005). A comparative analysis of adoptive family functioning with gay, lesbian, and heterosexual parents and their children. *Journal of GLBT Family Studies*, *1*, 43-60.

Elliott, P. (1996). Shattering illusions: Same-sex domestic violence. *Journal of Gay & Lesbian Social Services*, *4*, 1-8.

Elliott, S., & Umberson, D. (2008). The performance of desire: Gender and sexual negotiation in long-term marriages. *Journal of Marriage and Family*, *70*, 391-406.

Ellis, S. J. (2015). Lesbian psychology. In C. Richards & M. J. Barker (Eds.), *The Palgrave handbook of the psychology of sexuality and gender* (pp. 109-128). New York, NY: Palgrave Macmillan.

Elovitz, M. E. (1995). Adoption by lesbian and gay people: The use and misuse of social science research. In M. E. Elovitz and C. Schneider (Eds.), *Legal issues facing the nontraditional family* (pp. 172-191). New York, NY: Practicing Law Institute.

BIBLIOGRAPHY

Farr, R. H. (2017a). Does parental sexual orientation matter? A longitudinal follow-up of adoptive families with school-age children. *Developmental Psychology, 53*, 252-264.

Farr, R. H. (2017b). Factors associated with relationship dissolution and post-dissolution adjustment among lesbian adoptive couples. *Journal of Lesbian Studies, 21*, 88-105.

Farr, R. H., Forssell, S. L., & Patterson (2010). Parenting and child development in adoptive families: Does parental sexual orientation matter? *Applied Developmental Science, 14*, 164-178.

Farr, R. H., & Patterson, C. J. (2013). Lesbian-mother families formed through donor insemination. In A. E. Goldberg & K. R. Allen (Eds.), *LGBT-parent families: Innovations in research and implications for practice* (pp. 39-55). New York, NY: Springer.

Farr, R. H., Tasker, F., & Goldberg, A. E. (2016). Theory in highly cited studies of sexual minority parent families: Variations and implications. *Journal of Homosexuality, 64*, 1143-1179.

Fedewa, A. L., Black, W. W., & Ahn, S. (2015). Children and adolescents with same-gender parents: A meta-analytic approach in assessing outcomes. *Journal of GLBT Family Studies, 11*, 1-34.

Fedewa, A. L., & Clark, T. P. (2009). Parent practices and home-school partnerships: A differential effect for children with same-sex coupled parents? *Journal of GLBT Family Studies, 11*(1), 1-34.

Few-Demo, A. L., Humble, A. M., Curran, M. A., & Lloyd, S. A. (2016). Queer theory, intersectionality, and LGBT-parent families: Transformative critical pedagogy in family theory. *Journal of Family Theory & Review, 8*, 74-94.

Fitzgerald, B. (1999). Children of lesbian and gay parents: A review of the literature. *Marriage & Family Review, 29*, 57-75.

Flaks, D. K. (1993). *Lesbian couples and their children: Psychological and legal implications.* (Unpublished doctoral dissertation, Widener University, Chester, PA).

Flaks, D. K. (1994). Gay and lesbian families: Judicial assumptions, scientific realities. *William and Mary Bill of Rights Journal, 3*, 345-372.

Flaks, D. K., Ficher, L., Masterpasqua, F., & Joseph, G. (1995). Lesbians choosing motherhood: A comparative study of lesbian and heterosexual parents and their children. *Developmental Psychology, 31*, 105-114.

Folgero, T. (2008). Queer nuclear families? Reproducing and transgressing heteronormativity. *Journal of Homosexuality, 54*, 124-149.

Fomby, P., & Bosick, S. J. (2013). Family instability and the transition to adulthood. *Journal of Marriage and Family, 75*, 1266-1287.

Fomby, P., & Sennott, C. A. (2013). Family structure instability and mobility: The consequences for adolescents' problem behavior. *Social Science Research, 42*, 186-201.

Fond, G., Franc, N., & Purper-Ouakil, D. (2012). Homoparentalitie et development de l'enfant: Donnees actuelles. *L'Encephale, 38*, 10-15.

Francis, A. M. (2008). Family and sexual orientation: The family-demographic correlates of homosexuality in men and women. *Journal of Sex Research, 45*, 371-377.

Frank, N. (2016). Moving beyond anti-LGBT politics: Commentary on "Same-sex and different-sex parent households and child health outcomes: Findings from the National Survey of Children's Health". *Journal of Developmental and Behavioral Pediatrics, 37*, 24 5-247.

Frank, N. (2017). Comment on "Invisible victims: Delayed onset depression among adults with same-sex parents". *Depression Research and Treatment, 2016*, Article ID3185067, 1-2.

Freedner, N., Freed, L. H., Yang, Y. W., & Austin, S. B. (2002). Dating violence among gay, lesbian, and bisexual adolescents: Results from a community survey. *Journal of Adolescent Health*, *31*, 469-474.

Friedman, M. (1983). *Bright promises, dismal performance: An economist's protest and public opinion*. New York, NY: Harcourt, Brace, and Iovanovich.

Frisch, M., & Hviid, A. (2006). Childhood family correlates of heterosexual and homosexual marriages: A national cohort study of two million Danes. *Archives of Sexual Behavior*, *35*, 533-547.

Fulcher, M., Chan, R. W., Raboy, B., & Patterson, C. J. (2002). Contact with grandparents among children conceived via donor insemination by lesbian and heterosexual mothers. *Parenting: Science and Practice*, *2*, 61-76.

Fulcher, M., Sutfin, E. L., & Patterson, C. J. (2008). Individual differences in gender development: Associations with parental sexual orientation, attitudes, and division of labor. *Sex Roles*, *58*, 330-341.

Gabb, J. (2005). Lesbian m/otherhood: Strategies of familial-linguistic management in lesbian parent families. *Sociology*, *39*, 585-603.

Gailliot, M. T., & Baumeister, R. F. (2007). Self-regulation and sexual restraint: Dispositionally and temporally poor self-regulatory abilities contribute to failures at restraining sexual behavior. *PSPB*, *33*, 173-186.

Garofalo, R., Wolf, R. C., Kessel, S., Palfrey, J., &DuRant, R. H. (1998). The association between health risk behaviors and sexual orientation among a school-based sample of adolescents. *Pediatrics*, *101*, 895-902.

Gartrell, N. K. (1999). If this is Tuesday, it must be Dee... confessions of a closet polyamorist. *Journal of Lesbian Studies*, *3*, 23-33.

Gartrell, N., Banks, A., Hamilton, J., Reed, N., Bishop, H., & Rodas, C. (1999). The National Lesbian Family Study: 2. Interviews with mothers of toddlers. *American Journal of Orthopsychiatry*, *69*, 362-369.

Gartrell, N., Banks, A., Reed, N., Hamilton, J., Rodas, C., & Deck, A. (2000). The National Lesbian Family Study: 3. Interviews with mothers of five-year-olds. *American Journal of Orthopsychiatry*, *70*, 542-548.

Gartrell, N. K., & Bos, H. M. W. (2010). U.S. National Longitudinal Lesbian Family Study: Psychological adjustment of 17-year-old adolescents. *Pediatrics*, *126*(1), 28-36.

Gartrell, N. K., Bos, H. M. W., & Goldberg, N. G. (2011). Adolescents of the U.S. National Longitudinal Lesbian Family Study: Sexual orientation, sexual behavior, and sexual risk exposure. *Archives of Sexual Behavior*, *40*, 1199-1209.

Gartrell, N. K., Bos, H. M. W., & Goldberg, N. G. (2012). New trends in same-sex sexual contact for American adolescents? *Archives of Sexual Behavior*, *41*, 5-7.

Gartrell, N. K., Bos, H. M. W., Peyser, H., Deck, A., & Rodas, C. (2012). Adolescents with lesbian mothers describe their own lives. *Journal of Homosexuality*, *59*, 1211-1229.

Gartrell, N. K., Deck, A., Rodas, C., Peyser, H., & Banks, A. (2005). The National Lesbian Family Study: 4. Interviews with the 10-year-old children. *American Journal of Orthopsychiatry*, *75*, 518-524.

Gartrell, N. K., Hamilton, J., Banks, A., Mosbacher, D., Reed, N., Sparks, C. H., & Bishop, H. (1996). The National Lesbian Family Study: 1. Interviews with prospective mothers. *American Journal of Orthopsychiatry*, *66*, 272-281.

Gartrell, N. K., Rodas, C., Deck, A., Peyser, H., & Banks, A. (2006). The USA National Lesbian Family Study: Interviews with mothers of 10-year-olds. *Feminism & Psychology*, *16*, 175-192.

BIBLIOGRAPHY

Gates, G. J. (2011). Family formation and raising children among same-sex couples. *Family Focus*, FF*51*, F1-F4.

Gates, G. J. (2013a). Geography of the LGBT population. In A. K. Baumle (Ed.), *International handbook on the demography of sexuality* (pp. 229-242). New York: Springer Dordrecht.

Gates, G. J. (2013b). *LGBT parenting in the United States*. Los Angeles, CA: Williams Institute, UCLA School of Law.

Gates, G. J. (2015). Marriage and family: LGBT individuals and same-sex couples. *The Future of Children*, *25*, 67-87.

Gates, G. J., & Brown, T. N. T. (2015). *Marriage and same-sex couples after Obergefell*. Los Angeles, CA: Williams Institute, UCLA School of Law.

Gates, G. J., & Romero, A. P. (2009). Parenting by gay men and lesbians. In H. E. Peters & C. M. Kamp Dush (Eds.), *Marriage and family: Perspectives and complexities* (pp. 227-243). New York: Columbia University Press.

Gilmore, D. L., Esmail, A., & Eargle, L. A. (2016). Lesbian parents. In C. Shehan (Ed.), *The Wiley Blackwell encyclopedia of family studies* (Vol. 3, pp. 1287-1292). Malden, MA: Wiley Blackwell.

Golash-Boza, T. (2012). What does a sociology without borders look like? *Societies without Borders*, *7*, 397-404.

Goldberg, A. E. (2010). *Lesbian and gay parents and their children: Research on the family life cycle*. Washington, DC: American Psychological Association.

Goldberg, A. E., & Allen, K. R. (2013a). Conclusion: Reflections on the volume and visions for the future. In A. E. Goldberg & K. R. Allen (Eds.), *LGBT-parent families: Innovations in research and implications for practice* (pp. 359-365). New York, NY: Springer.

Goldberg, A. E., & Allen, K. R. (2013b). Donor, dad, or ....? Young adults with lesbian parents' experiences with known donors. *Family Process*, *52*, 338-350.

Goldberg, A. E., Downing, J. B., & Sauck, C. C. (2008). Perceptions of children's parental preferences in lesbian two-mother households. *Journal of Marriage and Family*, *70*, 419-434.

Goldberg, A. E., Gartrell, N. K., & Gates, G. (2014). *Research report on LGB-parent families*. Los Angeles, CA.: The Willliams Institute.

Goldberg, A. E., Kashy, D. A., & Smith, J. Z. (2012). Gender-typed play behavior in early childhood: Adopted children with lesbian, gay, and heterosexual parents. *Sex Roles*, *67*, 503-515.

Goldberg, A. E., & Kuvalanka, K. A. (2012). Marriage (in)equality: The perspectives of adolescents and emerging adults with lesbian, gay, and bisexual parents. *Journal of Marriage and Family*, *74*, 34-52.

Goldberg, A. E., Kinkler, L. A., Richardson, H. B., & Downing, J. B. (2012). On the border: Young adults with LGBQ parents navigate LGBTQ communities. *Journal of Counseling Psychology*, *59*, 71-85.

Goldberg, A. E., Moyer, A. M., Black, K., & Henry, A. (2015). Lesbian and heterosexual adoptive mothers' experiences of relationship dissolution. *Sex Roles*, *73*, 141-156.

Goldberg, A. E., Moyer, A. M., Kinkler, L. A., & Richardson, H. B. (2012). "When you're sitting on the fence, hope's the hardest part": Challenges and experiences of heterosexual and same-sex couples adopting through the child welfare system. *Adoption Quarterly*, *15*, 288-315.

Goldberg, A. E., & Smith, J. Z. (2013). Predictors of psychological adjustment in early placed adopted children with lesbian, gay, and heterosexual parents. *Journal of Family Psychology*, *27*, 431-442.

Goldberg, N. G., Bos, H. M. W., & Gartrell, N. K. (2011). Substance use by adolescents of the USA National Longitudinal Lesbian Family Study. *Journal of Health Psychology*, *16*, 1231-1240.

Goldberg, A. E., & Garcia, R. L. (2016). Gender-typed behavior over time in children with lesbian, gay, and heterosexual parents. *Journal of Family Psychology*, 30, 854-865.

Golombok, S. (2007). Foreword: Research on gay and lesbian parenting: An historical Perspective across 30 years. In F. Tasker & J. Bigner (Eds.), *Gay and lesbian parenting: New directions* (pp. xv-xxi). New York, NY: Haworth Press. Also published as volume 3, *Journal of GLBT Family Studies*.

Golombok, S. (2015). *Modern families: Parents and children in new family forms.* Cambridge, UK: Cambridge University Press.

Golombok, S. (2017). Parenting in new forms. *Current Opinion in Psychology*, *15*, 76-80.

Golombok, S., & Badger, S. (2010). Children raised in mother-headed families from infancy: A follow-up of children of lesbian and single heterosexual mothers, at early adulthood. *Human Reproduction*, *25*, 150-157.

Golombok, S., Blake, L., Slutsky, J., Raffanello, E., Roman, G. D., & Ehrhardt, A. (2017). Parenting and the adjustment of children born to gay fathers through surrogacy. *Child Development*, online advance publication.

Golombok, S., MacCallum, F., Goodman, E., & Rutter, M. (2002). Families with children conceived by donor insemination: A follow-up at age twelve. *Child Development*, *73*, 952-968.

Golombok, S., Mellish, L., Tasker, F., Jennings, S., Casey, P., & Lamb, M. E. (2014). Adoptive gay father families: Parent-child relationships and children's psychological adjustment. *Child Development*, *85*, 456-468.

Golombok, S., Perry, B., Burston, A., Murray, C., Mooney-Somers, J., Stevens, M., & Golding, J. (2003). Children with lesbian parents: A community study. *Developmental Psychology*, *39*, 20-33.

Golombok, S., Spencer, A., & Rutter, M. (1983). Children in lesbian and single-parent households: Psychosexual and psychiatric appraisal. *Journal of Child Psychology & Psychiatry*, *24*, 551-572.

Golombok, S., & Tasker, F. (1994). Children in lesbian and gay families: Theories and evidence. *Annual Review of Sex Research*, *5*, 73-100.

Golombok, S., & Tasker, F. (1996). Do parents influence the sexual orientation of their children? Findings from a longitudinal study of lesbian families. *Developmental Psychology*, *32*, 3-11.

Golombok, S., Tasker, F., & Murray, C. (1997). Children raised in fatherless families from infancy: Family relationships and the socioemotional development of children of lesbian and single heterosexual mothers. *Journal of Child Psychology and Psychiatry And Allied Disciplines*, *38*, 783-791.

Goodman, G. S., Emery, R. E., & Haugaard, J. J. (1998). Developmental psychology and law: Divorce, maltreatment, foster care, and adoption. In W. Damon, I. E. Sigel, & K. A. Renninger (Eds.), *Handbook of child psychology* (5th Ed., vol. 4, pp. 775-874). New York, NY: Wiley.

Gottlieb, A. R. (2003). Sons *talk about their gay fathers: Life curves.* Binghamton, NY:

BIBLIOGRAPHY

Harrington Park Press.

Gottman, J. M., Levenson, R. W., Gross, J., Frederickson, B. L., McCoy, K., Rosenthal, L., Ruef, A., & Yoshimoto, D. (2003). Correlates of gay and lesbian couples' relationship satisfaction and relationship dissolution. *Journal of Homosexuality*, *45*, 23-43.

Gray, J. (1992). *Men are from Mars, women are from Venus: A practical guide for improving communication and getting what you want in your relationships*. New York, NY: HarperCollins.

Green, A. I. (2010). Queer unions: Same-sex spouses marrying tradition and innovation. *Canadian Journal of Sociology*, *35*, 399-436.

Green, F. J., & Friedman, M. (2013). *Chasing rainbows: Exploring gender fluid parenting practices*. Bradford, Canada: Demeter Press.

Green, S. B. (1991). How many subjects does it take to do a regression analysis? *Multivariate Behavioral Research*, *26*, 499-510.

Greenan, D. E., & Tunnell, G. (2006). Sex, drugs, rock 'n' roll.... and children: Redefining male couples in the twenty-first century. In J. J. Bigner (Ed.), *An introduction to GLBT family studies* (pp. 223-243). New York, NY: Haworth Press.

Hamilton, B. E., Martin, J. A., Osterman, M. J. K., Curtin, S. C., & Mathews, T. J. (2015, December 23). Births: Final data for 2014. *National Vital Statistics Reports*, *64*(12), 1-64.

Haney-Caron, E., & Heilbrun, K. (2014). Lesbian and gay parents and determination of child custody: The changing legal landscape and implications for policy and practice. *Psychology of Sexual Orientation and Gender Diversity*, *1*, 19-29.

Harder, B. M. (2016a). Gay men's relationships in the United States. In C. Shehan (Ed.), *The Wiley Blackwell encyclopedia of family studies* (Vol. 2, pp. 896-901). Malden, MA: Wiley Blackwell.

Harder, B. M. (2016b). Lesbian relationships. In C. Shehan (Ed.), *The Wiley Blackwell encyclopedia of family studies* (Vol. 3, pp. 1292-1297). Malden, MA: Wiley Blackwell.

Harris, C. E. (2016). LGBT parenting. In K. L. Eckstrand & J. M. Ehrenfeld (Eds.), *Lesbian, gay, bisexual, and transgender healthcare* (pp. 115-124). Basel and Cham, Switzerland: Springer International Publishing.

Harter, S., & Pike, R. (1984). The pictorial scale of perceived competence and social acceptance for young children. *Child Development*, *55*, 1969-1982.

Hartz, C. L. (2010). Arkansas's unmarried couple adoption ban: Depriving children of families. *Arkansas Law Review*, *63*, 113-138.

Hatzenbuehler, M. L. (2013). Stigma as a fundamental cause of population health inequalities. *American Journal of Public Health*, *103*, 813-821.

Hatzenbuehler, M. L., Bellatorre, A., Lee, Y., Finch, R., Muennig, P., & Fiscella, K. (2014). Structural stigma and all-cause mortality in sexual minority populations. *Social Science & Medicine*, *103*, 33-41.

Hatzenbuehler, M. L., Bellatorre, A., Lee, Y., Finch, R., Muennig, P., & Fiscella, K. (2018). Corrigendum to "Structural stigma and all-cause mortality in sexual minority populations". *Social Science & Medicine*, online advance.

Hawkins, A. J., & Carroll, J. S. (2015). Beyond the expansion framework: How same-sex marriage changes the institutional meaning of marriage and heterosexual men's conception of marriage. *Ave Maria Law Review*, *13*, 219-235.

Hawkins, S. A. (2011). *Family relationships and adolescent behavior: A look at families headed by heterosexual, lesbian, and gay parents*. (Unpublished doctoral Dissertation, The Claremont Graduate University, Claremont, CA).

Hays, D., & Samuels, A. (1989). Heterosexual women's perceptions of their marriages to bisexual or homosexual men. *Journal of Homosexuality, 18*, 81-100.

Henehan, D., Rothblum, E. D., Solomon, S. E., & Balsam, K. F. (2007). Social and demographic characteristics of gay, lesbian, and heterosexual adults with and without children. *Journal of GLBT Family Studies, 3*, 35-79.

Henson, R. K., & Roberts, J. K. (2006). Use of exploratory factor analysis in published research: Common errors and some comment on improved practice. *Educational and Psychological Measurement, 66*, 393-416.

Hequembourg, A. (2007). *Lesbian motherhood: Stories of becoming*. New York, NY: Harrington Park Press.

Herek, G. M. (1991). Myths about sexual orientation: A lawyer's guide to social science research. *Law & Sexuality, 1*, 133-172.

Herek, G. M. (1998). Bad science in the service of stigma: A critique of the Cameron group's survey studies. *Psychological Perspectives on Lesbian and Gay Issues, 4*, 223-255.

Herek, G. M. (2006). Legal recognition of same-sex relationships in the United States. *American Psychologist, 61*, 607-621.

Herek, G. M. (2010). Sexual orientation differences as deficits: Science and stigma in the history of American psychology. *Perspectives on Psychological Science, 5*, 693-699.

Herek, G. M. (2014). Evaluating the methodology of social science research on sexual Orientation and parenting: A tale of three studies. *University of California-Davis Law Review, 48*, 583-622.

Hess, C., Milli, J., Hayes, J., & Hegewisch, A. (2015). *The status of women in the states: 2015*. Washington, DC: Institute for Women's Policy Research.

Hicks, S. (2005). Is gay parenting bad for kids? Responding to the "very idea of difference" in research on lesbian and gay parents. *Sexualities, 8*, 158-168.

Hicks, S. (2013). Lesbian, gay, bisexual, and transgender parents and the question of gender. In A. E. Goldberg & K. R. Allen (Eds.), *LGBT-Parent families: Innovations in Research and Implications for Practice* (pp. 149-162). New York, NY: Springer Science+Business Media.

Hirschman, D. (2016). Stylized facts in the social sciences. *Sociological Science, 3*, 604-626.

Hofmann, W., & Vohs, K. D. (2016). Desire and self-regulation. In K. D. Vohs & R. F. Baumeister (Eds.), *Handbook of self-regulation: Research, theory, and applications* (3rd Ed., pp. 76-94). New York, NY: Guilford Press.

Hooker, E. (1957). Adjustment of the overt male homosexual. *Journal of Projective Techniques, 21*, 1-31.

Hunter, J. E., & Schmidt, F. L. (2004). *Methods of meta-analysis: Correcting error and bias in research findings* (2nd Ed.). Thousand Oaks, CA: Sage.

Hunter, N. D., & Polikoff, N. D. (1976). Custody rights of lesbian mothers: Legal theory and litigation strategy. *Buffalo Law Review, 25*, 691-733.

Iantaffi, A. (2009). Houses full of love: Bringing up children in polyamorous relationships. In R. Epstein (Ed.), *Who's your daddy? And other writings on queer parenting* (pp. 283-290). Toronto, Canada: Sumach Press.

Infanti, A. C. (2014). The house of Windsor: Accentuating the heteronormativity in the tax incentives for procreation. *Washington Law Review, 89*, 1185-1233.

Ioannidis, J. P. A. (2005) Why most published research findings are false. *PLoS Medicine, 2*(8), e124.

BIBLIOGRAPHY

Israel, H., Buckhaber, E., & Weinmann, R. (1931). *A hundred authors against Einstein.* Leipzig, Germany: R. Voigtlander Verlag.

Jacobs, M. B. (2002). Micah has one mommy and one legal stranger: Adjudicating maternity for nonbiological lesbian coparents. *Buffalo Law Review, 50,* 341-391.

Jenny, C., Roesler, T. A., & Poyer, K. L. (1994). Are children at risk for sexual abuse by homosexuals? *Pediatrics, 94,* 41-44.

Javaid, G. A. (1993). The children of homosexual and heterosexual single mothers. *Child Psychiatry and Human Development, 23,* 235-248.

Jedzinak, J. A. (2004) Growing up in a lesbian family: a qualitative study of the adult daughter's experience. (Unpublished doctoral dissertation, Alliant International University, San Francisco Bay, California). *Dissertation Abstracts International, 65*(05), 2631B. UMI No. 3133453.

Jennings, S., Mellish, L., Tasker, F., Lamb, M., & Golombok, S. (2014). Why adoption? Gay, lesbian, and heterosexual adoptive parents' reproductive experiences and reasons for adoption. *Adoption Quarterly, 17,* 205-226.

Joos, K. E., & Broad, K. L. (2007). Coming out of the family closet: stories of adult women with LGBTQ parent(s). *Qualitative Sociology, 30,* 275-295.

Joyner, K., Manning, W., & Bogle, R. (2017). Gender and the stability of same-sex and different-sex relationships among young adults. *Demography, 54,* 2351-2374.

Jurich, A. P. (2008) *Family therapy with suicidal adolescents.* New York: Routledge.

Kaesar, G. (1999). *Love makes a family: Portraits of lesbian, gay, bisexual, and transgender parents and their families.* Amherst, MA: University of Massachusetts Press.

Kane, E. W. (2006). "No way my boys are going to be like that!" Parents' responses to children's gender noncomformity. *Gender & Society, 20,* 149-176.

Kaplan, R. A. (2015). "It's all about Edie, stupid": Lessons from litigating United States v. Windsor. *Columbia Journal of Gender and Law, 29,* 85-103.

King, G. (1986). How not to lie with statistics: Avoiding common mistakes in quantitative political science. *American Journal of Political Science, 30,* 666-687.

Kintner-Duffy, V. L., Vardell, R., Lower, J. K., & Cassidy, D. J. (2012). "The changers and the changed" 1: Preparing early childhood teachers to work with lesbian, gay, bisexual, and transgender families. *Journal of Early Childhood Teacher Education, 33,* 208-223.

Kirk, M., & Madsen, H. (1990). *After the ball: How America will conquer its fear & hatred of gays in the 90's.* New York, NY: Penguin.

Kirkpatrick, M., Smith, C., & Roy, R. (1981). Lesbian mothers and their children: A comparative survey. *American Journal of Orthopsychiatry, 51,* 545-55545-551.

Kline, R. B. (2011). *Principles and practice of structural equation modeling* (3rd Ed.). New York, NY: Guilford Press.

Knapp, S. J. (2009). Critical theorizing: Enhancing theoretical rigor in family research. *Journal of Family Theory & Review, 1,* 133-145.

Kuhar, R. (2015). Playing with science: Sexual citizenship and the Roman Catholic Church counter-narratives in Slovenia and Croatia. *Women's Studies International Forum, 49,* 84-92.

Kunin, J. D. (1998). Predictors of psychosocial and behavioral adjustment of children: A study comparing children raised by lesbian parents to children raised by heterosexual parents. (Unpublished doctoral dissertation, California School of Professional Psychology, San Diego, CA). *Dissertation Abstracts International, 59*/06, 3094B.

Kuran, T., & Sunstein, C. R. (1999). Availability cascades and risk regulation. *Stanford Law Review, 51*, 683-768.

Kurdek, L. A. (2001). Differences between heterosexual-nonparent couples and gay, lesbian, and heterosexual-parent couples. *Journal of Family Issues, 22*, 727-754.

Kurdek, L. A. (2004). Are gay and lesbian cohabiting couples really different from heterosexual married couples? *Journal of Marriage and Family, 66*, 880-900.

Kurdek, L. A. (2005). What do we know about gay and lesbian couples? *Current Directions in Psychological Science, 14*, 251-254.

Kurdek, L. A. (2006). Differences between partners from heterosexual, gay, and lesbian cohabiting couples. *Journal of Marriage and Family, 68*, 509-528.

Kuvalanka, K. (2013). The "second generation": LGBTQ youth with LGBTQ parents. In A. E. Goldberg & K. R. Allen (Eds.), *LGBT-parent families: Innovations in research and implications for practice* (pp. 163-175). New York, NY: Springer Science+Business Media.

Kuvalanka, K., & Goldberg, A. (2009). "Second generation" voices: Queer youth with lesbian/bisexual mothers. *Journal of Youth and Adolescence, 38*, 904-919.

Laird, R. D., Marks, L. D., & Marrero, M. D. (2011). Religiosity, self-control, and antisocial behavior: Religiosity as a promotive and protective factor. *Journal of Applied Developmental Psychology, 32*, 78-85.

Lamb, M. E. (2012). Mothers, fathers, families, and circumstances: Factors affecting children's adjustment. *Applied Developmental Science, 16*, 98-111.

Langbein, L., & Yost, M. A., Jr. (2009) Same-sex marriage and negative externalities. *Social Science Quarterly, 90*, 292-308.

Langbein, L., & Yost, M. A., Jr. (2015). Still no evidence of negative outcomes from same-sex marriage. *Econ Journal Watch, 12*, 161-163.

Langstrom, N., Rahman, Q., Carlstrom, E., & Lichtenstein, P. (2010). Genetic and environmental effects on same-sex sexual behavior: A population study of twins in Sweden. *Archives of Sexual Behavior, 39*, 75-80.

Lansford, J. E. (2009). Parental divorce and children's adjustment. *Perspectives on Psychological Science, 4*, 140-152.

Larson, J., & Micheels-Cyrus, M. (1986). *Seeds of peace: A catalogue of quotations.* Philadelphia, PA: New Society Publishers.

Lavner, J. A., Waterman, J., & Peplau, L. A. (2012). Can gay and lesbian parents promote healthy development in high-risk children adopted from foster care? *American Journal of Orthopsychiatry, 82*, 465-472.

Lavoie, S., Julien, D., & Fortier, C. (2006). The role of affirmation of homosexual identity in the parental experience of children with a gay father or lesbian mother. *Canadian Review of Mental Health, 25*, 51-65.

LeBlanc, A. J., Frost, D. M., & Bowen, K. (2018). Legal marriage, unequal recognition, and mental health among same-sex couples. *Journal of Marriage and Family, 80*, 397-408.

Lebow, J. L. (2014). Editorial: Overselling our findings. *Family Process, 53*, 175-178.

Leckey, R. (2014). Must equal mean identical? Same-sex couples and marriage. *International Journal of Law in Context, 10*, 5-25.

Lee, Y., Schumm, W. R., Lockett, L., Newsom, K. C., & Behan, K. (2016). An analysis of survivor data from the sinking of the HMT Birkenhead, the RMS Titanic, and the Korean ferry MV Sewol. *Comprehensive Psychology, 5*, 1-6.

BIBLIOGRAPHY

Legerski, E., Harker, A., Jeppsen, C., Armstrong, A., Dehlin, J. P., Troutman, K., & Galliher, R. V. (2017). Mormon mixed-orientation marriages: Variations in attitudes and experiences by sexual orientation and current relationship status. *Journal of GLBT Family Issues, 13*, 186-209.

Lesthaeghe, R. (2010) The unfolding story of the Second Demographic Transition. *Population and Development Review, 36*, 211-251.

Lesthaeghe, R. (2014) The Second Demographic Transition: A concise overview of its development. *PNAS, 111*(51), 18112-18115.

Lev, A. I. (2010). How queer! – The development of gender identity and sexual orientation in LGBTQ-headed families. *Family Process, 49*, 268-290.

Lewis, K. G. (1980). Children of lesbian parents: Their point of view. *Social Work, 25*, 198-203.

Lick, D. J., Schmidt, K. M., & Patterson, C. J. (2011). The Rainbow Families Scale (RFS): A measure of experiences among individuals with lesbian or gay parents. *Journal of Applied Measurement, 12*, 222-241.

Lick, D. J., Tornello, S. L., Riskind, R. G., Schmidt, K. M., & Patterson, C. J. (2012). Social climate for sexual minorities predicts well-being among heterosexual offspring of lesbian and gay parents. *Sexuality Research and Social Policy, 9*, 99-112.

Lin, T. E. (1999). Social norms and judicial decision-making: Examining the role of narratives in same-sex adoption cases. *Columbia Law Review, 99*, 739-794.

Lobaugh, E. R., Clements, P. T., Averill, J. B., & Olguin, D. L. (2006). Gay-male couples who adopt: Challenging historical and contemporary social trends toward becoming a family. *Perspectives in Psychiatric Care, 42*, 184-195.

Lubbe, C. (2007). Mothers, fathers, or parents: Same-gendered families in South Africa. *South African Journal of Psychology, 37*, 260-283.

Luntz, F. I. (2009). *What Americans really want…. really.* New York, NY: Hyperion.

Lytle, M. C., Foley, P. F., & Aster, A. M. (2013). Adult children of gay and lesbian parents: Religion and the parent-child relationship. *Counseling Psychologist, 41*, 530-567.

Mabry, C. R. (2005). Opening another exit from child welfare for special needs children: Why some gay men and lesbians should have the privilege to adopt children in Florida. *St. Thomas Law Review, 18*, 269-324.

Macatee, T. C. (2005). Psychological adjustment of adult children raised by a gay or lesbian parent. (Unpublished doctoral dissertation, Chestnut Hill College, Philadelphia, PA). *Dissertation Abstracts International, 68*, 03B.

MacCallum, F., & Golombok, S. (2004). Children raised in fatherless families from infancy: A follow-up of children of lesbian and single heterosexual mothers at early adolescence. *Journal of Child Psychology and Psychiatry, 45*, 1407-1419.

Malmquist, A., Mollerstrand, A., Wikstrom, M., & Nelson, K. Z. (2013). 'A daddy is the same as a mummy': Swedish children in lesbian households talk about fathers and donors. *Childhood, 21*, 119-133.

Manning, W. D., Brown, S. L., & Stykes, J. B. (2016). Same-sex and different-sex cohabiting couple relationship stability. *Demography, 53*, 937-953.

Manning, W. D., Fettro, M. N., & Lamidi, E. (2014). Child well-being in same-sex families: Review of research prepared for American Sociological Association amicus brief. *Population Research & Policy Review, 33*, 485-502.

Maranto, R., Redding, R. E., & Hess, F. (2009). The PC academy debate: Questions not asked. In R. Maranto, R. E. Redding, & F. Hess (Eds.), *The politically correct university* (pp. 3-14). Washington, DC: AEI Press.

Marks, L. (2012). Same-sex parenting and children's outcomes: A closer examination of the American Psychological Association's brief on lesbian and gay parenting. *Social Science Research, 41*, 735-751.

Marquardt, E., Glenn, N. D., & Clark, K. (2010). *My daddy's name is donor*. New York, NY: Institute for American Values.

Martin, J. A., Hamilton, B. E., Ventura, S. J., Menacker, F., & Park, M. M. (2002, February 12). Births: Final data for 2000. *National Vital Statistics Reports, 50*(5), 1-104.

Martin, J. A., Hamilton, B. E., Osterman, M. J. K., Curtin, S. C., & Mathews, T. J. (2015) Births: Final data for 2013. *National Vital Statistics Reports, 64*, 1, 1-65.

Martin-Storey, A. (2015). Prevalence of dating violence among sexual minority youth: Variation across gender, sexual minority identity and gender of sexual partners. *Journal of Youth & Adolescence, 44*, 211-224.

Martin-Storey, A., & August, E. G. (2016). Harassment due to gender nonconformity mediates the association between sexual minority identity and depressive symptoms. *Journal of Sex Research, 53*, 85-97.

Mason, K. (2018). "Won't someone think of the children?": Reproductive futurism and same-sex marriage in US courts, 2003-2015. *Sexuality Research & Social Policy, 15*, 83-98.

Maxwell, S. E. (2000). Sample size and multiple regression analysis. *Psychological Bulletin, 5*, 434-458.

McClellan, D. L. (2006). Bisexual relationships and families. In D. F. Morrow & L. Messinger (Eds.), *Sexual orientation and gender expression in social work Practice* (pp. 243-262). New York, NY: Columbia University Press.

McGraw, P. (2000). *Relationship rescue: A seven-step strategy for reconnecting with your partner*. New York, NY: Hyperion.

McGuire, J. K., Kuvalanka, K. A., Catalpa, J. M., & Toomey, R. B. (2016). Transfamily theory: How the presence of trans* family members informs gender development in families. *Journal of Family Theory & Review, 8*, 60-73.

McKerson, B. (2014). Raising the next generation: What's gender got to do with it? *Plaza: Dialogues in Language and Literature, 4*(2), 59-68.

McLaughlin, K. A., Hatzenbuehler, M. L., Xuan, Z., & Conron, K. J. (2012). Disproportionate exposure to early-life adversity and sexual orientation disparities in psychiatric morbidity. *Child Abuse & Neglect, 36*, 645-655.

McNeill, K. F. (1998). The lack of differences between gay/lesbian and heterosexual parents: A review of the literature. *National Journal of Sexual Orientation Law, 4*, 1-24.

Mellish, L., Jennings, S., Tasker, F., Lamb, M., & Golombok, S. (2013). *Gay, lesbian, and heterosexual adoptive families: Family relationships, child adjustment, and adopters' experiences*. London, UK: British Association for Adoption & Fostering.

Mezey, N. J. (2008). New *choices, new families: How lesbians decide about motherhood*. Baltimore, MD: John Hopkins University Press.

Mezey, N. J. (2015). *LGBT families*. Los Angeles, CA: Sage.

Miller, B. G., Kors, S., & Macfie, J. (2017). No differences? Meta-analytic comparisons of psychological adjustment in children of gay fathers and heterosexual parents. *Psychology of Sexual Orientation and Gender Diversity, 4*, 14-22.

BIBLIOGRAPHY

Miller, J. A., Jacobsen, R. B., & Bigner, J. J. (1981). The child's home environment for lesbian vs. heterosexual mothers: A neglected area of research. *Journal of Homosexuality, 7*, 49-56.

Miller, J. A., Mucklow, B. M., Jacobsen, R. B., & Bigner, J. J. (1980). Comparison of family relationships: Homosexual versus heterosexual women. *Psychological Reports, 46*, 1127-1132.

Moffitt, T. E., Arseneault, L., Belsky, D., Dickson, N., Hancox, R. J., Harrington, H., Houts, R., Poulton, R., Roberts, B. W., Ross, S., Sears, M. R., Thomson, W. M., & Caspi, A. (2011). A gradient of childhood self-control predicts health, wealth, and public safety. *Proceedings of the National Academy of Sciences USA, 108*, 2693-2698.

Moore, M. R., & Stambolis-Ruhstorfer, M. (2013). LGBT sexuality and families at the start of the twenty-first century. *Annual Review of Sociology, 39*, 491-507.

Morgan, P. (2014). *The Marriage Files: The purpose, limits, and fate of marriage.* London, UK: Wilberforce Publications.

Morse, C. N., McLaren, S., & McLachlan, A. G. (2007). The attitudes of Australian heterosexuals toward same-sex parents. *Journal of GLBT Family Studies, 3*, 425-455.

Mucklow, B. M., & Phelan, G. K. (1979). Lesbian and traditional mothers' responses to Adult Response to Child Behavior and self-concept. *Psychological Reports, 44*, 880-882.

Murray, P. D., & McClintock, K. (2005). Children of the closet: A measurement of the anxiety and self-esteem of children raised by a non-disclosed homosexual or bisexual parent. *Journal of Homosexuality, 49*, 77-95.

Murray, C. E., & Mobley, A. K. (2009). Empirical research about same-sex intimate partner violence: A methodological review. *Journal of Homosexuality, 56*, 361-386.

Mustanski, B., Kuper, L., & Greene, G. J. (2014). Development of sexual orientation and identity. In D. L. Tolman & L. M. Diamond (Eds.), *APA handbook of sexuality and psychology* (Vol. 1, pp. 597-628). Washington, DC: American Psychological Association.

Nazarinia Roy, R. R., Schumm, W. R., & Britt, S. L. (2014). *Transition to parenthood.* New York, NY: Springer.

Nock, S. L. (2001). Sworn affidavit of Stephen Lowell Nock. Ontario Superior Court of Justice. Between Hedy Halpern *et al.* and the Attorney General of Canada *et al.*: Court File No. 684/00.

Nungesser, L. G. (1980). Theoretical bases for research on the acquisition of social sex-roles by children of lesbian mothers. *Journal of Homosexuality, 5*(3), 177-187.

Nye, F. I. (1979). Choice, exchange, and the family. In W. R. Burr, R. Hill, F. I. Nye, & I. L. Reiss (Eds.), *Contemporary theories about the family: General theories/theoretical orientations* (pp. 1-41). New York, NY: Free Press.

Ocobock, A. (2018). Status or access? The impact of marriage on lesbian, gay, bisexual, and queer community change. *Journal of Marriage and Family, 80*, 367-382.

O'Connell, A. (1993). Voices from the heart: The developmental impact of a mother's lesbianism on her adolescent children. *Smith College Studies in Social Work, 63*, 281-299.

O'Connell, M. & Feliz, S. (2011). Same-sex couple household statistics from the 2010 Census. U.S. Bureau of the Census: Fertility and Family Statistics Branch, Social Economic, and Housing Statistics Division. Available at http://www.census.gov/hhes/samesex/

O'Donohue, W., & Redding, R. E. (2009). The psychology of political correctness. In R. Maranto, R. E. Redding, & F. Hess (Eds.), *The politically correct university* (pp. 99-119). Washington, DC: AEI Press.

O'Leary, D. (2010). Is the psychological adjustment of donor-conceived children of lesbians higher than that of other children? *The Linacre Quarterly*, *77*, 415-525.

Overby, L. M. (2014). Etiology and attitudes: Beliefs about the origins of homosexuality and their implications for public policy. *Journal of Homosexuality*, *61*, 568-587.

Patterson, C. J. (1992). Children of lesbian and gay parents. *Child Development*, *63*, 1025-1042.

Patterson, C. J. (1995a). Lesbian and gay parenthood. In M. H. Bornstein (Ed.), *Handbook of parenting: Status and social conditions of parenthood* (Vol. 3, pp. 255-274). Mahwah, NJ: Lawrence Erlbaum.

Patterson, C. J. (1995b). Lesbian mothers, gay fathers, and their children. In A. R. D'Augelli & C. J. Patterson (Eds.), *Lesbian, gay, and bisexual identities over the lifespan* (pp. 262-290). New York: Oxford University Press.

Patterson, C. J. (1996). Lesbian and gay parents and their children. In R. C. Savin-Williams & K. M. Cohen (Eds.), *The lives of lesbians, gays, and bisexuals: Children to adults* (pp. 274-304). Fort Worth, TX: Harcourt Brace.

Patterson, C. J. (2000). Family relationships of lesbians and gay men. *Journal of Marriage and the Family*, *62*, 1052-1069.

Patterson, C. J. (2001). Families of the lesbian baby boom: Maternal mental health and child adjustment. *Journal of Gay & Lesbian Psychotherapy*, *4*(3/4), 91-107.

Patterson, C. J. (2005). Lesbian and gay parents and their children: Summary of research findings. In American Psychological Association (Ed.), *Lesbian & gay parenting* (pp. 5-22). Washington, DC: American Psychological Association.

Patterson, C. J. (2006). Children of lesbian and gay parents. *Current Directions in Psychological Science*, *15*, 241-244.

Patterson, C. J. (2009a). Children of lesbian and gay parents: Psychology, law, and policy. *American Psychologist*, *64*, 727-736.

Patterson, C. J. (2009b) Lesbian and gay parents and their children: A social science perspective. In D. A. Hope (Ed.), *Contemporary perspectives on lesbian, gay, and bisexual identities: Nebraska Symposium on Motivation* (pp. 141-182). New York, NY: Springer Science and Business Media.

Patterson, C. J. (2013a). Children of lesbian and gay parents: Psychology, law, and policy. *Psychology of Sexual Orientation and Gender Diversity*, *1*(S), 27-34.

Patterson, C. J. (2013b). Family lives of lesbian and gay adults. In G. W. Peterson & K. R. Bush (Eds.), *Handbook of marriage and the family* (pp. 659-681). New York: Springer Science+Business Media.

Patterson, C. J. (2017). Parents' sexual orientation and children's development. *Child Development Perspectives*, *11*, 45-49.

Patterson, C. J., & Farr, R. H. (2016). Children of lesbian and gay parents: Reflections on the research-policy interface. In K. Durkin and H. R. Schaffer (Eds.), *The Wiley handbook of developmental psychology in practice: Implementation and impact* (pp. 121-142). Malden, MA: John Wiley & Sons.

Patterson, C. J., & Farr, R. H. (2017). What shall we call ourselves? Last names among lesbian, gay, and heterosexual couples and their adopted children. *Journal of GLBT Family Studies*, *13*, 97-113.

Patterson, C. J., & Friel, L. V. (2000). Sexual orientation and fertility. In G. R. Bentley & C. G. N. Mascie-Taylor (Eds.), *Infertility in the modern world: Present and future prospects* (pp. 238-260). New York, NY: Cambridge University Press.

BIBLIOGRAPHY

Patterson, C. J., & Goldberg, A. E. (2016). Lesbian and gay parents and their children. *National Council on Family Relations Policy Brief, 1* (1), 1-4.

Patterson, C. J., & Redding, R. E. (1996). Lesbian and gay families with children: Implications of social science research for policy. *Journal of Social Issues, 52*, 29-50.

Patterson, C. J., Sutfin, E. L., & Fulcher, M. (2004). Division of labor among lesbian and heterosexual parenting couples: Correlates of specialized versus shared patterns. *Journal of Adult Development, 11*, 179-189.

Paul, J. P. (1986). Growing up with a gay, lesbian, or bisexual parent: An exploratory study of experiences and perceptions. (Unpublished doctoral dissertation, University of California, Berkeley, CA). *Dissertation Abstracts International, 47*(07), 2756A.

Pelka, S. (2009). Sharing motherhood: Maternal jealousy among lesbian co-mothers. *Journal of Homosexuality, 56*, 195-217.

Pennington, S. B. (1987). Children of lesbian mothers. In F. W. Bozett (Ed.), *Gay and lesbian parents* (pp. 58-74). New York, NY: Praeger Publishers.

Peplau, L. A. (1993). Lesbian and gay relationships. In L. D. Garnets & D. C. Kimmel (Eds.), *Psychological perspectives on lesbian and gay male experiences* (pp. 395-419). New York, NY: Columbia University Press.

Peplau, L. A. (2003). Human sexuality: How do men and women differ? *Current Directions in Psychological Science, 12* (2), 37-40.

Peplau, L. A., & Beals, K. P. (2004). The family lives of lesbians and gay men. In L.Vangelisti (Ed.), *Handbook of family communication* (pp. 233-248). Mahwah, NJ: Lawrence Erlbaum Associates.

Peplau, L. A., & Fingerhut, A. W. (2007). The close relationships of lesbians and gay men. *Annual Review of Psychology, 58*, 405-424.

Peplau, L. A., Fingerhut, A. W, & Beals, K. P. (2004). Sexuality in the relationships of lesbians and gay men. In J. H. Harvey, A. Wenzel, & S. Sprecher (Eds.), *The handbook of sexuality in close relationships* (pp. 349-369). Mahwah, NJ: Lawrence Erlbaum Associates.

Perlesz, A., Brown, R., Lindsay, J., McNair, R., deVaus, D., & Pitts, M. (2006). Family in transition: Parents, children and grandparents in lesbian families give meaning to 'doing family'. *Journal of Family Therapy, 28*, 175-199.

Perrin, A. J., Cohen, P. N., & Caren, N. (2013). Are children of parents who had same-sex relationships disadvantaged? A scientific evaluation of the no-differences hypothesis. *Journal of Gay & Lesbian Mental Health, 17*, 327-336.

Perrin, A. J., Siegel, B. S., Dobbins, M. I., Lavin, A., Mattson, G., Pascoe, J., & Yogman, M. (2013). Promoting the well-being of children whose parents are gay or lesbian. *Pediatrics, 131*(4), e1374-1383.

Perrin, E. C. (2002). *Sexual orientation in child and adolescent health care*. New York, NY: Springer Science+Business Media.

Perrin, E. C., & Kulkin, H. (1996). Pediatric care for children whose parents are gay or Lesbian. *Pediatrics, 97*, 629-635.

Perrin, E. C., Pinderhughes, E. E., Mattern, K., Hurley, S. M., & Newman, R. A. (2016). Experiences of children with gay fathers. *Clinical Pediatrics, 55*, 1305-1317.

Peterman, L. M., & Dixon, C. G. (2003). Domestic violence between same-sex partners: Implications for counseling. *Journal of Counseling and Development, 81*, 40-47.

Peterson, G. W., & Bush, K. R. (Eds.) (2013). *Handbook of marriage and the family*. New York: Springer Science+Business Media.

Peterson, N. (1984). Coming to terms with gay parents. *USA Today*, April 30, at 3D.

Potter, D. (2012). Same-sex parent families and children's academic achievement. *Journal of Marriage and Family*, *74*, 556-571.

Potter, D., & Potter, E. C. (2017). Psychosocial well-being in children of same-sex parents: A longitudinal analysis of familial transitions. *Journal of Family Issues*, *38*, 2303-2328.

Powell, B., Hamilton, L., Manago, B., & Cheng, S. (2016). Implications of changing family forms for children. *Annual Review of Sociology*, *42*, 301-322.

Power, J. J., Perlesz, A., Brown, R., Schofield, M. J., Pitts, M. K., McNair, R., & Bickerdike, (2012). Bisexual parents and family diversity: Findings from the Work, Love, Play Study. *Journal of Bisexuality*, *12*, 519-538.

Puryear, D. (1983). A comparison of children of lesbian and single parent heterosexual mothers on three measures of socialization. *Dissertation Abstracts International*, *40*(07), 3418B-3419B.

Raley, J. A. (2013). Adolescents with same sex parents: Does it make a difference? *Adolescent Psychiatry*, *3*, 329-334.

Rambukkana, N. (2015). Open mon-monogamies. In C. Richards & M. J. Barker (Eds.), *The Palgrave handbook of the psychology of sexuality and gender* (pp. 236-260). New York, NY: Palgrave Macmillan.

Reczek, C., Spiker, R., Liu, H., & Crosnoe, R. (2016). Family composition and child health: does the sex composition of parents matter? *Demography*, *53*, 1605-1630.

Reczek, C., Spiker, R., Liu, H., & Crosnoe, R. (2017). The promise and perils of population research on same-sex families. *Demography*, *54*, 2385-2397.

Redding, R. E. (1999). Reconstructing science through law. *Southern Illinois University Law Journal*, *23*, 585-610.

Redding, R. E. (2001). Sociopolitical diversity in psychology: The case for pluralism. *American Psychologist*, *56*, 205-215.

Redding, R. E. (2002). Grappling with diverse conceptions of diversity. *American Psychologist*, *57*, 300-301.

Redding, R. E. (2008). It's really about sex: Same-sex marriage, lesbigay parenting, and the psychology of disgust. *Duke Journal of Gender Law & Policy*, *15*, 127-193.

Redding, R. E. (2012). Likes attract: The sociopolitical groupthink of (social) psychologists. *Perspectives on Psychological Science*, *7*, 512-515.

Redding, R. E. (2013). Politicized science. *Society*, *50*, 439-446.

Rees, R. (1979). *A comparison of children of lesbian and single heterosexual mothers on three measures of socialization.* (Unpublished doctoral dissertation). Berkeley, CA: California School of Professional Psychology.

Regnerus, M. (2012a). How different are the adult children of parents who have same-sex relationships? Findings from the New Family Structures Study. *Social Science Research*, *41*, 752-770.

Regnerus, M. (2012b). Parental same-sex relationships, family instability, and subsequent life outcomes for adult children: Answering critics of the New Family Structures Study with additional analyses. *Social Science Research*, *41*, 1367-1377.

Regnerus, M. (2017). Is structural stigma's effect on the mortality of sexual minorities robust? A failure to replicate the results of a published study. *Social Science & Medicine*, *188*, 157-165.

BIBLIOGRAPHY

Reiss, I. L. (2013). Exploring the relation of values, power, and advocacy in American sexual science. *International Journal of Sexual Health, 26*, 1-12.

Rich, T. S. (2016). Predatory publishing, open access, and the costs to academia. *Political Science & Politics, 49*, 265-267.

Richards, M. A., Rothblum, E. D., Beauchaine, T. P., & Balsam, K. F. (2017). Adult children of same-sex and heterosexual couples: Demographic "thriving". *Journal of GLBT Family Studies, 13*, 1-15.

Riggle, E. D. B., Rothblum, E. D., Rostosky, S. S., Clark, J. B., & Balsam, K. F. (2016). "The secret of our success": Long-term same-sex couples' perceptions of their relationship longevity. *Journal of GLBT Family Studies, 12*, 319-334.

Riley, M. (1975). The avowed lesbian mother and her right to child custody: A constitutional challenge that can no longer be denied. *San Diego Law Review, 12*, 799-864.

Ritenhouse, D. (2011). What's orientation got to do with it? The best interest of the child standard and legal bias against gay and lesbian parents. *Journal of Poverty, 15*, 309-329.

Rith, K. A., & Diamond, L. M. (2013). Same-sex relationships. In M. A. Fine & F. D. Fincham (Eds.), *Handbook of family theories: A content-based approach* (pp. 123-144). New York, NY: Routledge.

Ritter, M. J. (2010). Perry v. Schwarzennegger: Trying same-sex marriage. *The Scholar, 13*, 363-393.

Rivera, R. R. (1979, October 19). Lesbians' children – the legal issues. *Psychiatric News, 14*, 23.

Roberts, A. L., Glymour, M. M., & Koenen, K. C. (2013). Does maltreatment in childhood affect sexual orientation in adulthood? *Archives of Sexual Behavior, 42*, 161-171.

Robitaille, C., & Saint-Jacques, M-C. (2009). Social stigma and the situation of young people in lesbian and gay families. *Journal of Homosexuality, 56*, 421-442.

Rohrbaugh, J. B. (1992). Lesbian families: Clinical issues and theoretical implications. *Professional Psychology: Research and Practice, 23*, 467-473.

Ronner, A. D. (2010). When courts let insane delusions pass the rational basis test: The newest challenge to Florida's exclusion of homosexuals from adoption. *University of Florida Journal of Law and Public Policy, 21*, 1-85.

Rosario, M., & Schrimshaw, E. W. (2014). Theories and etiologies of sexual orientation. In D. L. Tolman & L. M. Diamond (Eds.), *APA handbook of sexuality and psychology* (Vol. 1, pp. 555-596). Washington, DC: American Psychological Association.

Rosato, J. L. (2006). Children of same-sex parents deserve the security blanket of the parentage presumption. *Family Court Review, 44*, 74-86.

Rosenfeld, M. J. (2010). Nontraditional families and childhood progress through school. *Demography, 47*, 755-775.

Rosenfeld, M. J. (2013). Reply to Allen *et al. Demography, 50*, 963-969.

Rosenfeld, M. J. (2014). Couple longevity in the era of same-sex marriage in the United States. *Journal of Marriage and Family, 76*, 905-918.

Rosenfeld, M. J. (2015). Revisiting the data from the New Family Structures Study: Taking family instability into account. *Sociological Science, 2*, 478-501.

Rosky, C. J. (2011). *Perry v. Schwarzenegger* and the future of same-sex marriage law. *Arizona Law Review, 53*, 913-983.

Rosky, C. J. (2013a). Fear of the queer child. *Buffalo Law Review*, *61*, 607-697.

Rosky, C. J. (2013b). No promo hetero: Children's right to be queer. *Cardozo Law Review*, *35*, 425-510.

Ross, H., Gask, K., & Berrington, A. (2011). Civil partnerships five years on. *Population Trends*, *145*, 172-202.

Ross, L. E., & Dobinson, C. (2013). Where is the "B" in LGBT parenting? A call for research on bisexual parenting. In A. E. Goldberg & K. R. Allen (Eds.), *LGBT-parent families: Innovations in research and implications* (pp. 87-103). New York, NY: Springer Science+Business Media.

Rostosky, S. S., Riggle, E. D. B., Rothblum, E. D., & Balsam, K. F. (2016). Same-sex couples' decisions and experiences of marriage in the context of minority stress: Interviews from a population-based longitudinal study. *Journal of Homosexuality*, *63*, 1019-1040.

Rothblum, E. D. (2009). An overview of same-sex couples in relation ships: A research area still at sea. In D. A. Hope (Ed.), *Contemporary perspectives on lesbian, gay, and bisexual identities* (pp. 113-139). New York: Springer Science + Business Media.

Rothblum, E. D., Balsam, K. F., & Mickey, R. M. (2004). Brothers and sisters of lesbians, gay men, and bisexuals as a demographic comparison group. *Journal of Applied Behavioral Science*, *40*, 283-301.

Rothblum, E. D., Balsam, K. F., & Solomon, S. E. (2008). Comparison of same-sex couples who were married in Massachusetts, had domestic partnerships in California, or had civil unions in Vermont. *Journal of Family Issues*, *29*, 48-78.

Rothblum, E. D., Balsam, K. F., Solomon, S. E., & Factor, R. J. (2006). Siblings and sexual orientation: Products of alternative families or the ones who got away? In J. J. Bigner (Ed.), *An introduction to GLBT family studies* (pp. 117-133). New York, NY: Haworth Press.

Rothblum, E. D., & Factor, R. (2001). Lesbians and their sisters as a control group: Demograhic and mental health factors. *Psychological Science*, *12*, 63-69.

Rouse, L. P. (2002). *Marital and sexual lifestyles in the United States: Attitudes, behaviors, and relationships in social context*. New York, NY: Haworth Clinical Practice Press.

Ruffini, A. (2017). Who's your daddy?: The marital presumption of legitimacy in the modern world and its application to same-sex couples. *Family Court Review*, *55*, 307-320.

Ruskola, T. (1996). Minor disregard: The legal construction of the fantasy that gay and lesbian youth do not exist. *Yale Journal of Law and Feminism*, *8*, 269-332.

Ruspini, E. (2016). Gay men as parents. In C. Shehan (Ed.), *The Wiley Blackwell encyclopedia of family studies* (Vol. 2, pp. 893-896). Malden, MA: Wiley Blackwell.

Russell, S. T. (2003). Sexual minority youth and suicide risk. *American Behavioral Scientist*, *46*, 1241-1257.

Ryan, S. (2007). Parent-child interaction styles between gay and lesbian parents and their adopted children. *Journal of GLBT Family Studies*, *3*, 105-132.

Saffron, L. (1997). *What about the children? Sons and daughters of lesbian and gay parents talk about their lives*. London, UK: Cassell.

Santilla, P., Wager, I., Witting, K., Harlaar, N., Jern, P., Johansson, A., Varjonen, M., & Sandnabba, N. K. (2008). Discrepancies between sexual desire and sexual activity: Gender differences and associations with relationship satisfaction. *Journal of Sex & Marital Therapy*, *34*, 31-44.

BIBLIOGRAPHY

Sarantakos, S. (1996a). Same-sex couples: Problems and prospects. *Journal of Family Studies*, *2*, 147-163.

Sarantakos, S. (1996b). Children in three contexts: Family, education, and social development. *Children Australia*, *21*, 23-31.

Sarantakos, S. (1998). Sex and power in same-sex couples. *Australian Journal of Social Issues*, *33*, 17-36.

Sarantakos, S. (2000). *Same-sex couples*. Sydney, Australia: Harvard Press.

Sarewitz, D. (2012). Beware the creeping cracks of bias. *Nature*, *485*, 149.

Sasnett, S. (2015). Are the kids all right? A qualitative study of adults with gay and lesbian parents. *Journal of Contemporary Ethnography*, *44*, 196-222.

Schlatter, E. (2012). *Anti-LGBT propagandist published again in academic journal*. Hatewatch blog, Southern Poverty Law Center, Montgomery, Alabama, September 20.

Schlatter, E., & Steinback, R. (2013). *10 myths about gay men and lesbians: Dissecting the claims used by the hard-line religious right to demonize the LGBT community*. Montgomery, AL: Southern Poverty Law Center.

Schofield, T. (2016). Knowing what we don't know: A meta-analysis of children raised by gay or lesbian parents. *The Winnower*, *3*: e147568.84110.

Schulenburg, J. (1985). *Gay parenting*. New York: Anchor Press/Doubleday.

Schumm, W. R. (1999) Satisfaction. In D. Levinson, J. J. Ponzetti, Jr., & P. F. Jorgensen (Eds.), *Encyclopedia of Human Emotions* (Vol. 2, pp. 583-590). New York, NY: MacMillan References.

Schumm, W. R. (2004a). What was really learned from Tasker and Golombok's (1995) study of lesbian and single parent mothers? *Psychological Reports*, *94*, 422-424.

Schumm, W. R. (2004b). Differential risk theory as a subset of social exchange theory: Implications for making gay marriage culturally normative and for understanding stigma against homosexuals. *Psychological Reports*, *94*, 208-210.

Schumm, W. R. (2004c). Response to Kirkpatrick (2004): Differential risk theory and lesbian parenthood. *Psychological Reports*, *95*, 1203-1206.

Schumm, W. R. (2004d) A reply to Belkin's argument that ending the "gay ban" will not influence military performance. *Psychological Reports*, *95*, 637-640.

Schumm, W. R. (2005). Empirical and theoretical perspectives from social science on gay marriage and child custody issues. *St. Thomas Law Review*, *18*, 425-471.

Schumm, W. R. (2008). Re-evaluation of the "no differences" hypothesis concerning gay and lesbian parenting as assessed in eight early (1979-1986) and four later (1997-1998) dissertations. *Psychological Reports*, *103*, 275-304.

Schumm, W. R. (2009). Gay marriage and injustice. *The Therapist*, *21*(3), 95-96.

Schumm, W. R. (2010a). Children of homosexuals more apt to be homosexuals? A reply to Morrison and to Cameron based on an examination of multiple sources of data. *Journal of Biosocial Science*, *42*, 721-742.

Schumm, W. R. (2010b). Evidence of pro-homosexual bias in social science: Citation rates and research on lesbian parenting. *Psychological Reports*, *106*, 374-380.

Schumm, W. R. (2010c). How science is done. *Marriage & Family Review*, *46*, 323-326.

Schumm, W. R. (2010d). Statistical requirements for properly investigating a null hypothesis. *Psychological Reports*, *107*, 953-971.

Schumm, W. R. (2010e). Comparative relationship stability of lesbian mother and heterosexual mother families: A review of evidence. *Marriage & Family Review*, *46*, 499-509.

Schumm, W. R. (2010f). "Adult attachment style dimensions in women who have gay or bisexual fathers": Response to Sirota. *Archives of Psychiatric Nursing, 24*, 371-372.

Schumm, W. R. (2010g). A comparison of citations across multi-disciplinary psychology journals: Case study of two independent journals. *Psychological Reports, 106*, 314-322.

Schumm, W. R. (2011a). Are two lesbian parents better than a mom and dad? Logical and methodological flaws in recent studies affirming the superiority of lesbian parenthood. *Ave Maria Law Review, 10*, 79-120.

Schumm, W. R. (2011b). Child outcomes associated with lesbian parenting: comments on Biblarz and Stacey's 2010 report. *Journal of Human Sexuality, 3*, 35-80.

Schumm, W. R. (2012a). Methodological decisions and the evaluation of possible effects of different family structures on children: The New Family Structures Survey (NFSS). *Social Science Research, 41*, 1357-1366.

Schumm, W. R. (2012b). Re-examining a landmark research study: a teaching editorial. *Marriage and Family Review, 48*, 465-489.

Schumm, W. R. (2013). The intergenerational transfer of parental sexual orientation and other "myths". *International Journal for the Jurisprudence of the Family, 4*, 267-434.

Schumm, W. R. (2014). Challenges in predicting child outcomes from different family structures. *Comprehensive Psychology, 3*, 10, 1-12.

Schumm, W. R. (2015a). Navigating treacherous waters – One researcher's 40 years of experience with controversial research. *Comprehensive Psychology, 4*, 24, 1-40.

Schumm, W. R. (2015b). Sarantakos's research on same-sex parenting in Australia and New Zealand: Importance, substance, and corroboration with research from the United States. *Comprehensive Psychology, 4*, 16, 1-29.

Schumm, W. R. (2015c). Legalizing same-sex marriage produces marital inequality. *International Journal of the Jurisprudence of the Family, 6*, 1-42.

Schumm, W. R. (2016a). A conservative's view from the academic trenches: Reply to Duarte, Crawford, Stern, Haidt, Jussim, and Tetlock (2015). *Journal of Behavioral and Brain Science, 6*, 149-166.

Schumm, W. R. (2016b). A review and critique of research on same-sex parenting and adoption. *Psychological Reports, 119*, 641-760.

Schumm, W. R., Bosch, K. R., & Doolittle, A. (2009) Explaining the importance of statistical variance for undergraduate students. *Psychology and Education – An Interdisciplinary Journal, 46*(3/4), 1-7.

Schumm, W. R., & Canfield, K. R. (2011). Statistically evaluating multiple comparisons among correlated measures: A practical example. *Psychology and Education, 48*(3/4), 51-55.

Schumm, W. R., & Crawford, D. W. (2015). Violations of fairness in social science research: The case of same-sex marriage and parenting *International Journal for the Jurisprudence of the Family, 6*, 67-113.

Schumm, W. R., & Crawford, D. W. (2018a). *(How) does a literature review matter? Evaluating the quality of literature reviews in the social sciences.* Working paper, School of Family Studies and Human Services, Kansas State University, March.

Schumm, W. R., & Crawford, D. W. (2018b). *Can social desirability be detected statistically at the macro-sociological level?* Working paper, School of Family Studies and Human Services, Kansas State University, March.

Schumm, W. R., Crawford, D. W., Childs, T., Ateeq, A. B., Koochel, E. E., & Alshalan, T. M. (2017). Reply to Cameron *et al.*: Mistakes were made. Can they be corrected?

Marriage & Family Review, *53*, 434-443.

Schumm, W. R., Landess, M., & Williams, G. (2014). *Assessing outcomes of same-sex parenting*. Paper presented at the Theory Construction and Research Methodology Workshop, National Council on Family Relations, Baltimore, Maryland, November 18.

Schumm, W. R., Pratt, K. K., Hartenstein, J. L., Jenkins, B. A., & Johnson, G. A. (2013). Determining statistical significance (alpha) and reporting statistical trends: Controversies, issues, and facts. *Comprehensive Psychology*, *2*, 1-6.

Schumm, W. R., Nazirinia Roy, R. R., & Theodore, V. (2012). Separation and divorce. In B. A. Moore (Ed.), *Handbook of counseling military couples* (pp. 157-181). New York: Routledge (Taylor & Francis).

Schumm, W. R., Seay, M., McClish, K., Clark, K., Asiri, A., Abdullah, N., & Huang, S. (2016). Assessing the history of exaggerated estimates of the number of children being raised by same-sex parents as reported in both legal and social science journals. *BYU Journal of Public Law*, *30*, 277-301.

Schumm, W. R., Southerly, W. T., & Figley, C. R. (1980). Stumbling block or stepping stone: Path analysis in family studies. *Journal of Marriage and the Family*, *42*, 251-262.

Schumm, W. R., Webb, F. J., Castelo, C. S., Akagi, C. G., Jensen, E. J., Ditto, R. M., Spencer-Carver, E., & Brown, B. F. (2002). Enhancing learning in statistics classes through the use of concrete historical examples: The space shuttle Challenger, Pearl Harbor, and the RMS Titanic. *Teaching Sociology*, *30*, 361-375.

Schwartz, L. B. (2012). Mixed-orientation marriages: Coming out, staying together. *Journal of GLBT Family Studies*, *8*, 121-136.

Sedlak, A. J., Mettenberg, J., Basena, M., Petta, I., McPherson, K., Greene, A., & Li, S. (2010). *Fourth National Incidence Study of Child Abuse and Neglect (NIS-4): Report to Congress*. Washington, DC: U.S. Department of Health and Human Services, Administration for Child and Families.

Selekman, J. (2007). Homosexuality in children and/or their parents. *Pediatric Nursing*, *33*, 453-457.

Shane, L., III. (2017, July 31). Top general blames unclear science in delay for transgender Troops. *Army Times*, *78*(14), p. 27.

Shechner, T., Slone, M., Lobel, T. E., & Shechter, R. (2013). Children's adjustment in non-traditional families in Israel: The effect of parental sexual orientation and the number of parents on children's development. *Child: Care, Health, and Development*, *39*, 178-184.

Shechory, M., & Ziv, R. (2007). Relationships between gender role attitudes, role division, and perception of equity among heterosexual, gay, and lesbian couples. *Sex Roles*, *56*, 629-638.

Sheff, E. (2010). Strategies in polyamorous parenting. In M. Barker & D. Langridge (Eds.), *Understanding non-monogamies* (pp. 169-181). New York: Routledge.

Shelley-Sireci, L. M., & Ciano-Boyce, C. B. (2002). Becoming lesbian adoptive parents: An exploratory study of lesbian adoptive, lesbian birth, and heterosexual adoptive parents. *Adoption Quarterly*, *6*, 33-43.

Sherkat, D. E. (2012). The editorial process and politicized scholarship: Monday morning editorial quarterbacking and a call for scientific vigilance. *Social Science Research*, *41*, 1346-1349.

Short, E., Riggs, D. W., Perlesz, A., Brown, R., & Kane, G. (2007). *Lesbian, gay, bisexual, and transgender (LGBT) parented families: A literature review prepared for the Australian Psychological Society*. Melbourne: Australian Psychological Society.

Sin, R., & Risman, B. J. (2016). Same-sex marriage in the United States. In C. Shehan (Ed.), *The Wiley Blackwell encyclopedia of family studies* (Vol. 4, pp. 1717-1723). Malden, MA: Wiley Blackwell.

Sirota, T. (1997). *A comparison of adult attachment style dimensions between women who have gay or bisexual fathers and women who have heterosexual fathers*. (Doctoral dissertation, New York University, New York, NY).

Sirota, T. (2009). Adult attachment style dimensions in women who have gay or bisexual fathers. *Archives of Psychiatric Nursing, 23*, 289-297.

Skinner, H. A., Steinhauer, P. D., & Sitarenios, G. (2000). Family assessment measures (FAM) and process model of family functioning. *Journal of Family Therapy, 22*210.

Smith, J. F. N. (2016). Same-sex marriage attitudes during the transition to early adulthood: A panel study of young Australians, 2008 to 2013. *Journal of Family Issues, 37*, 2163-2188.

Solomon, S. E., Rothblum, E. D., & Balsam, K. F. (2005). Money, housework, sex, and conflict: Same-sex couples in civil unions, those not in civil unions, and heterosexual married siblings. *Sex Roles, 52*, 561-575.

Sowell, T. (1993). *Is reality optional?: And other essays*. (Hoover Institute Press Publication No. 418). Stanford, CA: Stanford University.

Stacey, J. (2003). Gay and lesbian families: Queer like us. In M. A. Mason, A. Skolnick, & S. D. Sugarman (Eds.), *All our families: New policies for a new century* (2nd. Ed., pp. 144-169). New York, NY: Oxford University Press.

Stacey, J. (2004). Marital suitors court social science spin-sters: The unwittingly conservative effects of public sociology. *Social Problems, 51*, 131-145.

Stacey, J. (2011). *Unhitched: Love, marriage, and family values from West Hollywood to Western China*. New York, NY: New York University Press.

Stacey, J. (2013). LGBT-parent families: From abnormal to nearly normative, and ultimately irrelevant. In A. E. Goldberg & K. R. Allen (Eds.), *LGBT-parent families* (pp. v-viii). New York: Springer.

Stacey, J., & Biblarz, T. (2001). (How) does the sexual orientation of parents matter? *American Sociological Review, 66*, 159-183.

Steed, J. J., & Templer, D. I. (2010). Gay men and lesbian women with molestation history: Impact on sexual orientation and experience of pleasure. *Open Psychology Journal, 3*, 36-41.

Stettler, N. M., & Katz, L. F. (2017). Minority stress, emotion regulation, and the parenting of sexual-minority youth. *Journal of GLBT Family Studies, 13*, 380-400.

Stevens, J. (1992). *Applied multivariate statistics for the social sciences* (2nd. Ed.). Hillsdale, NJ: Lawrence Erlbaum Associates, Publishers.

Stevens, M., Perry, B., Burston, A., Golombok, S., & Golding, J. (2003). Openness in lesbian-mother families regarding mother's sexual orientation and child's conception by donor insemination. *Journal of Reproductive and Infant Psychology, 21*, 347-362.

Stober, J. (2001). The Social Desirability Scale-17 (SDS-17): Convergent validity, discriminant validity, and relationship with age. *European Journal of Psychological Assessment, 17*, 222-232.

Strassel, K. (2016). *The intimidation game: How the left is silencing free speech*. New York, NY: Twelve (Hachette Book Group).

Strasser, M. (2010). Adoption, best interests, and the Arkansas constitution. *Arkansas Law Review*, *63*, 3-29.

Straumsheim, C. (2013). A reviewer's conflict. *Inside Higher Education*, May 2.

Sullins, D. P. (2015a) Emotional problems among children with same-sex parents: Difference by definition. *British Journal of Education, Society, and Behavioural Science*, *7*, 99-120.

Sullins, D. P. (2015b). The unexpected harm of same-sex marriage: A critical re-appraisal, replication, and re-analysis of Wainright and Patterson's studies of adolescents with same-sex parents. *British Journal of Education, Society, & Behavioural Science*, *11*(2), 1-22.

Sullins, D. P. (2015c). Bias in recruited sample research on children with same-sex parents using the Strength and Difficulties Questionnaire (SDQ). *Journal of Scientific Research & Reports*, *5*(5), 375-387.

Sullins, D. P. (2016a). Truth and anti-truth: Faith, reason, and rhetoric in the public square. *The Catholic Social Science Review*, *21*, 207-217.

Sullins, D. P. (2016b). Invisible victims: Delayed onset depression among adults with same-sex parents. *Depression Research and Treatment*, *2016*, 2410392, 1-8.

Sullins, D. P. (2016c). Response to comment on "Invisible victims: Delayed onset depression among adults with same-sex parents". *Depression Research and Treatment*, *2016*, 6834618, 1-3.

Sullins, D. P. (2017). Sample errors call into question conclusions regarding same-sex married parents: A comment on "Family structure and child health: Does the sex composition of parents matter?" *Demography*, *54*, 2375-2383.

Sullivan, M. (2004). *The family of women: Lesbian mothers, their children, and the undoing of gender*. Berkeley, CA: University of California Press.

Sumontha, J., Farr, R. H., & Patterson, C. J. (2016). Social support and coparenting among lesbian, gay, and heterosexual adoptive parents. *Journal of Family Psychology*, *30*, 987-996.

Sutfin, E. L., Fulcher, M., Bowles, R. P., & Patterson, C. J. (2008). How lesbian and heterosexual parents convey attitudes about gender to their children: The role of gendered environments. *Sex Roles*, *58*, 501-513.

Sutton, S. A. (1980). The lesbian family: Rights in conflict under the California Uniform Parentage Act. *Golden Gate University Law Review*, *10*, 1007-1041.

Swain, C. M. (2015). Free speech, politics, and academia. *PS: Political Science & Politics*, *48* (S1), 100-107.

Swank, E., Woodford, M. R., & Lim, C. (2013). Antecedents of pro-LGBT advocacy among sexual minority and heterosexual college students. *Sex Research and Social Policy*, *10*, 317-332.

Tabatabai, A. (2016). *Lesbian, queer, and bisexual women in heterosexual relationships: Narratives of sexual identity*. New York, NY: Lexington Books.

Tan, T. X., & Baggerly, J. (2009). Behavioral adjustment of adopted Chinese girls in single-mother, lesbian-couple, and heterosexual-couple households. *Adoption Quarterly*, *12*, 171-186.

Tannen, D. (1991). *You just don't understand: Women and men in conversation*. New York, NY: Ballentine Books.

Tanturri, M. L. (2014). Why fewer babies? Understanding and responding to low fertility in Europe. In A. Abela & J. Walker (Eds.), *Contemporary issues in family studies: Global perspectives on partnerships, parenting, and support in a changing world.* New York: Wiley.

Tasker, F. (2013). Lesbian and gay parenting post-heterosexual divorce and separation. In A. E. Goldberg & K. R. Allen (Eds.), *LGBT-parent families: Innovations in Research and implications for practice* (pp. 3-20). New York: Springer.

Tasker, F., & Delvoye, M. (2015). Moving out of the shadows: Accomplishing bisexual motherhood. *Sex Roles, 73,* 125-140.

Tasker, F., & Golombok, S. (1991). Children raised by lesbian mothers: The empirical evidence. *Family Law, 21,* 184-187.

Tasker, F., & Golombok, S. (1995). Adults raised as children in lesbian families. *American Journal of Orthopsychiatry, 65,* 203-215.

Tasker, F., & Golombok, S. (1997). *Growing up in a lesbian family: Effects on child development.* New York, NY: Guilford Press.

Tasker, F., & Golombok, S. (1998). The role of co-mothers in planned lesbian-led families. *Journal of Lesbian Studies, 2,* 49-68.

Telingator, C. J., & Patterson, C. J. (2008). Children and adolescents of lesbian and gay parents. *Journal of the American Academy of Child and Adolescent Psychiatry, 47,* 1364-1368.

Titlestad, A., & Pooley, J. A. (2014). Resilience in same-sex-parented families: The lived experience of adults with gay, lesbian, or bisexual parents. *Journal of GLBT Family Studies, 10,* 329-353.

Tolman, D. L., & Diamond, L. M. (2014). Sexuality theory: A review, a revision, and a recommendation. In D. L. Tolman & L. M. Diamond (Eds.), *APA handbook of sexuality and psychology* (Vol. 1, pp. 3-27). Washington, DC: American Psychological Association.

Tomeo, M. E., Templer, D. I., Anderson, S., & Kotler, D. (2001). Comparative data of childhood and adolescence molestation in heterosexual and homosexual persons. *Archives of Sexual Behavior, 30,* 535-541.

Toomey, R. B., Ryan, C., Diaz, R. M., Card, N. A., & Russell, S. T. (2010). Gender-noncomforming lesbian, gay, bisexual, and transgender youth: School victimization and young adult psychosocial adjustment. *Developmental Psychology, 46,* 1580-1589.

Tornello, S. L., & Patterson, C. J. (2012). Gay fathers in mixed-orientation relationships: Experiences of those who stay in their marriages and of those who leave. *Journal of GLBT Family Studies, 8,* 85-98.

Tornello, S. L., & Patterson, C. J. (2016). Gay grandfathers: Intergenerational relationships and mental health. *Journal of Family Psychology, 30,* 543-551.

Tornello, S. L., Sonnenberg, B. N., & Patterson, C. J. (2015). Division of labor among gay fathers: Associations with parent, couple, and child adjustment. *Psychology of Sexual Orientation and Gender Diversity, 2,* 365-375.

Trandafir, M. (2014) The effect of same-sex marriage laws on different-sex marriage: Evidence from the Netherlands. *Demography, 51,* 317-340.

Trub, L., Quinlan, E., Starks, T. J., & Rosenthal, L. (2017). Discrimination, internalized Homonegativity, and attitudes toward children of same-sex parents: Can secure attachment buffer against stigma internalization? *Family Process, 56,* 701-715.

Turner, P. H., Scadden, L., & Harris, M. B. (1990). Parenting in gay and lesbian families. *Journal of Gay & Lesbian Psychotherapy, 1,* 55-66.

BIBLIOGRAPHY

Udry, J. R., & Chantala, K. (2005). Risk factors differ according to same-sex and opposite-sex interest. *Journal of Biosocial Science*, *37*, 481-497.

Umberson, D., Thomeer, M. B., Kroeger, R. A., Lodge, A. C., & Xu, M. (2015). Challenges and opportunities for research on same-sex relationships. *Journal of Marriage and Family*, *77*, 96-111.

U.S. Census Bureau. (2012) *The 2012 Statistical abstract*. Washington, DC: Author.

Ueno, K. (2010). Mental health differences between young adults with and without same-sex contact: A simultaneous examination of underlying mechanisms. *Journal of Health and Social Behavior*, *51*, 391-407.

VanderLaan, D. P., Gothreau, L. M., Bartlett, N. H., & Vasaey, P. L. (2011). Recalled separation anxiety and gender atypicality in childhood: A study of Canadian heterosexual and homosexual men and women. *Archives of Sexual Behavior*, *40*, 1233-1240.

Van Eeden-Moorefield, B., Few-Demo, A. L., Benson, K., Bible, J., & Lummer, S. (2018). A content analysis of LGBT research in top family journals 2000-2015. *Journal of Family Issues*, *39*, 1374-1395.

Vanfraussen, K., Ponjaert-Kristoffersen, I., & Brewaeys, A. (2002). What does it mean for youngsters to grow up in a lesbian family created by means of donor insemination? *Journal of Reproductive and Infant Psychology*, *20*, 237-252.

Vanfraussen, K., Ponjaert-Kirstoffersen, I., & Brewaeys, A. (2003). Family functioning in Lesbian families created by donor insemination. *American Journal of Orthopsychiatry*, *73*, 78-90.

Van Rijn-van Gelderen, L., Bos, H. M. W., & Gartrell, N. K. (2015). Dutch adolescents from lesbian-parent families: How do they compare to peers with heterosexual parents and what is the impact of homophobic stigmatization? *Journal of Adolescence*, *40*, 65-73.

Vittinghoff, E., & McCulloch, C. E. (2007) Relaxing the rule of ten events per variable in logistic and Cox regression. *American Journal of Epidemiology*, *165*, 710-718.

Vohs, K. D., & Baumeister, R. F. (2016). *Handbook of self-regulation: Research, theory, and applications*. New York, NY: Guilford Press.

Wainright, J. L., & Patterson, C. J. (2006). Delinquency, victimization, and substance use among adolescents with female same-sex parents. *Journal of Family Psychology*, *20*, 526-530.

Wainright, J. L., Russell, S. T., & Patterson, C. J. (2004). Psychosocial adjustment, school outcomes, and romantic relationships of adolescents with same-sex parents. *Child Development*, *75*, 1886-1898.

Wald, M. S. (2006). Adults' sexual orientation and state determination regarding placement of children. *Family Law Quarterly*, *40*, 381-434.

Waller, M. R., & McLanahan, S. S. (2005). "His" and "her" marriage expectations: Determinants and consequences. *Journal of Marriage and Family*, *67*, 53-67.

Walsh, C. F. (2016). Marriage equality in the United States. In C. Shehan (Ed.), *The Wiley Blackwell encyclopedia of family studies* (Vol. 3, pp. 1359-1361). Malden, MA: Wiley Blackwell.

Walters, M. L., Chen, J., & Breiding, M. J. (2013*). The National Intimate Partner and Sexual Violence Survey (NISVS): 2010 findings on victimization by sexual orientation*. Atlanta, GA: National Center for Injury Prevention and Control, Centers for Disease Control and Prevention.

Wardle, L. D. (1997). The potential impact of homosexual parenting on children. *University of Illinois Law Review*, *1997*, 833-919.

Wardle, L. D. (2004a). The curious case of the missing legal analysis. *BYU Journal of Public Law*, *18*, 309-370.

Wardle, L. D. (2004b). Adult sexuality, the best interests of children, and placement liability of foster-care and adoption agencies. *Journal of Law and Family Studies*, *6*, 59-99.

Wardle, L. D. (2005). A critical analysis of interstate recognition of lesbigay adoptions. *Ave Maria Law Review*, *3*, 561-617.

Wardle, L. D. (2015). The future of the family: The social and legal impacts of legalizing same-sex marriage. *Ave Maria Law Review*, *13*, 237-279.

Warner, R. M. (2008) *Applied statistics: From bivariate through multivariate techniques.* Los Angeles, CA: Sage.

Webb, S. N., & Chonody, J. (2014). Heterosexual attitudes toward same-sex marriage: The influence of attitudes toward same-sex parenting. *Journal of GLBT Family Studies*, *10*, 404-421.

Whatley, M. A., Cave, S. J., & Breneiser, J. E. (2016). The development of a scale to assess attitudes toward homosexual adoption: A preliminary investigation. *North American Journal of Psychology*, *18*, 107-121.

Wiik, K. A., Seierstad, A., & Noack, T. (2014). Divorce in Norwegian same-sex marriages and registered partnerships: The role of children. *Journal of Marriage and Family*, *76*, 919-929.

Wilkinson, L., & Task Force on Statistical Inference. (1999). Statistical methods in psychology journals: Guidelines and explanations. *American Psychologist*, *54*, 594-604.

Wittlin, W. A. (1983). Homosexuality and child custody: A psychiatric view-point. *Conciliation Courts Review*, *21*, 77-79.

Wolkomir, M. (2009). Making heteronormative reconciliations: The story of romantic love, sexuality, and gender in mixed-orientation marriages. *Gender & Society*, *23*, 494-519.

Ziegler, A., Conley, T. D., Moors, A. C., Matsick, J. L., & Runin, J. D. (2015). Monogamy. In C. Richards & M. J. Barker (Eds.), *The Palgrave handbook of the psychology of sexuality and gender* (pp. 219-235). New York, NY: Palgrave Macmillan.

Zrenchik, K., & Doherty, W. J. (2017). Confiding in the GLBT community about problems in marriage and long-term committed relationships: A comparative analysis. *Journal of GLBT Family Studies*, in press.

Zweig, R. (1999). The relationship among psychological androgyny and the well-being of adult children of traditional and nontraditional families of origin. (Unpublished Doctoral dissertation, Hofstra University, Hempstead, New York). *Dissertation Abstracts International*, *60*, 07B. UMI Number: 9936941.

APPENDIX A

LIST OF PUBLICATIONS BY PROFESSOR SCHUMM ON LGBT ISSUES
As of March 2018

Dr. Walter R. Schumm, Professor of Family Studies, Kansas State University,
schumm@ksu.edu

Schumm, W. R., & Crawford, D. W. (2018). How have other journals compared to "the top seven" journals in family social science with respect to LGBT-related research and reviews? A comment on "A content analysis of LGBT research in top family journals 2000-2015" An editorial analysis. *Marriage & Family Review, 56* (6), 521-530.

Schumm, W. R., Crawford, D. W., Childs, T., Ateeq, A. B., Koochel, E. E., & Alshalan, T. M. (2017). Reply to Cameron *et al.*: Mistakes were made. Can they be corrected? *Marriage & Family Review, 53*, 434-443.

Schumm, W. R. (2016). A review and critique of research on same-sex parenting and adoption. *Psychological Reports, 119*, 3, 641-760.

Schumm, W. R., Seay, M., McClish, K., Clark, K., Asiri, A., Abdullah, N., & Huang, S. (2016) Assessing the history of exaggerated estimates of the number of children being raised by same-sex parents as reported in both legal and social science sources. *BYU Journal of Public Law, 30*, 277-301.

Schumm, W. R. (2016) A conservative's view from the academic trenches: Reply to Duarte, Crawford, Stern, Haidt, Jussim, and Tetlock (2015). *Journal of Behavioral and Brain Science, 6*, 149-166.

Schumm, W. R. (2015) Legalizing same-sex marriage produces marital inequality. *International Journal of the Jurisprudence of the Family, 6*, 1-42.

Schumm, W. R., & Crawford, D. W. (2015) Violations of fairness in social science research: The case of same-sex marriage and parenting. *International Journal of Jurisprudence of the Family, 6*, 67-113.

Schumm, W. R. (2015) Sarantakos's research on same-sex parenting in Australia and New Zealand: Importance, substance, and corroboration with research from the United States. *Comprehensive Psychology, 4*, 16, 1-29.

Schumm, W. R. (2015) Navigating treacherous waters – one researcher's forty years of experience with controversial scientific research. *Comprehensive Psychology, 4*, 24, 1-40.

Schumm, W. R. (2014) Challenges in predicting child outcomes from different family structures. *Comprehensive Psychology, 3*, 10, 1-12.

Schumm, W. R. (2013) Intergenerational transfer of parental sexual orientation and other myths. *International Journal of the Jurisprudence of the Family, 4*, 267-433.

Schumm, W. R. (2012) Flawed evidence about gay marriage. In M. Cook (Ed.), *Same-sex marriage: dangers, difficulties, deceptions* (pp. 36-38). Van Nuys, CA: The New Media Foundation (Kindle edition).

Schumm, W. R. (2012) Re-examining a landmark research study: a teaching editorial. *Marriage and Family Review, 48*, 465-489.

This editorial was critiqued subsequently by:

Cameron, P., & Cameron, K. (2012) Re-examining Evelyn Hooker: Setting the record straight with comments on Schumm's (2012) editorial. *Marriage and Family Review, 48*, 491-523.

Schumm, W. R. (2012) Methodological decisions and the evaluation of possible effects of different family structures on children: The New Family Structures Survey (NFSS). *Social Science Research, 41*, 1357-1366.

Schumm, W. R. (2012) Lessons for the "devilish statistical obfuscator" or how to argue for a null hypothesis: A guide for students, attorneys, and other professionals. *Innovative Teaching, 1, 2* (online, 13 pages).

Schumm, W. R. (2011). Are two lesbian parents are better than a Mom and Dad? Logical and methodological flaws in recent studies affirming the superiority of lesbian parenthood. *Ave Maria Law Journal, 10*, 79-120.

Schumm, W. R. (2011) Child outcomes associated with lesbian parenting: comments on Biblarz and Stacey's (2010) report. *Journal of Human Sexuality, 3*, 35-80.

Schumm, W. R., & Canfield, K. R. (2011). Statistically evaluating multiple comparisons among correlated measures: A practical example. *Psychology and Education, 48* (3/4), 51-55.

Schumm, W. R. (2010) Criminal-justice sanctions minor and mostly against bisexual youth. *Pediatrics* (December 8), http://pediatrics.aapublication.org/cgi/eletters/127/1/49

Schumm, W. R. (2010) Comparative relationship stability of lesbian mother and heterosexual mother families: a review of evidence. *Marriage and Family Review, 46*, 499-509.

Schumm, W. R. (2010). Children of homosexuals more apt to be homosexuals? A reply to Morrison and to Cameron based on an examination of multiple sources of data. *Journal of Biosocial Science, 42* (6), 721-742.

Schumm, W. R. (2010) Statistical requirements for properly investigating a null hypothesis. *Psychological Reports, 107*, 3, 953-971.

Schumm, W. R., & Crow, J. R. (2010). Statistically evaluating multiple comparisons among correlated measures. *Psychology and Education, 47* (3/4), 27-30.

Schumm, W. R. (2011) Complexities of the social environment. *Pediatrics* (18 April). http://pediatrics.aapublications.org/cgi/eletters/peds.2010-3020v1 (accessed April 19, 2011).

Schumm, W. R. (2010) Lesbian parents. *Pediatrics* (June 8), http://pediatrics.aspublications/org/cgi/126/eletters/e01 (accessed June 8, 2010).

Schumm, W. R. (2010) How science is done. *Marriage and Family Review, 46*, 323-326.

Schumm, W. R. (2010). "Adult attachment style dimensions in women who have gay or Bisexual fathers": Response to Sirota. *Archives of Psychiatric Nursing, 24*, 371-372.

Schumm, W. R. (2010) Evidence of pro-homosexual bias in social science: citation rates and research on lesbian parenting. *Psychological Reports, 106*, 374-380.

Schumm, W. R. (2010) A comparison of citations across multi-disciplinary psychology journals: case study of two independent journals. *Psychological Reports, 106*, 314-322.

Schumm, W. R., Bosch, K. R., & Doolittle, A. (2009) Explaining the importance of statistical variance for undergraduate students. *Psychology and Education – An Interdisciplinary Journal, 46* (3/4), 1-7.

Schumm, W. R. (2009) Gay marriage and injustice. *The Therapist, 21* (3), 95-96.

Schumm, W. R. (2008) Re-evaluation of the "no differences" hypothesis concerning gay and lesbian parenting as assessed in eight early (1979-1986) and four later (1997-1998) dissertations. *Psychological Reports, 103*, 275-304.

APPENDIX A

Schumm, W. R., Akagi, C. A., & Bosch, K. R. (2008) Relationship satisfaction for heterosexual women compared to lesbians and heterosexual men in a sample of faith communities from Topeka, Kansas. *Psychological Reports, 102*, 377-388.

Schumm, W. R. (2005) Empirical and theoretical perspectives from social science on gay marriage and child custody issues. *St. Thomas Law Review, 18*, 2, 425-471.

Schumm, W. R. (2005) Making statistics come alive: a methods spotlight. Pp. 599-600 in V. L. Bengston, Acock, A. C., Allen, K. R., Dilworth-Anderson, P., & Klein, D. M. (Eds.), *Sourcebook of Family Theory and Research*. Thousand Oaks, CA: Sage.

Schumm, W. R. (2004) Differential risk theory as a subset of social exchange theory: implications for making gay marriage culturally normative and for understanding stigma against homosexuals. *Psychological Reports, 94*, 208-210.

Schumm, W. R. (2004). Response to Kirkpatrick (2004): Differential risk theory and lesbian parenthood. *Psychological Reports, 95*, 1203-1206.

Schumm, W. R. (2004) A reply to Belkin's argument that ending the "gay ban" will not influence military performance. *Psychological Reports, 95*, 637-640.

Schumm, W. R. (2004). What was really learned from Tasker and Golombok's (1995) study of lesbian and single parent mothers? *Psychological Reports, 94*, 422-424.

Commented on:

Kirkpatrick, M. (2004) Comments on Dr. Walter R. Schumm's paper "What was really learned from Tasker and Golombok's (1995) study of lesbian and single parent mothers?" *Psychological Reports, 94*, 1185-1186.

Schumm, W. R. (2000) Psychology of the scientist: LXXXIII – An assessment of Herek's critique of the Cameron group's survey studies. *Psychological Reports, 87*, 1123-1132.

Response:

Cameron, P., & Cameron, K. (2003) Psychology of the scientist: LXXXV. Research on homosexuality: a response to Schumm (and Herek). *Psychological Reports, 92*, 259-274.

Discredited?

Surely, some readers will recall that I have allegedly been "discredited" supposedly by some who are active on the Internet. As far as I am aware, I have never been discredited by genuine (Ph.D. university professor) scholars, though there are some internet gadflies that think they have found things with which to discredit me.

One professor once said that I was not well known. That may be true, but it more reflects my introverted nature and desire to avoid the limelight rather than being a reflection on the validity of my research. Lebow (2014) has argued that some scholars, in his opinion, seem to seek out media appearances. In contrast, I have generally avoided media appearances, partly because my schedule does not permit dedicating much time to that sort of thing – I have plenty to do without spending my time on media events.

Scott Rose once thought he had found an error in one of my reports (Schumm, 2012a), but I published a later paper that proved my statement to have been correct (Schumm, 2014). Some of my critics may claim that I had to pay to publish my papers, but many so-called "for pay" journals actually do not demand payment from every author for every paper. For example, Schumm (2015a, 2015b, 2016a) were published in journals that often assess page charges but because my contributions were invited by the editors, they waived the page charges, although peer reviews were required as usual.

At the 2008 Florida trial in which I was an expert witness, some say that the judge did not like me, but the court could not even get my academic rank correct, citing me as an assistant or associate professor when I had been a full professor for 18 years by then. Rosky (2011, p. 944) reported my name as "Walker Scrum" which is a pretty amazing way to botch up my name, given that my name was spelled correctly in an article citation in footnote 242 on the *same page* of Rosky's article. Some at the trial criticised me for reporting research results in which statistical significance was < .10, but a careful examination of the research published by those critics found that they had often done the very thing for which they had blamed me (Schumm *et al.*, 2013). Furthermore, the American Psychological Association now expects researchers to report all significance levels, even those that are > .05 (also see King, 1986, pp.683-684).

Some have criticised me for doing "unconventional" research and that is partly true – I have investigated a wide range of different topics, including Gulf War illness, Islam, various family relationships, methodological problems and challenges, premarital counselling, shipwrecks, and LGBT families, and I have applied statistics to some topics that are seldom assessed statistically (e.g., shipwrecks, such as the HMT Birkenhead; see Lee *et al.*, 2016). When considering the Florida trial and any apparent "discrediting" of myself, one should keep in mind that at the Florida trial both sides were told to produce all materials in writing weeks in advance of the trial, which the State did. The ACLU produced *nothing* in writing until after the trial had started, in direct contradiction of the court's order, but the court accepted that violation of the judge's orders as legitimate. Once the trial started, the ACLU was allowed to say anything they wanted about me, but I was not allowed to see what they had said about me. When I took the stand, they asked me what I thought about the ACLU's expert witnesses. Since I had no written information on what they had actually said about me or about their research, all I could say was that they had published a lot and were known as good scholars. That set up a comparison in which I praised them but they had denounced me, but it was an artifact of the trial process, rather than a fair debate on the merits in which each side gets to read or hear directly what the other side had said. In the end, I was told by the lawyers that both sides used my testimony to promote their causes. As I told the State's lawyers, I was going to only say what I felt was valid and if it did not help the State's cause, so be it. Later the ACLU claimed I had betrayed the State of Florida, although I did not think I was out to betray anyone, just to tell what I had found in the literature, just as I have tried to do with this book.

I recall that once someone thought I had made an error in my analysis by citing research on same-sex parenting in which the researchers had oversampled LGBT children of same-sex parents (Schumm, 2010a), but they overlooked the fact that I had tested my results for robustness, finding that my results would have remained significant even if I had made 20 errors in my measurement.

Some might accuse me of being a religionist. Yes, I was baptized and confirmed in the American Episcopal Church as an adolescent and I am currently a substitute pastor/preacher (with no seminary or formal theological training) at a non-denominational community church south of Manhattan, Kansas. I am not an official member of any church; it might be questionable if any of them would have me because I tend to reserve my rights to believe what I want, regardless of the church's particular doctrines. Because I might represent a security risk because of my controversial research, it might be unwise for any church to admit me as a member. At the Florida trial much was made of my discussion of the integration of religion and science. In my opinion, my analysis of the survival rates on the RMS Titanic is a good example of integrating religion and science, as the survival patterns seemed to follow a verse in Proverbs (30:9) better than most sociological theories about the power of the wealthy over the poor (Lee, Schumm, Lockett, Newson, & Behan, 2016; Schumm, Webb, Castelo, Akagi, Jensen, Ditto, Spencer-Carver, & Brown, 2002).

It is almost certain I will be criticised for having received summer research funding from the Witherspoon Institute and for this book being supported in a minimal way by an Anglican group from Britain (I will not be paid any royalties for this book). What I find amusing about such criticism is that pro-gay scholars can be funded by numerous pro-gay organisations and the question of credibility or bias is almost never raised. For example, Gartrell *et al.* (2006) acknowledged that "This study was funded in part by grants from the Arcus Foundation, the Susan A. and Donald P. Babson Charitable Foundation, the Bay Area Career Women's 'A Fund of our Own' administered by the Horizons Foundation, the California Wellness Foundation, The California Endowment, The Gill Foundation, the Horizons Foundation, the Joyce Mertz-Gilmore Foundation, the Lesbian Health Fund of the Gay and Lesbian Medical Association, the Roy Scrivner Fund of the American Psychological Association, and An Uncommon Legacy Foundation. The authors would like to thank the above mentioned organizations for their support...." (p. 189). But such researchers are seldom questioned about the sources of their funding and how that funding might have biased their research.

Some have criticised my research because much of it, though not all, has involved reviews of the literature. Elsewhere I have cited dozens of reviews of the literature by other scholars, who have seldom, if ever, been criticised for publishing such reviews (Schumm, 2008; Schumm & Crawford, 2018a). Furthermore, Hunter and Schmidt (2004) have stated that "At one time in the history of psychology and the social sciences, the pressing need was for more empirical studies examining the problem in question. In many areas of research, the need today is not for additional empirical data but for some means of making sense of the vast amounts of data that have been accumulated" (p. 16). Thus, even more now with the passing of 13 years since Hunter and Schmidt (2004) made that comment, reviews of the literature continue to be very important. If I have done nothing other than cite research that has been overlooked by previous scholars, that should be deemed at least a small contribution to social science. Certainly, I am not alone in publishing reviews of the literature in this area; our recent paper (Schumm & Crawford, 2018a) identified at least 72 reviews of the literature (not counting any by myself) on LGBT issues since 2001, not including any reviews published in medical, legal journals, or philosophy journals or reviews published by medical professionals, not to mention reviews published before 2001.

Fair Fight?

One of my "misfortunes" was perhaps that I was raised by a father who believed in debate, that it was a useful exercise to argue for positions with which we did not agree, to help ourselves better understand others. However, you might have wondered how it seems as though conservatives have lost most of the legal battles regarding same-sex marriage (SSM) and parenting (SSP), most notably with the *Obergefell* decision by the U.S. Supreme Court (Sin & Risman, 2016; Walsh, 2016). Others have written about political intimidation (Strassel, 2016) or political correctness in the university (Maranto, Redding, & Hess, 2009; O'Donohue & Redding, 2009; Redding, 1999, 2001, 2002, 2012), but here I want to mention specific examples of how one-sided the debate became over time in scholarly circles.

A few years ago, I was invited by the journal editor to submit a short article to a California family therapy journal as part of a two-sided debate on same-sex marriage. Although I did not go looking to submit such a paper, once asked, I agreed to do so and sent them a short paper, which was accepted (Schumm, 2009). Several other authors sent papers to represent a more conservative viewpoint. However, once the issue was published, the pro-SSM side was so upset that they demanded that the journal's editor retract the entire issue. You might think that retraction would have impacted both sides equally. However, the material printed for the pro-SSM side only represented reprints of already published articles, so they really could not be retracted. I do not think the editor really wanted to do that, but succumbed to the intense political pressure. My point is that retracting the entire issue might seem even-handed, but in fact it took away from the arguments against same-sex marriage far more than against the other side.

Another time, I was invited to present a paper at a symposium on SSM and SSP in California with a promise that my paper would be published as part of a journal issue derived from the symposium. At some point it occurred to the journal editors that publishing both sides might give some legitimacy to the conservative point of view, so they cancelled the issue for both sides. However, I think they eventually published some of the pro-SSM/SSP papers in a later issue. Again, on the surface, the cancellation might have seemed "fair" but the long-term result was to take away legitimacy of some of the more conservative arguments.

You might have heard about Professor Mark Regnerus of the University of Texas who published articles in *Social Science Research* in 2012. This raised an outcry against him in which over 200 scholars from several countries signed a petition for the article to be retracted. Later a reporter went to court to demand the names of the six scholars who had reviewed the paper before it was accepted. There were demands for the editor to resign. I do not know if it was natural turnover or something else, but the journal editor changed not long after. Numerous articles have been written to try to attack Regnerus's research (Adams & Light, 2015; Amato, 2012; Anderson, 2013; Ball, 2013, 2016; Barber & Schwartz, 2013; Becker & Todd, 2013; Bernstein, 2015; Blee, 2015; Cheng & Powell, 2015; Frank, 2016; Gates, 2015; Golash-Boza, 2012, p.403; Haney-Caron & Heilbrun, 2014; Harris, 2016; Herek, 2014; Hirschman, 2016; Infanti, 2014; Kaplan, 2015; Kuhar, 2015; Lebow, 2014; Mason, 2018; McKerson, 2014; Moore & Stambolis-Ruhstorfer, 2013; Perrin, Cohen, & Caren, 2013; Perrin, Siegel, Dobbins, Lavin, Mattson, Pascoe, & Yogman, 2013; Powell, Hamilton, Manago, & Cheng, 2016; Reczek, Spiker, Liu, & Crosnoe, 2016, p.1607; Reiss, 2013; Richards *et al.*, 2017; Schumm, 2012a; Sherkat, 2012; Sin & Risman, 2016; Strasser, 2012, p.312; Umberson, Thomeer, Kroeger, Lodge, & Xu, 2015). His work has been accused of being a work of hate speech (Schumm, 2015a, p.26) and as "fraudulent" (Rich, 2016, p.267, footnote 7). Blee (2015, p. 17) implicitly criticised Regnerus (2012b) for publishing research with adverse findings about gay parents, because such research would not benefit such sexual minorities. Swain (2015) noted how Regnerus was "roundly condemned by the media, and his university took the unusual step of issuing a press release distancing itself from the peer-reviewed article written by their colleague" (p.100). One recent report appears to blame the Regnerus study for a lesbian couple in Utah losing their infant foster daughter in 2015 (Whatley, Cave, & Breneiser, 2016). Umberson *et al.* (2015) stated that "the findings from this study have been largely discredited" (p.99). Mason (2018) opines that both Regnerus's

(2012a) and Sullins' (2015a) research "faced scrutiny from the wider scholarly community for their questionable methodologies and conflicts of interest" (p. 86). The main complaint about Regnerus's research was that he did not capture more than two or three lesbian or gay families that had been stable since the birth of the young adult respondent, leaving open the possibility that any issues with their lives might have been associated with family instability rather than family structure. Rosenfeld (2015) has made that sort of case in his reanalysis of the same data. Sullins (2016a) has discussed how Regnerus was vilified as well as other "nonconforming" (my term) research, noting that those who dare publish any results that don't support the "no difference" hypothesis may experience harm to their "career and reputation", be "publicly denounced and discredited, or quietly marginalized in your department or institution" (p. 215). Some have criticised me for having been on a planning session for the eventual NFSS study (New Family Structures Study) and not specifically mentioning my involvement when I critiqued Regnerus's study (Schumm, 2012a). I have helped plan a lot of research in my career, so that planning meeting did not strike me as much different than many other meetings with which I had been involved for planning research. Furthermore, having seen the start of the NFSS project and the conclusion might actually have placed me in a much better vantage point from which to discuss the pros and cons of the NFSS study rather than being a negative. In any event, if someone does not like my critique of the NFSS, you would be welcome to submit your "take" on it to either *Social Science Research* or to *Marriage & Family Review* and engage in even more public discussion about it.

However, it is not uncommon for researchers who study gay and lesbian families to find similar limitations. As discussed in detail elsewhere (Schumm, 2012a, 2013, pp. 427-430; 2014), many studies of same-sex parent families have featured family instability. Golombok, Spencer, and Rutter (1983, p. 569) indicated that 92% of the children of their lesbian mothers had lived in a heterosexual household for some time, 65% had lived therein for over two years, while 32% had lived therein for over five years. Golombok *et al.* (2003) included at least one family in her cluster of lesbian mother families in which the mother may have not entered a lesbian couple relationship until only a few months before her 9-10 year old child became part of the study, while some of the other children had been born into lesbian parent couple families; my concern is including both types of families in one group would seem to be mixing very different family types together. My own analysis of her data suggested that as many as half of her lesbian parent-couple families may have involved at least one caregiver transition and that up to half of the child's life may have been spent in something other than a lesbian parent couple family (Schumm, 2014). Jedzinak (2004, pp. 69-72) interviewed seven daughters (ages 18 to 27) of lesbian mothers and found that five daughters had lesbian mothers who had been partnered with a nonheterosexual partner for part of the daughter's life (two lesbian mothers lived as single parents, one of whom had given birth to their daughter with a gay father who, with his partner, continued to see the daughter); those five families had experienced at least two stable lesbian parents as follows: age one to thirteen (only 13 years), birth to three (only 3 years); birth to nine months (less than one year) and later eight years with a different lesbian partner; age 11 to 16 (only 6 years or less), and a biological mother who had raised her daughter with multiple female partners but was now living with one other woman; Jedzinak did not find a single stable lesbian couple family, but no one has been out to discredit *her* research. Another example is reported by Robitaille and Saint-Jacques (2009) in which they interviewed eleven adult children, ages 15 to 29 (average age of 21.4 years), from lesbian and gay families. Notably their criterion for having belonged to a gay or lesbian family was clear: having lived a minimum of 8 days per month for at least one year, whereas Regnerus's study featured many children who had lived with same-sex parents for many years, at least four months out of each year. However, despite their ages, the average time spent in a lesbian or gay household among these eleven children was only 5.73 years (SD = 2.9 years), meaning that on average each child had spent only 32% of their life (18 or younger) within a nonheterosexual household. The longest time spent in a nonheterosexual family was in a gay male/lesbian household for 11 years; the shortest time spent in a lesbian or gay household was two years. Bos, Knox, van Rijn-van Gelderen, & Gartrell (2016) reported that of a random national representative U.S. study, 29.5% (41/139) of the focal children (ages 6-17 years old) with lesbian mothers and 52.9% (9/17) of the focal children of gay fathers had experienced a parental divorce or at least one family transition sometime earlier in their family life. Elsewhere, I have cited numerous research studies in which the children of same-sex parents had been initially born into a heterosexual relationship (Schumm, 2013, pp. 427-430). My point is that I have not seen any criticism of the methodology of Golombok *et al.* (1983) or of Robitaille and Saint-Jacques (2009) even though some to nearly *all* of their participants came from unstable families with quite a mixture of longer and shorter times spent in nonheterosexual households. Even though these studies had many of the same limitations as the NFSS, did you see hundreds of scholars attacking them? Perhaps you might wonder why not (Redding, 2013).

A scholar, with an earned Ph.D., was on the staff of a major Christian university in California, and was supported by a grant for several million dollars a year, which you might have thought would have protected his position from political interference. He made the "mistake" of speaking out against same-sex marriage at a country outside the United States. When he returned, as soon as he came back to his office, the very first hour, he was told he had an hour to retrieve his personal stuff from his office because he had been fired. Do you realise the long reach of the other side's "law"? He was at what I think is an evangelical Christian university and spoke overseas, not in California or elsewhere inside the United States. It was not like he was given a final year before being terminated or a week to clean out his office, he was fired on the spot in an instant with no explanation needed or really given (from what I understand, recognising I was not there at that time). He was not even allowed to pull research data from his computer, data that had no relationship to same-sex marriage or parenting. Appeals from his funding agency were, apparently, rebuffed. When you can get an academic with multi-million dollar grants fired in an instant, that is what I call some serious political clout.

Another professor published an article that featured a negative outcome for children of same-sex parents but somewhere one protester had a sign that mentioned that article. Consequently, the journal editor had the published article flagged in a cautionary way, not quite a retraction. I have to wonder: since when does an anonymous protester someplace have so much power that they can nearly get an article retracted for merely mentioning it? In my opinion this is not how science should be done.

I was at a conference in the US and was listening to a plenary speech by two well-known researchers. They referenced my "disagreeable" research in their speech and the audience was waiting to see what I might say back. However, comments at the microphone were limited to two minutes which was not sufficient time to deal with the issues, so I did not say anything then. At a smaller session later, I challenged their research. After a time, one of the other scholars present just could not stand it any longer and got up and screamed at me that I did not know *anything* about *any* type of research. I asked another scholar to explain that emotional reaction because I had only earned a Ph.D. from Purdue University, had been a professor for nearly 30 years, and had published hundreds of articles, which made such a criticism silly as well as baseless. He told me that, as a lesbian mother, she probably saw any disagreement about same-sex parenting as a threat to her retaining custody of her children and that made me, emotionally, enemy #1 for that moment. Later that day there was a meeting of older scholars and I sat down to see if anyone would sit with me. No one did at first. Remarkably the President of the association and some of his friends eventually came over and sat down with me, because we had both done research on military families for many years.

At a different symposium in California, I had been invited to present comments on a paper, if I recall correctly, on the increase in State taxes that would accrue to States that allowed same-sex weddings. Since it was not my area of expertise, my comments were pretty plain and I thought non-controversial. But in my whole life, I do not think I have ever seen an audience so full of obviously apparent hate against me, even before I had said a word.

Another time I had allowed Dr. Paul Cameron to publish a critique of myself in my journal, *Marriage & Family Review*. That did not mean I agreed with the critique or with Cameron *per se*, but showed that I believe in free discourse, even more so if the issues or persons are controversial (Knapp, 2009). Yet, this upset the Southern Poverty Law Center (SPLC), which considers Cameron's Family Research Institute to be a hate group

(Schlatter, 2012). The SPLC did not contact me to discuss it, but went over my head to the publisher, to whom I gladly explained my editorial policies. Recently, Cameron and two of his associates again criticised me and I allowed them to discuss their criticisms in the journal (Cameron *et al.*, 2017), although I and some of my graduate students (Schumm *et al.*, 2017) rebutted them strongly. I am waiting to see if the SPLC will complain again or if Cameron will be able to address our criticisms in detail and explain the difficulties we detected in his research.

On another occasion I was teaching a doctoral graduate course on advanced research methodology with several graduate students. It is my habit to criticise many journal articles in the process of teaching such classes. However, one day I happened to criticise an article by lesbian scholars and one student took great exception, so much so that the student convinced several professors to demand that every student drop the class. At least one student has told me that he did not want to drop it but was forced to do so against his will. Then, on the premise that I had failed to perform my teaching duties because of the class being cancelled, I was given a written letter of reprimand, which is a rarity for college professors. The letter said that no matter how well I did in teaching, research, administration, or grants over the whole year, I would be guaranteed a bad evaluation overall because of this one day's incident. Since I was a witness at a federal trial on SSP at the time, this intimidation tactic could easily have been construed as an attempt to intimidate a witness at a federal trial (I am told that is a felony), but I did not push it. However, the "lesson" was clearly that criticism of anything about same-sex families or written by LGBT scholars was henceforth to be off limits in classroom discussion, even at the Ph.D. level, for myself or any of our other faculty, if they did not want to take the same risks. I might have hoped that the University might have taken a stand and said that "Any professor here is free to criticise any journal article" but that is not what happened.

Another example occurred when I testified as a citizen about a non-discrimination law that the city council of Manhattan, Kansas was debating. The main provision I did not like was that the law granted unelected, untrained citizens the power to legally fine those accused (not convicted by a court or judge) of anti-LGBT discrimination up to $50,000 per case. To me, it is one thing for a highly trained, experienced judge to render such a decision, but it is totally another for an untrained person with no accountability to anyone whatsoever to do so. Nonetheless, students at a rally at my own university called for me to be fired because of my views, an attempt to shame me in front of the public, one must suppose.

You might wonder why it seems conservative scholars are often late to the party. For example, last year I published a 120-page paper on same-sex parenting; but that paper had been in the review process for many years, in a nearly perpetual revise and resubmit status. Keeping a paper in that status is almost worse than just having it rejected because it ties up the paper and keeps you from submitting to another journal. At the same time, I was and am grateful for the many helpful comments I received over the years that did help to improve the final published article.

Another issue is that many pro same-sex parenting scholars will not release their data to other scholars for independent re-examination. This enables them to hide behind their data. In contrast, Professor Regnerus made his data available to anyone who wanted it and at least two pro-SSP scholars got the data and re-analysed it so they could criticise Regnerus's research (2012a, b). In real life, most data has flaws such as outliers that do not make sense (an age of 134 years, having had 54 children, having sex 70 times a week, an adult weighing 22 pounds, etc.). Some scholars eliminate the entire case, some eliminate the particular value, while others retain it as part of the random error involved in every study. No matter what you do, it can be criticised, *unless* you do not make your data available to other scholars or use data whose access is restricted by the U.S. government (one site demands a $20,000 fee for access, which is prohibitive for many scholars and makes replication attempts of such data analyses virtually impossible).

Even progressive scholars have come under intense scrutiny if they stray from the "no difference" hypothesis. For example, Stacey and Biblarz (2001) have been criticised by other progressive scholars for their mere suggestion that the "no difference" hypothesis might not be completely true in some areas of same-sex parenting (Golombok *et al.*, 2003, p.21; Hequembourg, 2007, p.132; Herek, 2006, p.613; Hicks, 2005, pp.162-163; Ball, 2003). Ball (2003) went so far as to call Stacey and Biblarz's (2001) conclusion not only essentially unfounded but "both useless and dangerous" (p. 703). Second, some scholars have come under pressure to "retract" their findings if those findings appeared to reject the "no difference" hypothesis. In one case, a scholar had found a very significant ($p < .001$) difference of say, 30% versus 3% (revised slightly to protect their identity) in sexual orientation between children of same-sex parents versus heterosexual parents, but that person came under pressure to retract their results. If such a difference does not really mean anything, then perhaps *nothing* in social science can mean anything. Sometimes scholars will attempt to excuse such a finding by claiming that some unmeasured variable was responsible, but speculation is not sufficient in science to ignore significant and substantial findings. I could contend that a high level of divorce among same-sex parents might have caused the 30% versus 3% difference but, unless I have measured that and controlled for it statistically, it is just speculation. If scientists were to allow mere speculation to determine or override facts, we would be in some serious trouble as a profession. I think that speculation should at least be based on some credible theory and I am not aware of any social science theory that would suggest that parental divorce (for either heterosexual, mixed marriage, or same-sex parents) would usually be associated with a 30% or greater rate of having children who would identify as LGBT or use illegal drugs. Speculation should not be some magic wand you wave to dismiss any results that you do not like. While I have criticised the infrequent measurement and control for social desirability in much of the research on same-sex parenting, I have specifically discussed the types of scales and items that might be used to measure different types of social desirability (Schumm, 2016b, p. 40). But I have not denied the evidence that is clear – if you ask lesbian mothers how their children are doing psychologically, you will (on average) be told that they are doing very well. I am suggesting you would have a much stronger test of the "no difference" theory if you measured and controlled for the appropriate types of social desirability when comparing reported psychological outcomes for the children of same-sex and heterosexual parents, as well as controlling for other pre-existing family differences in socioeconomic status, education, number of children, or per-capita household income.

Another type of indirect pressure or bias to which both conservative and progressive scholars can be exposed is the bias in citation rates of articles that depends on their conclusions more than their findings (Redding, 2013). One example of this involves three published articles that had used pretty much the same data, from the same university, from some of the same graduate students or professors. One article (Miller, Mucklow, Jacobsen, & Bigner, 1980) reported some adverse information about lesbian parents while two other articles reported more positive information (Miller, Jacobsen, & Bigner, 1981; Mucklow & Phelan, 1979). The first article indicated that a significant percentage of the lesbian mothers hated men. Likewise, Golombok, Spencer, and Rutter (1983, p. 559) found that 18% (3/17) of their lesbian mothers had "definitely negative" current feelings toward men while another 29% were "indifferent". When I first published a report on this (Schumm, 2010b), the first article (Miller *et al.*, 1980) had been cited twice while the other two papers had been cited 65 times. As of late February, 2018 Google Scholar reported 14 citations (of which six were in articles by myself) for Miller *et al.* (1980) compared to 188 citations for the other two articles. Accounting for the 2-1 number of articles, the less favourable article was nearly seven times less likely to have been cited than the more favourable articles. If one were to discount the six times I cited each of the three articles, the less favourable article was eleven times less likely to have been cited. Since then, we have also found that the chances of a research report being cited by other scholars was as much a result of what the research found (i.e., politically correct results) as it was of the quality of that research (Schumm & Crawford, 2018b).

Another more recent example of this issue concerns Schumm (2010e), in which I reviewed the literature on the relative stability of same-sex parent couples versus opposite-sex parent couples, with a focus on four comparison studies. That paper, according to Google Scholar (as of February 28th, 2018), has been cited 29 times in the past eight years. However, it is not clear that a single progressive scholar has ever cited it. Yet Biblarz and Stacey (2010a) were willing to conclude that lesbian parent couples had lower rates of stability, based on a single source of evidence (MacCallum & Golombok, 2004), while Schumm (2010e) cited at least four studies that featured similar evidence, including MacCallum and Golombok (2004). Notably, Biblarz and Stacey (2010a) has been cited 447 times while Stacey and Biblarz (2001) has been cited 813 times (my most cited article, according to Google Scholar was cited 810 times, and was one of the least controversial papers I have ever published). It would appear that progressive scholars may have a tendency to turn a "blind eye" toward research results with which they disagree or about which they feel uncomfortable (e.g., Schumm, 2010e). That is not to say that some conservative researchers might not have a similar tendency. It ultimately boils down to which type of source seems to look at the overall research landscape in more detail.

Since the impact or even quality of articles is often judged by their citation rates, the normal tendency of scholars would be to focus on the highly cited papers rather than the less often cited paper, even if the qualities of the articles were similar. This type of bias has the potential to distort how social science literature is reviewed and summarised. If scholars depend on reviews and do not do their own in depth analyses, such reviews may lead them astray.

Another type of pressure on scholars can come from lawyers for opposing sides. There are a number of clever schemes to destroy a professor's credibility aside from their actual academic competence. Some professors do not have the time or stomach for this sort of thing and will either never go there or will bail out before going to a trial as an expert witness. One scheme for example would be to ask the potential expert witness if they read every word in an article (or have read every reference at the back of the article or in the footnotes). If they say yes, then grill them until their memory fails or fatigue sets in and they make a mistake – and accuse them of lying and use that mistake to destroy their credibility or at the very least to make them doubt themselves as a potential witness. If they say no, then they use that answer to destroy their credibility as if (which isn't the case) that every other scholar in the world reads every word and has read every reference, so *ergo* they must be one of the worst scholars in the world. It does not have to be true, just enough to shake their confidence in themselves enough that they will give up on any idea of being an expert witness. With any luck, the lawyer will not only dissuade them from ever serving as an expert witness but may break their confidence in general so they give up being an academic altogether. Please note that it does not matter what answer they give; any and all answers will be used against them, regardless of their accuracy.

Another example is when at your pre-trial deposition, the other side's lawyers will ask a question like "When did you first discuss topic X with Dr. Y?" – an event that may have happened three or four years before. You must realise that it is quite possible no one cares what your answer is at that moment – it is just a trap. A year later, at the trial, when that event is now over five years ago, then they will ask the same question. If you say you do not recall, then your testimony will be discredited because clearly your memory has faded or is unreliable. If you say something different than what you said at the deposition, then you will be discredited for either being stupid or for lying or for having unreliable testimony. No matter what you say, it will be used against you. Even if you give the same and correct answer, then if you make any mistake on anything else, you will be challenged on how you can remember one event so well but not some other issue as well. If you give the same answer, you may be asked if you re-read your deposition before the trial and if you say "yes", then that may be held against you. In other words, it is not a "let's find the truth here" process but a process of "how can we destroy, by any means, the value of this expert witness?"

Clearly, the process isn't about getting at some "truth" but at destroying any legal opposition. Many questions cannot be answered truly with a "yes" or a "no", so to tell the truth you would have to give a more complex answer but if that is ruled out of order, you can be discredited for trying to tell the truth (when it is more complex). A judge might demand a "yes" or "no" answer and force you to perjure yourself in the sense of not being able to tell the truth fully. One possible escape hatch might be to say that you have sworn an oath to tell the truth, not to give only yes or no answers. If the truth cannot be told with a yes or no answer, then you may have to decline to comment to avoid being forced to testify to a falsehood as if it were true. Whomever your side's lawyers may be, it is essential that they help you navigate the legal hurdles, or you had better be prepared for the other side's lawyers to turn you into intellectual mincemeat. I say that to highlight the importance of being prepared for depositions and court testimony with the careful guidance of your own side's lawyers, especially if you are on a conservative side of an issue. If you do choose to serve as an expert witness, expect that any mistakes you make will probably be sported all over the internet in an attempt to embarrass you to the utmost, possibly even with your own colleagues or any other religious or fraternal association with which you may be associated.

I should add that "repentant" conservatives can be forgiven sometimes. At one annual conference of a national organisation, a year or two after I was told I knew nothing about research, a speech was made by an ACLU representative concerning the same Florida trial at which I had testified. The speaker claimed that in the middle of the trial I had betrayed the State of Florida and had come out in favour of same-sex parenting. I am not sure what led to her saying that, but I had tried to say what I thought was true, regardless of which side it might seem to help. After that, many of the LGBT scholars at that conference warmed up to me considerably and were once again willing to speak to me, at least as a matter of courtesy. However, my "betrayal" at the trial did not seem to impress most of the media analysis of the trial, although at one blog site, the gay fathers involved actually, in a very class act, defended me against some of the criticisms that were being tossed around about me. For that I have to commend them because they were taking some risk to do that, at least going against the grain of most of the discussions about the trial. I hope this helps you understand the types of pressure that conservative, and even progressive, scholars are up against if they stray from the politically correct order with respect to same-sex marriage and/or same-sex parenting. If you are interested in more details on these issues, please consult Schumm (2005, 2013, 2016a) or Redding (2013), which all contain more references for further study.

Basic Research Issues

Science Often Done Incorrectly
It would be impossible to discuss research on same-sex parenting without a quick primer on how research can be biased by various methodological decisions. For more details than presented here with respect to low quality research methods and implications for policy-making, see Schumm (2016b, pp. 644-648) or Allen (2015) or Marks (2012).

First, a review of the literature should be comprehensive. An example of this not occurring is when Sarantakos, an Australian professor, came under fire for one of his articles (1996b)(e.g., Herek, 2014; Patterson, 2005). Not only did most of his critics omit any discussion of effect sizes in his results and that some of the results favoured the children of same-sex parents (limiting the claims that teacher bias was accounting for all of the adverse results), but virtually none of his critics mentioned his other research with same-sex couples and families (Sarantakos, 1996a, 1998, 2000). Sarantakos published a great deal of material, including a number of textbooks on family life and research methodology; nearly 40 articles or books by Sarantakos have been reported (Schumm, 2015b). If you selectively criticise one article by an author and do not mention any other works, it could lead readers to believe that the author was not much of a scholar, having done little else in the particular area or perhaps little anywhere else, supporting the likelihood that your criticisms are valid. If I have done this with any family scholar in this book, I apologise in advance, but my habit has been to examine *multiple* publications by scholars in the same-sex parenting area. Nonetheless, in my review of Sarantakos's research on same-sex families, I showed the extent to which he did or did not find results that paralleled findings by other scholars in other parts of the world, so readers could see how Sarantakos's results did or did not fit with comparable examples of research. I hope readers agree that my approach represents a better approach to scholarship than simply picking one of a scholar's many reports and hammering it to death as if it was the only thing that scholar had ever done.

As part of being comprehensive, you will most likely run across research results that do not support whatever your position might be (I have tried to mention quite a few cases that do seem to support the "no difference" hypothesis in this area). If you have never detected any such counter results, it is likely that you have not dug very deeply into the research literature. For some courts, pro-LGBT scholars have argued that they had considered all the research that did not support their side of the case, but when they did not present more than one or two such studies, they actually weakened their case in the eyes of researchers used to doing comprehensive literature reviews. The odds of only finding one or two contradictory results in a large field of literature are pretty small. There is a chance you may even encounter an argument that no research should be done on minorities of any type if it leads to "negative conclusions" (Blee, 2015, p. 17) about them, including "gay parents" (Blee, 2015, p. 17) because such results might not benefit those minorities.

Second, if you wish to compare two groups on a variable, such as parental sexual orientation, the general scientific plan is to make the two groups as equivalent as possible prior to your comparison. This is why we have classes of athletic competition. You wouldn't think it "fair" to have a 90 pound 12-year-old wrestle against a 200 pound 20-year-old. In the same way, it is not fair to compare these two groups: same-sex parents making hundreds of thousands a year, with one child, with a paid nanny, with graduate degrees, with low levels of depression, anxiety, and parental stress, versus heterosexual parents, making half as much, with five children, without any child care support, with high school degrees, and high levels of anxiety, parental stress, and psychological depression. If you did compare those groups and found the results in terms of child outcomes to be equal, you might well conclude that same-sex parenting was a negative factor overcome by all of the other positive differences. For example, Golombok, Tasker, and Murray (1997) compared heterosexual two-parent (N = 41) and single-parent heterosexual (N = 42) families with 30 lesbian mother families. The heterosexual families were significantly worse off than the lesbian families in terms of younger age, lower social class, and larger family size. At the same time, the two-parent heterosexual mothers reported higher levels of depression and lower levels of maternal warmth compared with the lesbian mothers. The children of the lesbian mothers reported greater peer acceptance at school. Yet in spite of these many disadvantages, when their children were asked about their cognitive competence and physical competence at school, the children of the heterosexual two-parent families reported significantly higher levels (Schumm, 2015b, p.9). Do you understand what has been done? You have different groups of parents in which one group is better off economically and in terms of mental health and the groups' children are compared – with the most disadvantaged children, those of the heterosexual two-parent families, faring much better in school despite lower peer acceptance! Had proper statistical controls been applied, perhaps the sexual orientation of the parents might have revealed an adverse impact (that was compensated for by the lesbian mothers' other advantages). I also think it is important to understand that demographic factors seldom have a significant direct effect on any outcome if you control for enough other variables, whether control variables or mediating variables. If you work hard enough at it for long enough, a good statistical analyst can probably make any independent variable such as same-sex parental status look harmless once you control for enough other variables.

A further issue with group comparisons is that the groups should be mutually exclusive; otherwise, you may not know who you are comparing. For example, in research cited by some courts or amici briefs as "gold standard", Wainright and Patterson (2006) allegedly compared children from 44 same-sex and 44 heterosexual parents. However, Patterson herself admitted (2009b) and Sullins (2015b) reaffirmed that only 17-18 of the 44 "same-sex" families were really lesbian mother families, which is only 39% of the reported 44 families. This was also true with respect to Evelyn Hooker's (1957) research on homosexuality as she compared groups of men alleged to be homosexual versus heterosexual but in fact each group included 10% bisexual men; although the composition of the groups was contaminated by the same percentage of bisexual men, having bisexual men in the mix made a pure comparison of homosexual versus heterosexual men impossible (Schumm, 2012b). Other researchers have included bisexuals in their "heterosexual" parent groups, rendering their comparisons with lesbian parents more questionable.

Third, if you wish to use parents' answers to questions about their children's mental health or related variables, you should measure and control for tendencies to report socially desirable results that match the nature of the outcome variables. For example, Gartrell, Hamilton, Banks, Mosbacher, Reed, Sparks, and Bishop (1996) noted that same-sex parents "might wish to present themselves and their families in the best possible light" and consequently "the study findings may be shaped by self-justification and self-presentation bias" (p. 279). Other scholars have discussed the potential for socially desirable responding by parents when asked about their children (Goldberg, 2010, p. 169; Golombok, MacCallum, Goodman, & Rutter, 2002, p. 965). This is especially true if you are comparing a hand-picked group of same-sex parents (who are probably not blind to the purposes of the study) and compare them to a subgroup of heterosexual parents from a nationally representative sample (who had no idea their answers would be compared to those of same-sex parents). You need to select a measure of social desirability response bias that corresponds to the outcome variable – individual social desirability, romantic relationship social desirability, or parental social desirability are just three possibilities (Schumm, 2016b, p. 40).

Fourth, if you study parents (this applies equally to same-sex and to heterosexual parents) who are basically wealthy, it is not correct to generalise results to parents who are not wealthy. Lamb (2012) is probably correct in citing "the availability of economic and socio-economic resources" (p. 106) as one factor that predicts the adjustment of children and adolescents. To generalise results from families with such resources to those without them is not correct scientifically. While, as discussed previously, it is not proper scientifically to compare wealthy and poor groups as if their socioeconomic status did not matter, it is also not proper to study wealthy families and assume that your findings will apply equally to all families, including poor families. As has been discussed at length, many of the studies that compared heterosexual and same-sex adoptive families involved extremely high levels of household annual income (often more than $200,000 a year). Some people have criticised adoptive families (some within my own family circle) that had, say, eleven or twelve adopted or foster children, with annual household incomes of perhaps $75,000 (at most $5,400 per year per family member); that sort of situation is simply not comparable to an adoptive family with one child and an annual income of $300,000 a year ($100,000 per member) – a ratio of per capita income of nearly nineteen! Treating such families as if they were equally capable of supporting children economically is not how science should be done. If the far less advantaged family did more poorly or experienced more stress would it be any surprise?

Fifth, social science is complex, kind of like a vegetable soup with many different ingredients. For example, you might compare parents with a broken leg versus parents without a broken leg. I would not be surprised if you found that if you predicted parenting success from how much love the children feel from their parents, that the "broken leg" variable might not predict child outcomes. You might well draw a statistical conclusion that broken legs do not matter, but does that really mean it would be acceptable to break a lot of legs just "because"? Would any parent want to volunteer for a broken leg? What I am saying is that a broken leg is most likely a bad experience that no one would want, but you could probably whitewash it statistically to show it did not matter at all. Likewise, could you save lives by statistically controlling for the effects of bullets and show that guns were mostly harmless (after you controlled for the number of bullets fired, impacting, and the inflicted damage)? Are the dead going to rise up because of your statistical analysis? Not at all. If the soup tasted too salty, you could save the situation statistically by saying, well, if you control for the amount of salt added, then the salty taste would disappear. But it is hard to get the salt out, right? It is not enough to say that there were no differences in variable Y, after controlling for variable X, as a function of variable Z. The ideal scientific approach would be to use X as a mediating variable between Y and Z, testing both the direct and indirect effects of Z on Y. Another approach to washing out a variable X, is to simply include dozens of other variables along with it in your statistical model. Sooner or later, you can make just about any variable fade in apparent importance if you include enough covariates.

Sixth, science does not operate by fiat. I should not be able to say that variable X is either related to Y or unrelated to Y without some evidence. My opinion, no matter how great of a scholar I might be, should not count for evidence. If one scholar says that X and Y have not been related in any research ever done, then that statement can be disproven by only one counter-example. If the other scholar comes back and produces a hundred studies showing no differences (all effect sizes below .20), that might suggest that the "several studies" were an artifact of statistics (5% of studies will be significant by chance alone). But if the scholar shows that of the hundred studies, 50 actually did show a difference (some effect sizes greater than .20) in addition to the "several studies", then one might conclude that there really was a difference. But my key point is that the process is supposed to be evidence-driven, not "pronouncement" driven. For example, Lamb (2012) made a pronouncement that "these differences have nothing to do with psychological adjustment" (p. 104) without citing any scholarly evidence. Herek (2014) criticised the Regnerus (2012a, b) study and two other articles (including Sarantakos, 2016b) but without any real data to disprove what had been presented, largely more speculation about what might have been going on. As an individual you are free to speculate however you want; but if you present your view as scientific, you should back it up with evidence. That is not to say that scientists cannot be free to speculate; of course, they should be free to do so, but such speculations should not be expected to count as genuine evidence.

Seventh, social science is cumulative in knowledge and an ongoing enterprise. I would suggest one be very careful if a scholar cites 30 or 40 year old articles as the basis for a conclusion about how X and Y are related today. For example, Lamb (2012) cited studies between 30 and 40 years old in order to provide evidence that "children in nontraditional families sometimes have more flexible views of sex-roles" (p. 104). In social science, things can change over the decades, so that reliance upon older studies is risky; older findings may not remain valid for today's cultures or societies. It is possible that what was a correct assessment of facts fifty years ago might not be a correct assessment today. Thus, if you read scholars today quoting *only* studies from 30 or 40 years ago, I would recommend that you be skeptical with respect to accepting their conclusions.

An eighth concern is scientific bias. Sarewitz (2012) has stated recently that "Alarming cracks are starting to penetrate deep into the scientific edifice. They threaten the status of science and its value to society.

And they cannot be blamed on the usual suspects – inadequate funding, misconduct, political interference, an illiterate public. Their cause is bias, and the threat they pose goes to the heart of research" (p. 149). Stacey and Biblarz (2001) identified ideological preferences as an important danger in the area of same-sex parenting specifically.

In some respects, one way to look at this issue is whether science has become a servant to politics and thus, in my opinion, biased. I am reminded of a story that appeared in our local newspaper, though I have never been able to pin down the source. A native American chief once told a white man that Native Americans and the White man operated differently. Native Americans had experts in law, science, and religion as did the White man. But Native American leaders relied upon their experts to help them find the will of the Great Spirit and to do it. But White men look at their experts differently, the chief said. In your case, the White leader makes up his mind about what to do, independently of the Great Spirit's will, and then calls upon his experts as his servants to explain and justify his prior decisions giving those decisions the *apparent* (but not real) approval of the Great Spirit, law, science, and religion. One example of this process might well be represented by the Challenger disaster in which the space shuttle blew up after launch in 1986. Good science would have determined (see Schumm *et al.*, 2002, for details) that the launch was a very risky action that should have been delayed until the weather had improved. But rather than considering themselves as independent agents capable of telling truth to power when that is what the science demanded, the scientists caved to the political pressures to get the shuttle launched with no further delays. In another example, in 1996 some researchers had found data from 1992 that indicated that certain subgroups of soldiers were at a very high risk of divorce (70% over two years) if they had deployed to the first Persian Gulf War (Schumm, Nazarinia Roy, & Theodore, 2012). But the leadership of the scientific institute decided that telling the truth would get the press too deep into the issue and they blocked release of the "bad news" for at least 16 years. This is not an example of science helping locate military subpopulations that might have needed more relationship or legal support but of the suppression of science – science being treated as the servant rather than the leader.

What is often missing from Science

For a long time, effect sizes were seldom reported in same-sex parenting research, but about 2008 that began to change, even though the American Psychological Association had been calling for the reporting of effect sizes since at least 1994. However, some scholars continue to not report effect sizes, acting as if the only thing that matters is significance levels. That omission is important because effect sizes tell you how substantial a possible association between two variables may be. With smaller samples, substantial effects may not be statistically significant and too easily dismissed while with larger samples trivial effects may be statistically significant and given too much credence (Borenstein, Hedges, Higgins, & Rothstein, 2009, pp. 297-302).

Second, another missing piece of the research on same-sex parenting is an almost total omission of mediating variables, otherwise known as indirect effects. When combined with a refusal to release original data, scholars are greatly handicapped in understanding how the data tie together. In one study, for example, it was noted that same-sex parents were more stressed than heterosexual parents and that high levels of stress greatly reduced parenting effectiveness. But the mediating role of stress between same-sex parenting and parenting effectiveness was not reported; it is quite possible that same-sex parenting might have had a significant indirect effect on parenting effectiveness (Bos, Knox, van Rign-van Gelderen, & Gartrell, 2016). A related omission, related to the lack of testing of indirect or mediating factors, is a lack of complex model testing in the arena of same-sex parenting research. There is so much that could be done here and it is largely absent from the traditional research in this area; more complex model testing would certainly be welcome, regardless of the findings.

Third, another major omission from the research involves variables that might be related to delayed gratification skills. We know that if a small child can delay gratification, they are more likely to be a productive, non-destructive citizen at age 30 or older (Moffitt, Arseneault, Belsky, Dickson, Hancox, Harrington.... & Caspi, 2011). Yet, I cannot recall seeing a direct test of delayed gratification skills or attitudes as a function of parental sexual orientation. There are some hints but no direct tests. It is as if one of the most important things a parent does – to help their children learn to delay personal gratification for the greater good of society – has been forgotten by most researchers in the same-sex parenting arena.

Lessons learned at trial(s)

Ball (2016) seems to revel in the inability of conservatives to present any evidence about differences between same-sex parents and heterosexual parents at three major U.S. trials regarding same-sex marriage (p. 140). If the trials had been set up as fair debates, I might laud Ball for noticing this outcome. But he does not realise that the context of the trials involved deliberate attempts to suppress expert witnesses who might have been able to testify against the "no difference" hypothesis. Ball also seems to not realise that absence of evidence can occur for a variety of reasons not related to the scientific status of a field. Nor does he seem to realise that inequity might be the basis for making distinctions among different family types rather than some nefarious idea of harming the children of same-sex parents. Nor is it clear that marriage access will benefit the children of same-sex couples; that will take a few years at least to determine by comparing outcomes for children of married same-sex parents with outcomes for children of never married or divorced same-sex parents (assuming the groups are made equivalent on other key factors before the comparisons on sexual orientation differences are made). Ball argued that the Obergefell decision "was a victory for principles of fairness, equality, common sense, and rationality" (p. 144), but I would contend that it undermined equality and succeeded at the expense of tossing science under the bus, regardless of any other positive outcomes. Furthermore, it is clear that Ball will not be satisfied until all family forms, married or otherwise, are granted the same legal privileges and benefits now provided for married couples (same-sex or different-sex) as he clearly does not like the idea that marriage was privileged by the U.S. Supreme Court (pp. 144-145). Likewise, Mezey (2015) argues that "There is no reason to think that LGBT families will be the last frontier of new family forms.... In fact, there is evidence that those in polygamous relationships in the United States are drawing on the marriage-equality platform from the LGBT movement to argue for legal recognition of their relationships as well" (p. 64). Thus, I think there may have been a substantial disconnect between the way courts have functioned in the United States and the way good science operates. Now, I will discuss some more specific ways that I believe this occurred.

Weak research allowed to go unquestioned
(hence, making it appear undeservedly "sound")

Suppose you have an expert witness. The "expert" will come to the stand and promise to tell the truth, nothing but the truth, and the whole truth. They will be asked about their credentials and the goal is for their side to be able to say that "Here is professor XYZ who is a highly distinguished professor from this highly distinguished university who could never possibly be wrong about anything." Then they will ask professor XYZ about the issue at hand and if the goal is to prove a "no difference" hypothesis (about any topic) then they will ask questions to get to where the lawyers can say "Professor XYZ, who is highly distinguished from a highly distinguished university who can't be wrong about anything says that there is total scientific consensus in favour of the "no difference" hypothesis and anyone who disagrees with him has been discredited within the scientific community." News flash: this isn't science, folks! This *is* pure and simple pontification for effect, much noise without much meaning, designed to impress those who are too easily impressed.

Let us try an example. Suppose a highly distinguished professor XYZ from highly distinguished university XYZ has done a piece of research that alleges to show that the relationship stability of married same-sex parents is the same as married heterosexual parents, that is, after applying numerous statistical controls. Most of the time, that will be allowed to stand, because, after all, professor XYZ must know what their research says and they are from a distinguished university. What is ignored is that even highly distinguished professors (dare I say judges, too?) are human and vulnerable to confirmation bias (Schumm, 2015a, p.2), no matter what robes they may be figuratively (or literally) wearing. What is most likely to happen is that the court accepts that professor XYZ is highly distinguished and from a highly distinguished University and has published a few articles on the relevant topic, so what he or she is saying must be 100% correct. What is not likely to happen, unfortunately, is this scenario:

Examiner: "Professor XYZ, what is the gold standard in science for response rates in surveys?" If XYZ is truthful, XYZ will say that the U.S. Census gets rates around 75% by mail and most researchers strive for response rates of 50% or better. Then ask what response rate XYZ got. XYZ will have to admit that it was only 13%. It can be pointed out that Professor Herek (1998) once criticised Dr. Paul Cameron for a research study on the basis that it had only a 20% response rate. Bos, van Balen, & van den Boom (2007) surveyed lesbian and heterosexual parents in the Netherlands and obtained 56% and 21% response rates, respectively. I think it can be demonstrated that 13% is not a very good rate to which Professor XYZ will have to agree.

Examiner: "Professor XYZ, how did you determine whether the couples in your 4 year longitudinal study were stable?" Now this might seem like a silly question because stable would mean they did not get divorced, right? Until XYZ, if truthful, says that nearly 100 couples were counted as stable because one or both of the partners had died over the four year period of time between the two waves of the study used for the analysis. The point is that whatever the analysis was that had been presented, it needs to be redone without the dead folks being counted (technically, partner A could have murdered partner B and that couple would have been counted as "stable").

Examiner: "Professor XYZ, how did you determine that couples were heterosexuals?" Again this might sound silly, but it is a serious issue. In the study, all persons in an opposite-sex relationship were deemed heterosexuals, even though in the actual data set, hundreds of these "heterosexual" relationships included at least one partner who either identified as gay, lesbian, or bisexual or revealed such attractions. Do you see how this muddies the meaning of the research? The study did not use as a comparison group those who were heterosexuals both in relationship status and identity/attraction.

Examiner: "Professor XYZ, how did you determine that couples were 'married'?" Again, you might think this was a useless question. But upon further questioning, XYZ will have to admit that marriage was not determined legally but by the subjective evaluation of the respondent. That is, a cohabiting unmarried (legally) heterosexual woman who felt she was married, got credit for being "married". A heterosexual couple who were legally married got credit only for being married, thus, in some sense, equating legal marriage with nonmarital cohabitation. This, of course, was also true for cohabiting gay men or lesbians who felt they were married. If that was not enough, you could show how many heterosexual women who are cohabiting feel they are married while at the same time their partner (when asked) will tell the researcher that he has no intention of ever marrying her and thinks she is crazy for feeling married. You could discuss how legal marriage is different in so many ways from "felt" marriage (e.g., more difficult to leave it, more expensive to leave it, has an imposition of some legal duties, has some benefits not available to the unmarried, children born to it will be deemed more legitimate in some respects by some). I hope that it would be clear upon further investigation that claiming that this type of "marriage" makes for stability may reflect little more than if you think you are committed, then you may act more committed – which doesn't prove that if you could become legally committed you would get legally married and thus accrue the differences thereby afforded.

Examiner: "Professor XYZ, after taking the 'dead' stable couples out of the data, how many 'married' same-sex parents did you have in your study, compared to how many similarly placed heterosexuals?" XYZ will have to tell you 'four' and 'over 400'. XYZ will have to tell you, if truthful, that the instability rates or break-up rates were 25% and 8%, respectively. XYZ will have to admit that among living couples, "married" same-sex parent couples had a break-up rate that was over three times higher than compared to the equivalent group of heterosexuals.

Examiner: "Professor XYZ, after all this is looked at in detail, are you not taking a break-up rate that is three times higher and trying to tell this court that there is no difference in stability between 'married' same-sex parents and 'married' heterosexual parents? Is this not like trying to convince this court that 3=1?"

Can you not see the problems here? Stable doesn't really mean stable. Marriage does not really mean marriage. Thousands of cases really means four cases. Not significant really means you cannot compare four cases to anything because the statistical power is so low. Multivariate statistical controls may obscure more than they reveal; you have to look at the actual raw data to see what is happening. If you don't, pontification is going to win out.

I would be glad to be proven wrong, but see for yourself. Did this type of detailed, almost hostile "deconstruction" of progressive research ever occur at any trial related to same-sex marriage or parenting issues? I think not; but perhaps I could be proven wrong.

Experts disqualified because of religious views (and fatigue)
But on the other hand, this type of attack on conservative expert witnesses did occur. One trick of lawyers is to fatigue those testifying so they don't think clearly due to fatigue. One expert was asked at the end of a long day in court if he believed that all homosexuals would go to hell. A "yes" or "no" answer was demanded. The simplest answer would have been "that type of decision is above my pay grade, so it would be inherently misleading or incorrect to answer it" or "I think you need an expert witness who is an ordained clergy person to answer that type of question, it is outside my area of expertise for which I have been brought before this court". If the judge demanded a "yes" or "no" answer, I would recommend "no" for these reasons:

You need to "demand" that the lawyer explain what is meant by "homosexual" and by "hell". Just because you think he has a concept in his mind and you have a concept in your mind does *not* mean that you agree on the definition of the concept. "Homosexual" is a scientific term often defined by attraction, behaviour, or identity but capable of up to four other dimensions (e.g., fantasy) and can be defined relative to not merely heterosexuality but relative to asexuality and bisexuality (Rosario & Schrimshaw, 2014, p.559). The lawyer should be required to explain what is meant. "Hell" is a complex term that could have many meanings (a "felt" hell, like a "felt" marriage; hell as in *sheol* in the Torah or Prophets or Psalms or hell as in Gehenna in the Gospels or hell as in Dante or as hell in the current "whatever" popular culture?).

If that is not enough to tie the lawyer in knots, bring up issues like these: Demographic variables in social science usually have relatively little effect on outcomes after you control for intervening variables of a "process" nature. A classic example is that if you compare cohabiting and legally married heterosexual couples but control for their "felt" love for each other, there might not be much left unexplained directly in relationship satisfaction. That would make it look like cohabitation without marriage was harmless until you examined the significance and effect size of the indirect effect instead of just looking at the direct effect. With relationships, it is even more challenging because each person in the relationship or family can have a different report of "love" as well as a different report of "satisfaction". Differences in reported "love" across family members might also influence reported satisfaction levels, even after you controlled for the correct types of social desirability (yes, there are several types of social desirability that might or might not be biasing satisfaction reports).

If there are parallels between social science research and spiritual situations, one might expect that any effect of "being homosexual" (whatever that means) might have no direct impact on ultimate eternal destiny (whatever that means) without taking into account intervening variables such as religious faith or experience (however those are defined). In other words, any person – no matter what labels they might attach to themselves or have attached to themselves by others – might avoid "hell" (whatever that means) through intervening processes (of whatever the effective types might be). But that would not "prove" that there were no indirect effects whereby the probabilities (whatever they were) of going to hell (whatever that meant) were not unrelated to the established initial condition (whatever that might be, including whatever was meant by "homosexual").

Now what does the Bible say? It suggests that some people who make a habit of engaging in some sins are more likely to go to hell but that virtually anyone can be saved by faith and avoid hell. Hence, I would suggest the best answer ultimately would be "no". But that does not mean that there are no potential favourable or unfavourable consequences to some behavioural or self-definitional aspects or versions of homosexuality.

Unbalanced trial procedures

If you want to get at any issue, I think having a fair, civil debate between the sides is one way to try to understand. However, I have seen situations in which lawyers are so intent on "winning" that they (at least to me) appear to deliberately create imbalances that favour their side. In my experience at the Florida trial, both sides were told to prepare manuscripts that made their case, weeks in advance of the trial so the judge and each side could study the opinions of both sides. This was fair enough in my view. But what happened was that one side submitted hundreds of pages and the other side presented nothing – as in zero pages. In my view of science, this should have been like a football game where the score was 60-0. One side prepared, the other side did not. But that is not how it "went down". One side followed the court's orders and the other did not, but that proved to not be a problem, of course, for the side with no pre-trial submissions.

One side hired experts to critique every detail of what our side had submitted. That was not hard to do. I had asked my lawyers how strict I needed to be on my submissions. They told me "rough draft" was OK, presumably to save the State of Florida from higher costs associated with producing nearly perfect papers. Only one such critic (of the six witnesses in favour of same-sex adoption) was asked how much time and money had been expended to critique my work. It came to $14,000 or 70 hours at $200 an hour. It was not asked of the other five critics as best as I can recall. Trust me, you give me a chance to put 70 hours into critiquing someone's rough draft and I will find lots of problems, even if I do it *pro bono*. Keep in mind the expert had all the advantages of their university office, library, internet, and colleagues to assist in this effort to deconstruct my literature review.

So when our side went to trial, we had nothing to review, much less critique. At trial, then, the other side presented some research in writing that should have been presented weeks before and given to our side in advance. It was not that I could not have critiqued it, but I was told to stay at my hotel until my turn to testify came and not visit other libraries, use the internet, etc. In other words, once away from my office and internet connections, I did not have the same resources with which to check out what the other side had said. I don't even recall being asked to comment on it, anyway. But in terms of process, the other side presented their written evidence, which the court accepted in spite of being in violation of the court's own orders, and it accepted their critiques of my paperwork even though I was never allowed to read, much less rebut their critiques. I suggested to my lawyers the sequence of questions they might ask me to best explore my papers' content (or even questions dealing with rebuttals to what my lawyers knew about what my critics had said about me), but at the trial they asked a different sequence which did not help me explain things and frankly confused me (why are you changing up the sequence, did I miss something?). Neither side was allowed to present a précis of their testimony, only to answer questions. The net result was that the other side had full opportunity and advantage to challenge our side, but our side had virtually no opportunity to know in advance what their arguments were, much less to have time to challenge their arguments. I know I am not a lawyer but does that process sound balanced and fair to you? As another consideration, Florida law apparently forbade lawyers from using a person's religious affiliation or views to discredit their testimony at a trial but that was also done, which apparently did not disturb the appeals courts either. At a later trial against the State of New Jersey, the State tried to switch up the pattern and not present any testimony before the trial, but that did not seem to work either. They asked me to study patterns of city councils dealing with nondiscrimination laws but I did nothing on that, because it was so far outside of my expertise (I didn't charge them anything for what advice I did give).

As a minor point, perhaps, during my deposition I was told by the State to not bring any notes, paperwork, articles, etc. So I did not. The other side got really upset with me for not having such things because I had to rely entirely on an imperfect memory, but it was not that I didn't want to be able to answer more precisely, I was kept from being able to do so. Also, there was this psychological war going on whereby when I needed to go to the bathroom (as it turned out I probably was suffering from cancer at the time that exacerbated my condition of old age) the other side forbade me from doing so. My lawyers acceded to their prohibitions. I suppose I should have played "mule" and refused to continue testimony, but I had not anticipated this little "war". My nephew, who has been a lawyer for decades, says he would not have tolerated such nonsense. I also had not fully anticipated the games that would be played whereby you would be asked the same question, sometimes in slightly different ways, over and over again until one might want to scream something like "I have answered that 65 times already, enough!" I suggest that some enterprising law student compare the intensity with which I was grilled at my deposition with the intensity with which Dr. Michael Lamb or Dr. Susan Cochran were grilled by the State and see if my perceptions – of a difference there – is actually so from an outsider's viewpoint. Again, I am fine with intense grilling; if the scales of justice are balanced, it ought to be equally intense for both sides.

Politics of personal destruction at work

It seemed to me that the whole point of the lawyers in favour of same-sex marriage was to destroy the credibility of any conservative witnesses, preferably at the first trial in which they appeared. It was pretty much the politics of personal destruction. Unfortunately in some ways, I don't believe in that sort of treatment of people because, as I mentioned in my deposition for the Florida trial, I think God wants us to love everyone, regardless of their demographic or religious profiles. Even conservative lawyers were apprehensive that I had been discredited at the Florida trial so they were not eager to involve me in further trials. At the same time, the depositions and examinations of witnesses in favour of same-sex marriage were usually pretty tame affairs, meaning that they were seldom "discredited". The net effect was that at each new trial one side had highly experienced witnesses who had testified at many trials before and were being paid very well because of their experience, while the other side usually had witnesses who had seldom ever testified at more than one trial before and were probably being paid much less because they had much less such experience. This created an imbalance in evenhandedness that I suspect most courts did not take into account.

Implications

Statues of Justice show her blindfolded and with equal scales. But if bad research is allowed to go unquestioned or without any serious questions, that is not being "blind" in a good way. If experts are disqualified on things other than their area of expertise for which they came to court, then are the scales really balanced? If research is presented by both sides, it should be presented on equal terms with equal expectations and equal requirements. My recommendation is that experts should be allowed to question other experts because lawyers often do not have the technical expertise to ask the questions that need to be asked. At the very least, the lawyer should be allowed to have an expert at his side to suggest questions.

Each side should be allowed to present a précis of their arguments so both sides can see what the basic lines of argument are. The expert witnesses should be able to read (not just hear about it secondhand from lawyers who may not understand the statistical issues involved) what the other experts are saying about them before they are called to testify or allowed to rebut. I think that judges have a duty to ensure fairness in trials and should not just assume fairness but perhaps ask each side, including their expert witnesses, if they think it is fair.

With respect to legislation, sometimes I wonder if all legislators actually think before they pass it. In Florida, they passed a law that banned all gay or lesbian persons from adopting children. There were so many holes in this legislation or the way it was implemented that one might have a hard time counting or explaining all of them. First, the way the law was implemented was that the application form had a question to which you could answer yes or no as to whether you were a homosexual. First, there was no guarantee that folks wouldn't lie about their sexual orientation with little chance of ever being "caught". There was therefore some doubt if the law would be enforced. Second, some folks might not understand the term homosexual and guess that it meant you were human and sexual, so they would check "yes" incorrectly (in terms of what the legislature meant). Third, it is doubtful the legislature understood that homosexuality is defined in at least three and possibly seven or more dimensions. Which one(s) did they mean? One question is not going to capture all of that. Some people identify as gay or lesbian but have never had sex ever. Some engage in same-sex sex but never identify as gay or lesbian. Some may have same-sex sexual attractions but never have sex ever. The dimensions do not always line up and the law did not specify which dimensions were intended for the ban.

Once the State allowed folks to lie on the form and also adopt, then that suggested unequal enforcement of the law if the State cracked down on any particular "homosexual" applicant. Once Lawrence v. Texas was put forth by the U.S. Supreme Court, I doubt asking about private (same-sex or heterosexual) sexual behavior would pass muster with courts. To be specific, suppose a lesbian woman is pondering the question on the adoption application form: "Are you a homosexual?" She could refuse to answer because she felt the question itself was discriminatory. She could answer no for many plausible reasons: the question was biased, the term homosexual is obsolete, she defines herself as a lesbian not as a homosexual, homosexual is often identified with gay men rather than lesbians, she identifies as lesbian but has no sexual partners. I could go on for hours about the practical problems with the law from a logical and scientific point of view, but I shall spare you.

But don't laugh. The next major issue may be polyamory. Gartrell (1999), a leading same-sex parenting researcher, stated that as of 1999 she was committed, not only to a lesbian lifestyle, but to a polyamorous way of life as well. She was hopeful that society would someday accept her polyamory as much as her lesbianism. Polyamory has become a frequent topic of discussion in academic circles (Rambukkana, 2015). So perhaps some new law will be proposed to ban polyamorists from adopting. However, I can see that running into problems because some people have lots of visitors who want to save on housing and stay with relatives when visiting nearby tourist sites. Some people may rent out rooms or apartments to many different people throughout a year. I think the "rub" would come if a person who wanted to adopt was boastful about giving the future child a chance to have several different mothers each year. That is different than having several different sexual partners (that is private by U.S. Supreme Court definition). However, telling your child that she has a new "mother" every few months may not be private since the child is free to tell everyone at public school about each new mother, as well as the idea that being a mother is a public type of information (e.g., schools need to know who the parents may be in case of an emergency; if there are two parents, they probably want information on both since the first parent they try to contact might be unavailable). The remedy might be to demand that the adopter not define sexual partners with high turnover as a new parent, only as a friend. But would that somehow represent interference with free speech? I think that our culture teaches children that parents are (nearly) forever and most children come to expect some degree of stability (this is a researchable question, I could be proven incorrect).

We know that at least one lesbian mother in Gartrell's *et al.*'s study (2006) had at least six sexual partners or co-mothers over the ten years after she broke up with the initial lesbian co-mother. So we know that the phenomenon exists. What we do not know is if it is actually harmful to the child – and some say polyamory is not! (Conley, Ziegler, Moors, Matsick, & Valentine, 2012; Iantaffi, 2009; Sheff, 2010; see Schumm, 2013, pp. 341-342 for more details). But it remains an avenue for future research. I am just saying that no matter what category of person or interpersonal process a legislature might want to "ban" from adopting, a highly resourced effort to overturn that ban might well be successful due to the ambiguities associated with nearly everything in social science (that is, it has not been researched enough, or the research is mixed, or maybe the research did not examine this particular type of issue, etc.). If the burden of proof rests upon those who want to "ban", then it will be most difficult, no matter what the group of interest may be. Beyond polyamory, the next stage may be where the government favours homosexuality in children, regardless of what their parents think, because homosexuality (not bisexuality) is a sure way to reduce early or unwanted pregnancies (Rosky, 2013a, b) which may lead to welfare expenses, etc., a cost to the government.